WITHDRAWN
HARVARD LIBRARY
WITHDRAWN

Mild Contraction

*Evaluating Loss of Information
due to Loss of Belief*

Mild Contraction

*Evaluating Loss of Information
due to Loss of Belief*

Isaac Levi

CLARENDON PRESS · OXFORD

OXFORD
UNIVERSITY PRESS

Great Clarendon Street, Oxford OX2 6DP

Oxford University Press is a department of the University of Oxford.
It furthers the University's objective of excellence in research, scholarship,
and education by publishing worldwide in

Oxford New York

Auckland Bangkok Buenos Aires Cape Town Chennai
Dar es Salaam Delhi Hong Kong Istanbul Karachi Kolkata
Kuala Lumpur Madrid Melbourne Mexico City Mumbai Nairobi
São Paulo Shanghai Taipei Tokyo Toronto

Oxford is a registered trade mark of Oxford University Press
in the UK and in certain other countries

Published in the United States
by Oxford University Press Inc., New York

© Isaac Levi 2004

The moral rights of the author have been asserted
Database right Oxford University Press (maker)

First published 2004

All rights reserved. No part of this publication may be reproduced,
stored in a retrieval system, or transmitted, in any form or by any means,
without the prior permission in writing of Oxford University Press,
or as expressly permitted by law, or under terms agreed with the appropriate
reprographics rights organization. Enquiries concerning reproduction
outside the scope of the above should be sent to the Rights Department,
Oxford University Press, at the address above

You must not circulate this book in any other binding or cover
and you must impose this same condition on any acquirer

British Library Cataloguing in Publication Data
Data available

Library of Congress Cataloging in Publication Data
Data available

ISBN 0-19-927070-8

1 3 5 7 9 10 8 6 4 2

Typeset by Kolam Information Services, Pvt. Ltd, Pondicherry, India
Printed in Great Britain on acid-free paper by
Biddles Ltd., King's Lynn, Norfolk.

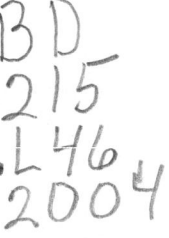

For Judith

Preface

I was initially stimulated to write this essay by a brief conversation I had with Hans Rott and an oral report he gave at a Swedish-German Workshop on Belief Revision held in Leipzig early in May 1996. He informed me of work he had done with Maurice Pagnucco that argued for a recipe for contraction quite similar to the one I had just a few months earlier concluded was more consonant with my own way of thinking than the view I had advanced in *Fixation of Belief and Its Undoing* and had reiterated in *For the Sake of the Argument*. Both Rott and Pagnucco commented on the July 1996 draft of this essay and subsequently sent me a draft of their ideas on contraction that were published as "Severe Withdrawal (and Recovery)" in *The Journal of Philosophical Logic* in 1999. I have sought here to explain how I came to change my mind and recommend mild contractions (the severe withdrawals in the title of the Rott and Pagnucco paper). A confession of my past errors would in itself be of little interest. However, mild contraction is rationalized in a different way than severe withdrawal. Because I think there is some philosophical interest in the differences, I have decided finally to publish my own version of these ideas.

I owe Rott and Pagnucco a debt of gratitude for the useful exchanges we have had. I am also grateful to Horacio Arló Costa for insightful discussions of the topics of this essay and to Teddy Seidenfeld for his helpful advice on technical issues pertaining to Chapter 6.

Isaac Levi

New York
29 December 2002

Contents

1. **Supposition and Belief Change**   1
   - 1.1. Belief, Doubt and Inquiry   1
   - 1.2. Doxastic Commitment and Performance   3
   - 1.3. Certainty and Probability   8
   - 1.4. Parmenidean Epistemology and the Corrigibility of Full Belief   10
   - 1.5. Types of Change in States of Full Belief   13
   - 1.6. Contraction and Corrigibility   18
   - 1.7. Conditional Modal Judgment and Supposition   24
   - 1.8. Prospectus   38
   - Appendix to Chapter 1   41

2. **Cognitive Decisions**   44
   - 2.1. How to Contract as a Decision Problem   44
   - 2.2. Expansion Strategies   46
   - 2.3. Potential Contractions   55
   - 2.4. Partial Meet Contractions   61
   - 2.5. The Commensuration Requirement   68
   - 2.6. Options in Cognitive Decision-Making   73

3. **Deliberate Expansion**   76
   - 3.1. Seek Valuable Information! Shun Error!   76
   - 3.2. Undamped Informational Value in Expansion   80
   - 3.3. Epistemic Utility as the Utility of New Error-Free Information   86

Contents

    3.4. Maximizing Expected Epistemic Utility   86
    3.5. Stable Inductive Expansion   88
    3.6. Degrees of Surprise and Belief (Plausibility)   89
    3.7. Context Dependence   95

4. Informational Value in Contraction   98

    4.1. Probability Measures as Determiners of Informational and of Expected Value   98
    4.2. Indeterminacy in Probability and Utility   102
    4.3. Undamped Informational Value in Contraction   106
    4.4. Weak and Strong Positive Monotonicity   112
    4.5. Why Losses in Undamped Informational Value ought not to be Minimized   115
    4.6. The Damping Constraint   125
    4.7. Damped Informational Value: Version 1   130
    4.8. Damped Informational Value: Version 2   140

5. Contraction, Rational Choice and Economy   148

    5.1. Choice Functions and Selection Functions   148
    5.2. Informational Economy, Indifference, Strict Preference and Weak Preference   163
    5.3. Contraction and Plausibility   172
    5.4. Embedding Preference in Prior Plausibility   175
    5.5. Plain Belief   179
    5.6. Plausibility as Informational Value   180
    5.7. Severe Withdrawal = Mild Contraction   181
    5.8. Revision and Recovery   186
    5.9. Entrenchment and Incorrigibility   191
    5.10. A Dogma Vindicated (Sort of)   199
    5.11. Categorial Matching   202
    5.12. Indeterminacy in Informational Value   204
    5.13. Fallbacks   211

6. Some Problems with Infinity 214

   6.1. Infinite Ultimate Partitions: Finite Intervals   214
   6.2. Countably Infinite Ultimate Partitions   220
   6.3. Estimating a Real Valued Parameter
       Lying on the Real Line   225

7. Base Contraction and the Filtering Condition 227

References   237
Index   241

Supposition and Belief Change   1

Some philosophers have imagined that to start an inquiry it was only necessary to utter a question or set it down on paper, and have recommended us to begin our studies with questioning everything! But the mere putting of a proposition into the interrogative form does not stimulate the mind to any struggle after belief. There must be a real and living doubt, and without this all discussion is idle (Charles S. Peirce, "The Fixation of Belief").

1.1. Belief, Doubt and Inquiry

Peirce's summary dismissal of Cartesian methodological skepticism is an expression of a wholesale rejection of Cartesian epistemology. The "paper doubts" that Peirce derides as the essential tools of methodological skepticism are not "real and living doubts". Did Saddam Hussein's Iraq have "weapons of mass destruction" in 2003? Bush, Cheney and Rumsfeld did not seem to harbor any "real and living doubts". The matter was settled. There was no point in inquiring as to whether it is so because there was no serious possibility that it is otherwise. Insofar as one cares to destroy these chemical and biological stockpiles, efforts should be made to find them; but these efforts are not undertaken to find out whether such stockpiles exist.

Supposition and Belief Change

According to Bush, Cheney, Rumsfeld *et al.* that there are such stockpiles is perfectly free from doubt.

Most of the participants in the debate that raged prior to the Iraq war agreed that Iraq had had some stocks of chemical and biological agents usable as weapons in military conflict. Bush and Rumsfeld were joined by Chirac and Vuillepin on this point. Not only was there no real and living doubt according to the points of view of a few individuals but there was consensus on this point among many of the participants in the debate.

Here we have an example of a full belief that many individuals endorsed in late 2002 and early 2003—to wit that Saddam Hussein's regime had possession of weapons of mass destruction. From the point of view of any individual X adopting such a view, there is no *serious possibility* that Saddam Hussein did not have possession of such weapons. No "real and living doubt" is present. Feigning such doubts by paper doubts does not warrant a serious inquiry.

The moral of the story is this. X at the given time when X has no doubt that Hussein had weapons of mass destruction does not stand in need of a justification of X's full belief that Hussein has weapons of mass destruction. At least X does not need to justify X's conviction *to* X. Bush did not need to justify his belief to himself.[1]

---

[1] Of course, Y, who disagrees with X, will require a reason to come to agree with X's view. Bush, Cheney, Rumsfeld *et al.* may seek to justify their claims to doubting Thomases in the UN and to their fellow citizens. This does not mean that there are two distinct modes of justification: X justifying belief that h to X and X justifying belief that h to Y. If X is to justify X's conviction to Y, X must show that Y is warranted, given the information already available to Y in coming to believe that h. That is to say, X must furnish Y with information that enables Y to justify X's convictions to Y. X and Y may have different information about X's beliefs and this will impact on their judgments as to what X is warranted in inferring. Nonetheless, Y should invoke the same standards in determining whether X would be justified in coming to believe that h that X does. That is to say, Y should make a determination of the information available to X and of any other judgments (such as judgments of probability and value) that may be relevant to determining whether X is justified in coming to believe that h) and determine whether X is warranted on that basis in coming to believe that h. Y may be convinced that the information available to X is rife with error. But Y should still acknowledge that X came to believe that h justifiably.

Supposition and Belief Change

According to Cartesian epistemology, however, X's current beliefs require a justification even to X.[2] Indulging in paper doubts is defended because such doubts provide a means of approaching the task of justifying beliefs that are current and, hence, not subject to doubt. Peirce turned his back on this basic requirement of Cartesian *and* contemporary epistemology. I have followed Peirce in this since the early 1970s and continue to do so here.

Current beliefs do not require justification. This does not mean that self-critical individuals should not be concerned with justification at all. The point is that the *scope* of the *demand* for justification is more modest than many epistemologists have thought. Justification is demanded only when *change* in belief is on offer. Sometimes the inquirer needs to justify making the change or to justify programs for making changes in response to external stimuli.

1.2. Doxastic Commitment and Performance

According to Peirce, an inquirer's beliefs are free of any real and living doubt. I prefer to tone down the florid rhetoric. No doubt all of us experience fits of doxastic conviction and doubt of varying degrees of intensity. But an inquirer may have moments of anxious doubt concerning matters about which he or she is convinced. The pangs of uncertainty may prompt a search for solace in the medicine or liquor cabinet or in the moral support of one's friends. But inquirers should not automatically recognize the *angst* as a legitimate occasion for inquiry.

---

[2] The plausibility of the Cartesian methodology may be due to the pervasive prejudice that insists that if X and Y disagree, X owes a justification of X's view to Y (and vice versa). If X claims to be an authority and lays a claim that his expert testimony should be accepted automatically, Y surely can reasonably demand that X provide *bona fides* for his claim to be an authority. But such a justification is not a case of X justifying X's current belief to X.

Peirce himself seems to backslide on this point. He takes for granted that those who follow the "method of authority" get into trouble when authorities disagree. Peirce, however, was making the point that if X followed the method of authority the appeal to authority would be incapable of resolving conflicts between authorities. And this seems to be right-minded.

Supposition and Belief Change

Peirce, like Bain before him and Ramsey afterwards, thought of beliefs as habits or dispositions to manifest fits of doxastic conviction, assent and other types of behavior in response to appropriate prompting. Doubts are other such doxastic dispositions. Under suitable prompting, such doubts are manifested by attacks of anxiety or by types of linguistic behavior. But even this is not quite right.

If there are dispositions to these kinds of behavior, the behaviors manifested in the dispositions are a function not only of the agent's beliefs but of X's values, desires, preferences and other attitudes. Of course, by the same token, it is doubtful if a useful notion of a purely conative disposition without beliefs among the initiating conditions is available. Some authors have concluded from this kind of reflection that there are neither beliefs nor desires but only "besires" that can be treated as dispositions to behavior. But such a view fails to take into account that *changes* in besires may be due to changes in beliefs alone or changes in desires or values alone or, perhaps, in other attitudes. None of these factors can be dispositions to behavior where the inputs and outputs are publicly observable behavior.

A model of X's psychology might be entertained as a candidate for the status of an empirically adequate and theoretically satisfactory account of X's behavior useful for prediction and explanation in which attitudes of belief, desire, valuing, supposing, hoping, etc. figure as theoretical primitives axiomatically characterized by principles of rational belief, desire, preference or value and choice. But the adequacy of the model would depend on whether the agent X is perfectly rational according to the principles specified. The adequacy of such a model as a predictive and explanatory theory is, however, in serious jeopardy. Not only are we not perfectly rational, we are not even approximately or "by and large" rational. No one is "logically omniscient" or perfectly self-aware. No one makes probability judgments fully conforming to the requirements of the calculus of probability. No one avoids cycles in judgments comparing prospects as better or worse. And our failures are dramatic owing to our lack of an infinite or indefinitely large memory and our vulnerability to emotional disturbances.

Supposition and Belief Change

We do better, I think, to take beliefs in the central sense to be commitments or undertakings in concert with other attitudinal commitments to having dispositions of various kinds. In that case, X's beliefs in the sense of doxastic commitments obligate X to have beliefs qua psychological attitudes that satisfy principles for rational full belief and cohere with X's commitments to judgments of value according to principles of rationality that constrain such coherence.

A model of X's psychology is then used as a standard for measuring the extent to which X is behaving in a manner that fulfills X's commitments. We seek to rationalize X's behavior rather than explain it. We do not predict X's behavior unconditionally but only on the presupposition that X will fulfill X's commitments.

Suppose X utters "The cat is on the mat". It is entertainable that this is a simple reflex of no significance whatsoever. But it may be a response to a question about the cat's whereabouts. If X wants to be truthful in X's response, X will be seeking to fulfill X's doxastic commitment. X may fail due to some sort of confusion. Or X may succeed. Either way, X's response is interpreted as an unsuccessful or successful partial fulfillment of a doxastic commitment.

Of course, the commitment to linguistic behavior involved here depends not only on X's doxastic commitments but on X's being committed to being truthful. So the disposition to which X is committed that is counted a doxastic disposition and in that sense a "belief" is correctly so classified only on the assumption that the commitment to truthfulness is fairly constant over a variety of contexts where X attempts linguistic communication.

X's doxastic commitments may be said to incur obligations not only to dispositions to various behaviors in concert with other attitudinal commitments characterizing X's goals and values and other relevant attitudes but to having attitudinal states of belief, desire or value. Such commitments need not figure at all in a model of X's biological and physical constitution used in an empirically adequate and theoretically satisfactory explanation of X's behavior. But they should figure in a model that would be empirically adequate and theoretically satisfactory were X perfectly rational along the lines suggested a few paragraphs back.

Supposition and Belief Change

Thus, if X fully believes that h in the sense of doxastic commitment, X fully believes in the sense of doxastic commitment that hvf. If X were perfectly rational, X would fully believe hvf in the sense of partially fulfilling that commitment by being disposed to respond affirmatively to a question as to whether hvf is true on the supposition that X wanted to respond sincerely and was rational. What X is committed to when committed to fully believing that h is (1) satisfying requirements of doxastic rationality such as, among other things, fully believing the logical consequences of what X fully believes and being consistent and (2) fully believing that X fully believes that h. X is committed to believing the logical consequences of X's beliefs even though X is incapable of perfectly fulfilling that commitment. X is committed to being fully informed both as to what X believes and does not believe in spite of X's incapacity to satisfy this demand completely. X has in this sense doxastic commitments to doxastic commitments that are dictated by normative principles of rational belief. X may go part of the way towards fulfilling such commitments. X is not obliged to go further than X can, but X should hunt out ways and means of improving X's capacities to be rational—costs and opportunities permitting.

So freedom from real and living doubt as to whether h is true or false is not, in the sense in which I understand such freedom, freedom from anxious insecurity concerning the truth of h. Nor is it equivalent to having dispositions to manifestations of doxastic conviction or lack of conviction that h. It is having the commitment to have such dispositions. The extent to which X fulfills X's doxastic commitments varies with the capacities and temperament of X. X may fully believe that h in the sense of having the doxastic commitment yet fail to behave in a manner that fulfills the commitment and, in that sense, fail to believe that h.

This means that change in belief can be understood in two ways: As change in doxastic commitment and as change in doxastic performance, i.e. change in the extent to which doxastic commitments are satisfied.

Jack has answered the questions put to him by the program he is using to prepare his income tax return. He has to list all sources of

Supposition and Belief Change

income. Having the documents before him, Jack knows for each source what the amount earned is. But he lets the tax program compute the sum. In an important sense, upon finding out the sum, Jack has changed his beliefs. But changes of this kind are not of primary concern in this essay. Jack has changed his doxastic *performance*; but he has not changed his doxastic *commitment*. He was already committed to fully believing the value of the sum before the computation is made.³ Inquiry as I am conceiving it focuses on efforts to change doxastic commitments. Explicating the implications of the commitments we already have or otherwise overcoming the impediments to recognizing the implications of these commitments is also a kind of doxastic change. It is not the kind of change that is of central concern in this essay.

Thus, the real and living doubts that an inquirer seeks to eliminate on the reinterpretation of Peirce I favor are the doubts embedded in the state of full belief that characterizes X's *commitments* as to what to believe true, what to believe false and what to leave in suspense. Doubts as to whether X is fulfilling X's doxastic commitments are at least as vivid to the X. We spend fortunes on devices to enhance our memory, improve our computational capacity and escape from the disabilities of depression and other emotional difficulties. The contributions of computer scientists and clinical psychologists among others engaged in helping disciplines are of first-rate importance to efforts to enhance performance.

Doubts about performance and performance capacity are not my concern here. I am exploring doxastic commitments and changes in such commitments. Computer scientists and mathematicians who develop devices that enhance our computational capacities and psychologists and therapists who seek to help us overcome our

---

³ Some authors seem to think that Jack is committed to requirements of rationality such as deductive closure of full belief without being committed to believing the information about the sum. If $h \vdash g$ and X believes that h but does not believe g, it is widely held that X is obligated either to believe g or to cease believing h. On the view I am proposing, X is committed to believing g as well as h. That X is committed to obeying deductive closure with respect to full belief is a doxastic commitment that does not change. That X is committed to fully believing h and its consequences is a commitment that does.

Supposition and Belief Change

disabilities need conceptions of belief and doubt in the sense of doxastic commitment constrained by the principles of rationality that give structure to these conceptions in order to direct their own efforts to improve the doxastic performances of their clients. But their gaze is on changing doxastic and other attitudinal performance. There is no need to justify current doxastic commitments even though there is excellent reason to improve doxastic performance when it falls short of such commitment. Change in doxastic commitment is not an effort to narrow the gap between the current commitment and performance. The issue is whether one should retain or abandon the commitments one currently has in favor of alternative commitments.

1.3. Certainty and Probability

Inquirers are never free from doubt on all issues. No ideal of rationality requires an agent to be perfectly opinionated on every issue that might conceivably arise. But agents should be perfectly opinionated on some issues.

I was convinced in late 2002 and early 2003 that Iraq had weapons of mass destruction. I am convinced beyond any doubt that London is the largest city in England. Later in 2003 I continued to be convinced about London's size but came to doubt the allegations about weapons of mass destruction in Iraq. I had come to have good reasons to cease being certain about the presence of weapons of mass destruction in Iraq. That is not true of my conviction about London. In the absence of a good reason for modifying my view about London, I do not need justification for retaining that conviction. As far as I am concerned, there is no serious possibility that I am wrong.

The absolute certainty that I attributed to my conviction about Iraq's weapons of mass destruction in late 2002 and my view about London's population then and now is absolute certainty in the same respect. In the period when I was convinced about the truth of both claims, there is no relevant respect in which one differed from the other with respect to how certain I was about them or with respect to the possibility of their being false. This absolute certainty should not be confused with high probability, with probability infinitesimally different from 1 or some other index of near certainty.

If I were to assign the claim about London a non-standard valued probability infinitesimally near to 1, I would, nonetheless, be acknowledging the serious possibility that London is not the largest city in England. I would do the same if I were to assign standard valued probability 1 to the hypothesis that London is the largest city in England in the sense of almost certainty but not absolute certainty. I, of course, do no such thing.

Probability judgments are intended to be fine-grained discriminations between serious possibilities. Instead of distinguishing between what might be and what is impossible, the might-be's are distinguished from one another in terms of how probable they are.

There are other ways to structure such discriminations than in terms satisfying the requirements of the calculus of probability. Such alternative ways have different intended applications. Probabilistic discriminations are used in deliberation when the expected values of alternative courses of action are being calculated. To assign positive probability less than 1 to h is to presuppose that both h and ~h are serious possibilities. That is commonly acknowledged. This is also true when the probability is 0 or 1 as long as certainty is understood as "almost certainty".[4] If X is absolutely certain that h is true, the probability that f given ~h is not well defined. If X is only almost certain that h is true, the conditional probability can be well defined.

---

[4] For example, if X were to face a fair lottery with a countable infinity of tickets, each ticket would have an equal probability of 0 of winning. (I assume here that probability judgment is finitely but not countably additive.) The conditional probability that ticket m will win given that m or n will win is equal to 0.5 even though the unconditional probability that m or n will win is 0. Conditional probability is well defined as long as the condition is a serious possibility. In that case, it is *almost certain* that neither ticket m nor ticket n will be drawn but it is not *absolutely certain*, i.e. it is not impossible. If X comes to believe fully that m or n will win, X becomes absolutely certain that this is so. Such a change in view requires justification for adding new information to the state of full belief. It does not require ceasing to believe that neither m nor n would win. X did not initially fully believe that proposition to be true even though X assigned it probability 1 at that time.

Probability conditional on a logical contradiction or mathematical falsehood such as that $2 = 1$ is not well defined. So X is committed to being absolutely certain that $2 \neq 1$.

The moral of the story is that there is no escaping commitment to full belief by moving to judgments of probability or some other index of uncertainty. Probability does after all presuppose absolute certainty.

1.4. Parmenidean Epistemology and the Corrigibility of Full Belief

Someone might insist that reasonable inquirers ought always to be radical skeptics of the sort who equate serious possibility with logical, mathematical or conceptual possibility. X ought not to fully believe that h unless h is a logical, mathematical or conceptual truth. According to this view, there would then be no need for an account of inquiry justifying changes in doxastic commitments. There is exactly one state of full belief to which inquirers ought to be committed. On that view, I should never have fully believed that Iraq had weapons of mass destruction. Indeed, I should not now (in May 2003) fully believe that the United States and the United Kingdom invaded and conquered Iraq.

Advocates of such Parmenidean epistemology insist that they still recognize changes in belief. What they mean is that they substitute for belief change and change in judgments of serious possibility changes in probability judgment. Full belief and serious possibility is the Permanent One. Probability judgment is the flux.

Parmenideans engage in persuasive definition. Belief always comes in degrees and changes in belief are nothing more than changes in degrees of belief. Probabilists think that such degrees are degrees of belief-probability. Others favor non-probabilistic measures.

But the difference between serious possibility and absolute certainty is not a matter of degree. I grant that so-called judgments of degree of belief can change and such changes ought to be subject to critical scrutiny. But I also insist that the very distinction between

Supposition and Belief Change

serious possibility and impossibility and, hence, between full belief and uncertainty is subject to change. This point is the nub of my dissent with Parmenidean epistemology.

Parmenidean epistemology is accompanied by the view that if inquirer X is certain or fully believes that h, X can have no good reason to come to doubt that h. From X's point of view, X's belief that h is incorrigible or immune to revision. Consequently, X should not be prepared to become certain of a proposition and, hence, committed to judging it true without opportunity for revision unless X can be provided with some hyperbolic guarantee that X will not be deceived. Parmenidean epistemologists are rightly skeptical of efforts to satisfy this demand.

Parmenidean epistemology may seem compelling if one thinks that X is obliged to justify current beliefs as well as changing beliefs as Cartesian foundationalists, Hegelian coherentists and reliabilists or wanna-be naturalized epistemologists all require in differing ways. According to so-called "foundationalist" versions of this view, there must be "first premises" that are self-justified in the sense that once they are recognized they cannot lose this property. Coherentists are no better. They avoid first premises but retain first principles of coherence whose status is indiscernible from the status of first premises.

Naturalized epistemologists seek to explain why we have the attitudes we do. Perhaps, the way attitudes are acquired may be explained within the frameworks of biological and physical theory under some description or other. I doubt very much that they can be explained under descriptions of them as propositional attitudes. In any case, such explanation is no substitute for the justification of the acquisition of belief when such justification is required.

I do not seek to rebut the diverse versions of pedigree epistemology (Levi, 1980). I prefer to turn my back on such views and urge others to do likewise in the hope of shifting from degenerating research programs to projects that may be more rewarding.

Once the demand that all current views should be justified is given up and attention is refocused on the problem of justifying changes in doxastic commitments, then the thesis that full beliefs must be immune to being given up becomes plainly question-begging.

But Parmenidean epistemologists might insist that advocates of the variant of the Peircean belief-doubt model I favor need to furnish an account of when one is justified in ceasing to be certain that h given that one initially fully believed that h. It is not enough to provide accounts of legitimate "expansion" via induction (Levi, 1967, 1980, 1984 (ch. 5), 1991, 1997). Justifying ceasing to be certain that h is especially urgent. This is especially so precisely because inquirer X needs to justify or otherwise legitimate giving up full belief that h from a vantage point prior to surrendering the conviction when X is certain that h is true. To cease being certain that h incurs increased doubt or loss of information without increasing confidence that one is avoiding error. Surely, so the Parmenidean epistemologist might argue, this is a form of cognitive self-immolation.

To cease to be certain that some proposition is true is to *contract* one's state of full belief according to jargon I introduced in the early 1970s (Levi, 1984 (ch. 8) and 1997 (ch. 6)).[5] To justify coming to be certain that a proposition is true is to justify what I called an *expansion*. I took the position (Levi, 1980 and 1991 and the essays just cited) that providing an account of justifying expansions and justifying contractions would secure my contention that inquirers can be certain of extralogical and extra conceptual claims while recognizing the serious possibility that they may eventually have to be revised for good reason. Both the first and the second objection coming from the direction of Parmenidean epistemology would have been refuted.

However, my own efforts to give an account of legitimate contraction in Levi, 1991 and 1996 were flawed. This essay seeks to identify the flaws, to show why they are, indeed, flaws, and to propose a remedy.

---

[5] The paper in Levi, 1997 was originally published in 1974. The paper in Levi, 1984 was published first in 1983 but was read in more or less its published form as early as 1971 at the University of Pittsburgh, Rockefeller University and the University of Michigan.

1.5. Types of Change in States of Full Belief

Expansions and contractions are intended to be changes in states of full belief understood as states of doxastic commitment. We can obtain a better idea of what sorts of changes expansion and contraction amount to by taking a closer look at the commitments incurred by being in state **K**.

One of the types of commitment undertaken by being in a given state **K** of full belief is the judging true of all and only those potential states of full belief that are *consequences* of **K**. A potential state **K'** is judged false if and only if all potential states having both **K** and **K'** as consequences are judged false. Of course, at least one potential state is judged true by the inquirer—to wit, the inquirer's current state **K**. At least one is judged false—to wit, the complement $\mathbf{K}^c$ of the current state. Let K be the set of all potential states of full belief.[6]

Formally, we have begun with two primitive ideas, the potential states of full belief and a relation of one state being a consequence of another. The inquirer X is in some state **K** in K and shifts to another **K'**. If **K'** is a consequence of **K**, X has moved to a less informative or weaker state and has ceased being certain of some of the consequences of **K**. If **K** is a consequence of **K'**, X has moved to a more informative or stronger state and has become certain of consequences of **K'** that are not consequences of **K**.

Suppose we attribute belief that h to X at t. On the model I am proposing, we are alleging that X is in a state of doxastic commitment **K** that has as a consequence another potential state expressed by sentence "h". To the extent that regimented language L has the resources to express potential states in K, a potential state **K** may be represented by a deductively closed set K of sentences in L.

Thus, if inquirer X should expand X's state of full belief **K** by coming to full belief that h, the change in doxastic commitment is representable in suitable L by K_h^+. This is the set of deductive consequences of $K \cup \{h\}$. The new belief state is $\mathbf{K}_h^+$. (If "h" expresses potential state **H**, this belief state is $\mathbf{K} \wedge \mathbf{H}$.)

---

[6] See the appendix to Chapter 1 for a brief summary of the notational conventions and terms of art frequently used but unexplained in the text.

Supposition and Belief Change

Suppose X were to contract the potential state expressed by K by removing g. When g is in K, there is no single way of removing it and obtaining a deductively closed set in L as we shall see. As a consequence, there is no univocal way to define a contraction removing g from K that is determined by g and K in the way there is a unique way of defining K_h^+ from K and h. This is a topic that will occasion the problem of central attention in this essay. For the present, I wish to bracket it and assume that we have somehow identified an acceptable way to characterize K_h^- and the belief state $\mathbf{K}_h^-$ it expresses.

I have identified two ways of changing a state of full belief:

(1) By expansion through coming to be certain that h.
(2) By contraction through ceasing to be certain that g.

But we can consider other types of change as well. X can start with K that contains ∼h (and, hence, entails ∼h) and shift to a belief state that *replaces* ∼h with h. I have called this *replacement*. Formally, a replacement may be defined in terms of expansion and contraction:

Replacement: If K ⊢ ∼h, the replacement of K by adding h = $[K_{\sim h}^-]_h^+$

Finally, suppose as before that K entails k. X contracts by removing k and then expands by adding g consistent with K_k^-. The result is a *residual shift*.

Residual Shift: If K ⊢ k and g is consistent with $[K_k^-]$, $[K_k^-]_g^+$ is a residual shift.

Replacement and residual shifting are both decomposable as the definitions indicate into contractions and expansions.

A self reflective and critical inquirer X is not required to justify X's current state of full belief **K** represented by K. But if X contemplates an expansion by adding h, a contraction by removing g, a replacement of ∼h with h or a residual shift removing k and adding g, justification is called for.

This brings us to an important question about justifying change in state of full belief. Suppose that X is in state K that entails ∼h. We know that replacement of ∼h by h is *formally* decomposable into contraction removing ∼h followed by expansion by adding h. But this does not mean necessarily that replacement involves two

Supposition and Belief Change

changes of belief state, i.e. two changes in doxastic commitment rather than one, three or n. It is entirely entertainable that replacement of $\sim$h by h is not justifiable when the replacement represented as a single change but is justifiable indirectly when it is conceived as a sequence of justifiable contractions and expansions in some order or other.

Suppose X is concerned to avoid importing false beliefs into X's point of view *where truth and falsity are as judged from the point of view when a change is contemplated*. If justification is sought for direct replacment of $\sim$h by h in K at the next step, X must make the case knowing for certain that by replacing $\sim$h by h, X will import false belief. If X cares to avoid error, X should regard such a move as unacceptable.

But suppose that X merely contracts K by removing $\sim$h. X avoids importing false belief in taking this step. To be sure, X will risk importing error subsequently; but when attempting to justify changing X's doxastic commitments, X may be concerned to avoid error in implementing the *next* change and not with possibilities of avoiding error subsequently. I call those who seek to avoid error at the next step *secular realists* (Levi, 1991). A secular realist can sometimes justify replacement of $\sim$h by h by justifying a sequence of contractions and expansions but cannot do so in one step.

Visionary realists are concerned to avoid error not only at the next change but take into account the risk of importing false belief at later stages. *Messianic realists* hope to obtain at the End of Days a system of full beliefs that is not only free of error but complete in the sense that all doubt about every issue is removed. Visionary and Messianic realists should find justifications of replacement of $\sim$h by h at the next step or change and through a sequence of contractions and expansions unacceptable as the Messianic realist, Karl Popper, did do.

Secular realists (in contrast to Visionary and Messianic realists) can maintain that the concern to import false belief at the next stage is not an impediment to contraction. In that sense, from secular realist X's point of view prior to contraction, removing $\sim$h from K incurs no risk of error.

Supposition and Belief Change

Once that contraction is implemented, the inquirer no longer is certain that h is false. X may then, perhaps, find a justification for expanding by adding h that takes into account of risk of error. The net effect is a justification of the replacement of ~h by h that is not direct and, hence, does not require indifference to the possibility of importing error at the next step that choosing direct replacement would require.

Thomas Kuhn claimed that in scientific revolutions, scientists "convert" from one paradigm or theory to another *incommensurable* with it. In such cases, it seems that inquirers shift from one perspective to another incompatible with it. But to do so is to deliberately import beliefs one is initially convinced are false into one's state of full belief. The incommensurability of the rival views precludes shifting to a "neutral" perspective relative to which one might seek to adjudicate the dispute without begging questions. To contract K representing **K** by removing ~h does not yield a belief state. Removing ~h must be accompanied by the addition of some g that implies h. In algebraic terms, incommensurability implies that incommensurable **K** and **K'** lack a *join*. There is no state **K** ∨ **K'** accessible to the inquirer. If there were such a state, then there would be a potential state of full belief that would lack h and ~h as consequences.

The claim that two rival points of view are incommensurable in the sense that the issue between them cannot be investigated except by begging the question in favor of one or the other view ought not to be endorsed without demonstration. The default attitude ought to be that all issues of fact are open to inquiry. Roadblocks ought not to be thrown up gratuitously. The requirement that the set *K* of potential states of full belief constitutes a Boolean Algebra is a formal expression of this attitude and, in effect, the commensurability thesis (Levi, 1991, p. 65). The commensuration requirement (Levi, 1991, p. 65) presupposes the commensurability thesis. It stipulates that a justification of a change of state of full belief must decompose the change into a sequence of contractions and expansions and show that each step is legitimate.

According to an approach made famous by Alchourrón, Gärdenfors and Makinson (1985), a *revision* $\mathbf{K}_h^*$ of belief set or corpus K expressing a belief state **K** that adds h to K expresses a potential state of belief $\mathbf{K}_h^*$ expressible by K_h^*.[7] K_h^* is definable as follows:

AGM Revision:

(1) If $K \vdash \sim h$, K_h^* is the replacement of $\sim h$ by h in K.
(2) If not-$[K \vdash \sim h]$, $K_h^* = K_h^+$.

Since $K_h^+ = K$ if $K \vdash h$ and $K_{\sim h}^- = K$ when $\sim h$ is not a consequence of K, it follows that $K_h^* = [K_{\sim h}^-]_h^+$ whether $\sim h$, h or neither is a consequence of K.

AGM (1985) does not give an account of justification of theory changes. Neither does Gärdenfors (1988). We are not told, for example, when expanding K by adding h is legitimate but merely what properties the new state K_h^+ should have. But Gärdenfors does say (1988, p. 52) that revisions occur when epistemic "inputs" into a belief state contradict the beliefs already there. He seems to suggest that in such cases, the inputs ought to be retained and at the expense of items in the initial belief state. If the input is consistent with K, then the change is an expansion.

This view does not show due respect for the concern to avoid error at least at the next step. If the input is a conjecture presented to us for our consideration, we should refuse to replace any element of the old doctrine we are certain is true by the input that we know is false. At the very best, we may open up our mind and shift to a position of suspension of judgment between the input and its contradictory. This will call for contracting the initial belief state but will not require replacing what is initially judged certainly true by something judged certainly false. That is neither replacement nor revision. It is contraction.

If a program judged antecedently to be reliable for acquiring new beliefs in response to sensory input is used, it is possible for the inquirer to form a new belief incompatible with his or her initial belief state. As long as the antecedent expectation of importing error in this way is sufficiently low, this practice is quite acceptable. But it

---

[7] According to my practice revision is defined for all consistent **K** but is undefined for the inconsistent belief state $\mathbf{K}_\perp$. Alchourrón, Gärdenfors and Makinson define revision for all **K**. See the appendix to this chapter and the related discussion in the text.

can lead to inadvertent stumbling into inconsistency. This is not an AGM revision.

To be sure, the inquirer should somehow retreat from inconsistency. Consider the net effect of stumbling into inconsistency plus retreating. The retreat might lead to retaining the input and giving up some elements of the initial state of belief. The result is a reasonable facsimile of an AGM revision. But that is not the only possibility (see Hansson, 1991 and Levi, 1991, ch. 4). The net effect of expanding into inconsistency and then contracting might be that the input is given up. The net effect will then (roughly speaking) be return to the *status quo ex ante*. The final alternative is that both the input and some elements in the background will be given up. The net effect will be (roughly speaking) contraction from the initial state. Neither Gärdenfors (1988) nor AGM (1985) provides an account of the conditions under which one choice or another should be made between these alternatives.

Thus, there are contexts where AGM revisions are net results of sequences of belief changes that can be rationalized in keeping with the commensuration requirement. But in all such cases, the fundamental kinds of changes to be justified are contractions and expansions and most especially contractions. Without an account of justified contractions and justified expansion, there can be no legitimate AGM revisions understood as justifiable changes in belief that respect the desideratum of avoiding error at the next step.

1.6. Contraction and Corrigibility

According to the approach to justifying changes in belief I favor, justification of a change of belief attempts to show that the change proposed best promotes the goals of the given inquiry. In this sense, all such justification is "pragmatic". There is no rift between theoretical and practical rationality. There is no separate theoretical standard of rationality.

In another sense, however, there is an important difference between the theoretical and practical. Although the aims of diverse

Supposition and Belief Change

efforts to improve beliefs are quite different, there are certain features that these aims *ought* to share even though it is clear that they often do not. On the one hand, they ought to be concerned to maximize the amount of valuable information acquired. On the other hand, they ought to seek to minimize risk of error.

The Parmenidean skeptic (for example, Jeffrey, 1965 and Spohn, 1988) who insists that once X fully believes that h, X can have no warrant for contracting, may wish to cast doubt on whether contraction of full beliefs can ever be justifiable or legitimate.

In contraction, the skeptic may rightly note, there can be no risk of error in the relevant sense. From X's point of view when in state **K** expressed by K every consequence of **K** is true. Every sentence in K is true in L. Contraction removes beliefs. It does not add them. Hence, contracting K cannot import false sentences into X's new corpus. Contracting the state of belief **K** cannot add false beliefs.

On the other hand, contraction does incur a loss of valuable information. What incentive could there be to contract rather than to refuse to contract? Contraction does, indeed, amount to a form of self-immolation. This is the challenge of the Parmenidean skeptic.

We have already noted that sometimes an inquirer inadvertently expands into inconsistency and is compelled to contract because his or her belief state can no longer serve to distinguish between what is possibly true and not possibly true. This can happen when the inquirer legitimately relies on the testimony of experts or reliable witnesses or trusts in the testimony of his or her senses aided by reliable instruments of observation and measurement. Yet, the results of relying on such trustworthy oracles contradict what the inquirer initially takes for granted.

Jack is convinced that he has at least two more hours to work on the speech he is to deliver at 5.00 p.m. But he wants to ascertain how much more than two hours he has. He then looks at his watch and reads 4.30. In this case, Jack has inadvertently expanded into inconsistency and is compelled to contract. Inconsistency is, as Gärdenfors (1988) put it, "epistemic hell". The inconsistent state of full belief is unacceptable. Jack needs to be extricated from it. The challenge is not *whether* to contract but *what* to contract.

Supposition and Belief Change

In such cases, the usual response would be to check the watch again or look at another timepiece. That type of response reveals that Jack has come to doubt that it is before 3.00 p.m. He also is doubtful as to the reliability of his watch or of his initial reading. So he undertakes a test. But Jack might have refused to take in the reading on his watch and remained convinced that it was still before 3.00. Or Jack might have given up the claim that it is before 3.00 and accepted the conviction that it is 4.30 or thereabouts.

Officially the contraction is from the inconsistent state of full belief $K_\perp$ or the inconsistent corpus $K_\perp$. But each of the three contraction strategies I described yields net results of one of three varieties.[8]

(a) If the testimony of the oracle that h is true is retained in K, then the net result is that ∼h is removed from the initial K and is replaced by h. The change is a *replacement* or *revision* of K by adding h.
(b) If the testimony of the oracle that h is given up, then the net result is reverting to the initial K—unless the reliability of the procedure for consulting the oracle is also called into question.
(c) If both h and ∼h are given up, the net effect is contraction of K by removing ∼h—unless the reliability of the procedure for consulting the oracle is also called into question.

Contraction strategy (c) yields a weaker state of full belief than either of the alternatives. If the inquirer bases his or her decision on minimization of loss of information, (c) will never be chosen. But (c) is often favored—especially in cases where there is not much difference in the value of the information yielded by (a) and (b).

In such cases, it is widely though not universally agreed that one should move to a "skeptical" position where one adopts of a posture of suspense with regard to the items of information that are controversial. I have always endorsed this view. But maximizing the *information* yields a result in conflict with this idea.

Perhaps, however, we should not worry that (c) yields less information than either (a) or (b). We do discriminate between

---

[8] On this accounting, I ignore the acquisition of the information that the oracle did make such and such a report.

Supposition and Belief Change

alternatives with respect to the *value* of the information carried. And perhaps (c) carries as much *valuable* information as (a) and (b) even though it carries less information. If a case for this view can be made out, then recommending (c) over the other two alternatives might be favored on the grounds that, when confronting equally optimal belief states to which one may move, one should always choose the weakest among them.

I adopted a similar point of view concerning expansion in the 1960s and have endorsed a similar attitude when confronting contraction. Unfortunately the way I previously conceived of informational value in the context of contraction (Levi, 1991, 1996) is defective in some other critical respects even though it satisfies this demand.

Assuming that a reasonable account of informational value that will allow for the skeptical response (c) when there is no difference in the value of the information obtained by options (a) and (c) is available, it still remains the case that no matter which option is chosen, the result will yield less information than is found in $\mathbf{K}_\perp$. Yet the contraction from inconsistency is legitimate because the inconsistent belief-state is epistemic hell. We are compelled to leave it.

Thus, there are circumstances where giving up information through contraction is not an act of cognitive self-immolation. So it is not true that once one becomes certain that h, one cannot be justified in removing it as the Parmenidean insists. There are, however, two objections to this riposte.

One is that the inquirer cannot coherently identify and choose between the three options for contraction (a), (b), (c). It is not so much that there are other options; but that no matter what the options are, the agent cannot coherently deliberate on them in the inconsistent state (see Olsson, 2003. Kevin Kelly has also been persistent in pressing this point[9].)

---

[9] Apologists for paraconsistent logics may wish to protest the allegation of incoherence. I do not. When it comes to the structure of states of full belief in the sense of doxastic commitment, an inconsistent belief-state is one that has every potential belief-state as a consequence. Since the doxastic performances of agents do not measure up to their doxastic commitments, it becomes a question as to which of agent X's performances

21

Supposition and Belief Change

I now think that the inquirer should be regarded as committed beforehand to contingency plans for addressing inadvertent expansion into inconsistency so that the retreat from inconsistency should be regarded as a product of choices made (commitments undertaken) prior to such expansion. The appraisal of the various contingency plans can be coherently made from this prior point of view (Levi, 2003).

With this understood I continue to think that the account of what to remove to retreat from inconsistency that I offered in Levi, 1991 may remain substantially the same.

The second response open to the Parmenidean epistemologist complains that the defense I have just offered shows at best that contraction is justified only when the inquirer expands into inconsistency. The Parmenidean may conclude that inquirers should take steps to avoid expanding into epistemic hell. Inquirers should avoid acquiring new information via the testimony of the senses and of reliable witnesses. Some Parmenideans (Jeffrey, 1965; Spohn, 1988) are happy to endorse this attitude. However, as long as programs for routine expansion are accompanied with a bolt-hole allowing for escape along the lines suggested above, there is no need for such drastic Parmenidean remedies in order to sooth worries about epistemic hell.

In any case, there are alternative grounds for contraction. An inquirer may deliberately contract K and incur loss of information because doing so allows the inquirer to give a serious hearing to some important conjecture without begging the question either in favor of or against the conjecture or current doctrine. Regard for delayed gratification is the order of the day. By giving a hearing to the conjecture that is currently judged false yet also judged to have attractive properties (such as being a candidate explanation for an otherwise anomalous phenomenon) that enhance its informational

---

are and are not fulfillments of X's commitments. The problem here is how to compartmentalize X's inconsistent doxastic performances so that some are fulfillments of commitments and others not. Paraconsistent logicians may have something to contribute to this topic. But in the context of this discussion, inconsistency in doxastic commitment and not in doxastic performance is the order of the day. In that setting, inconsistency is, indeed, hell.

Supposition and Belief Change

value, one might increase the expectation that in subsequent inquiry one will end up in a potential state of belief that gratifies demands for understanding to a higher degree than currently achieved. In this case, the choice is between giving up ∼h in K or refusing to give the putatively important conjecture h a hearing.

When Einstein offered a statistical mechanical prediction and explanation of an entropy reversal in Brownian motion, advocates of phenomenological thermodynamics as a fundamental physical theory had to give up their view that entropy reversal never occurs if they were to entertain the conjecture that Boltzmannian theory is true. If they opened their minds to the Boltzmann theory, they lost the explanatory power of their theory. But the Boltzmannian theory promised to explain more than phenomenological thermodynamics. This circumstance did not justify converting to it. To do so would be to replace a theory the inquirer is certain is true with one the inquirer is certain is false. That practice disregards the demand that error be avoided.

On the other hand, the prospects of obtaining an explanatorily more satisfactory theory in subsequent developments might act as an incentive for opening up one's mind. The inquirer X does not risk importing false belief at the next stage of belief (although there is a risk of importing error at later stages). X does have the opportunity to inquire further and possibly reap the benefits of greater explanatory power.

This approach is consonant with seeking to avoid error at the next change (but not being concerned with avoiding error at subsequent stages) while taking a longer-range perspective when it comes to informational value.

My aim here has been a modest one. I mean to show how a rational inquirer concerned to avoid error (at the next stage of inquiry) might have good reason to give up current full beliefs or certainties. That is all that is necessary to undermine that widely prevalent dogma that certainty entails incorrigibility. Once this dogma is undermined so is the Parmenidean skepticism that is based on it.

The answer remains, nonetheless, incomplete. I have argued that coerced contraction sometimes renders it moot *whether* one should contract but raises only the issue as to which of the conflicting

Supposition and Belief Change

alternatives injecting inconsistency ought to be removed. On the other hand, sometimes the question of *what* to contract is settled provided only the issue of whether to contract in order to give an alternative a hearing can be decided.

In both cases, however, a third question needs to be settled. We need to determine for each proposition h that is a candidate for being given up from a given state of full belief **K** *how* to contract by removing h. Because there are several alternative ways to contract that successfully remove h from **K**, a principled method of selecting between them needs to be specified.

The determination of how to contract is the only element of an account of justified contraction for which AGM offers an answer. As we shall see, AGM requires the adoption of a *partial meet contraction*. For this reason, this element of the AGM approach will be considered more closely in later chapters.

AGM has virtually nothing to say about whether a given context is one where X should contract or not (the question of whether to contract) and given that one should contract, what to contract. It also has nothing to say about justified expansion. Nor does AGM pretend to do so. The circumscribed scope of AGM's ambition cannot, of course, be an object of complaint. But it should be emphasized that AGM does not exhaust the topic of justified belief change. Nonetheless, AGM has much of importance to say about how to contract and this issue remains of concern.

Explaining how to contract is critical to showing that ceasing to be absolutely certain is justifiable without self-immolation. This in itself should warrant attending to the topic. There is, however, a second excellent reason for interest in contraction. Examining how to contract is relevant to providing a sensible account of conditional or suppositional modal judgment.

1.7. Conditional Modal Judgment and Supposition

An inquirer X's state of full belief draws a distinction between what X judges certainly true, judges certainly false and judges possibly true and possibly false. In this sense, X's state of full belief is X's "picture of reality".

If X has a clear sense of reality, X does not confuse fact with fiction, fantasy or, more generally, what X supposes to be true for the sake of the argument.

Distinguishing fact from fiction is distinguishing what one judges true from what one judges true on a supposition. Alternatively, it is distinguishing what one judges seriously possible unconditionally from what one judges possible conditional on the truth of such a supposition.

Thus, X may be in suspense as to whether Iraq had weapons of mass destruction. X might argue: "Suppose that Iraq did have weapons of mass destruction. In that case, the 'coalition forces' would have found them."

In supposing that Iraq has weapons of mass destruction, X is not changing X's state of full belief. X remains in suspense. But X entertains or supposes that a certain proposition is true purely for the sake of the argument. And the judgment expressed by "The coalition forces would have found them" is a modal judgment. It rules out as impossible that the coalition forces fail to find the weapons given the supposition. To dispute this modal judgment, one might say "the coalition forces might not have found them".

The supposition on which the modal judgment is conditioned represents a transformation of X's state of full belief to a potential state of belief. The transformed state of full belief is represented by a potential corpus that is a transformation of the corpus representing the current state. The supposition operates on the current state (or corpus) to yield the transformation. The suppositional transformation does not, however, constitute the endpoint of a genuine change in X's state of doxastic commitment. The supposition is invariably for the sake of the argument.

Nonetheless, relative to such transformed belief states, distinctions between possibility and impossibility are drawn just as relative to the current state of full belief. These conditional judgments of modality are expressed in English in certain forms of "if"-sentences and variant articulations of conditional judgment.

Thus, X might say "If Hussein had weapons of mass destruction, coalition forces would have found them by now." Let Y dissent from X's judgment. Y would then say: "If Hussein had weapons of mass destruction, coalition forces might not as yet have found them." X's judgment is a judgment of impossibility (that the weapons remain undiscovered) conditional on a supposition (that Hussein had weapons of mass destruction). Y's judgment is a judgment of possibility (that the weapons remain undiscovered) conditional on the same supposition.

Obviously the potential states of full belief X and Y obtained by using the same supposition are different. The difference could be due to a difference between X's state of full belief expressed by K_X and Y's state of full belief expressed by K_Y. But, even if X and Y share the same state of full belief, they might use somewhat different transformations of the same state to derive different suppositional states or corpora. Either way, it is of philosophical interest to know what kinds of transformations of an inquirer's state of full belief yield the suppositional state relative to which judgments of conditional possibility and impossibility are made.

Let "h > g" express the conditional modal judgment that ~g is impossible on the supposition that h. This might be expressed by "if h had been true, g would have been true". " ~(h > ~g)" expresses the judgment that g might be true on the supposition that h.

The account of modal judgment conditional on a supposition sketched above is encapsulated in the following schemata:

Positive Ramsey Test:

h > g is supported by K if and only if the suppositional corpus $T(K, h)$ obtained by successfully adding h to K contains g.

Negative Ramsey Test:

~(h > g) is supported by K if and only if the suppositional corpus $T(K, h)$ obtained by successfully adding h to K does not contain g.

We have already taken note of the fact that AGM revision plays a relatively minor role in the investigation of justified change of full belief. Justified expansion and contraction are far more central. It is

Supposition and Belief Change

at least *prima facie* entertainable that AGM revision is a more useful tool in discussing suppositional reasoning.

We might think of substituting the AGM revision K_h^* for $T(K, h)$ in the Ramsey Test Schema formulated above to yield the following:

AGM revision-based Ramsey Test:

(1) h > g is supported by K if and only if the AGM revision K_h^* by h has g as a consequence. (Positive)
(2) ~(h > g) is supported by K if and only if the AGM revision K_h^* does not have g as a consequence. (Negative)

Recall that AGM revision does not state the conditions under which an inquirer is justified in shifting through a sequence of legitimate expansions and contractions from K to K*. This is appreciated by rehearsing AGM revision in slightly more detail.

If both h and ~h are serious possibilities according to K (the "open" case), $K_h^* = K_h^+$. AGM does not state conditions under which X is justified in shifting from K to its expansion by adding h in the open case.

When h is already in K (the belief conforming case), $K_h^* = K_h^+ = K$ so that there is no need for justification since there is no change.

In the belief-contravening case where h is inconsistent with K and, hence, is judged impossible, the shift from K to K_h^* is never directly justifiable if the inquirer X seeks to avoid deliberately importing false belief into X's corpus. However, if X has shifted from K to $K_\perp$ inadvertently by adding h to K via routine expansion, it is possible that the legitimate extrication from inconsistency is a revision K_h^* by adding h. In this one case, by no means the typical one, revision plays a significant role in belief change. But even here, neither AGM (1985) nor Gärdenfors (1988) has anything to say concerning when such net revision is legitimate.

In all three cases, the AGM revision transformation is construed as representing a change in doxastic commitment. In such a setting, AGM revision requires justification. AGM is silent about this matter.

The AGM revision-based Ramsey test specifying necessary and sufficient conditions for a state of full belief or the corpus expressing it to support or warrant the making of conditional modal judgments

Supposition and Belief Change

does not interpret the AGM revision transformation as a representation of a change in doxastic commitment. In this setting, the question of justifying change is no longer relevant. In suppositional reasoning, the inquirer *stipulates* or *supposes* for the sake of the argument that the supposition h is true. Such supposing requires removing ∼h if it is present in K. Once this is done, supposition according to AGM revision requires that $K^-_{\sim h}$ be expanded by adding h. There is no need for justification of removing ∼h and adding h. Supposing that h does not involve changing one's point of view but exercising one's imagination. In fantasy, we feign having points of view we do not endorse (Levi, 1996).

The kind of supposition under discussion is consistency-preserving supposition where both the initial corpus K and the supposition h are consistent. Whether or not K and h are consistent with each other, the corpus obtained by supposition is required to be consistent. Logical, mathematical and, if there be such, conceptual truths cannot be supposed false and their negations cannot be supposed true in the consistency-preserving sense. (A consistency-preserving "counterlogical" supposition in Goodman's sense would be an oxymoron.)

But consider supposing that logical, mathematical or conceptual truths are true. AGM revision K^*_T of K by any such sentence is K itself. Hence, T > h is supported by K just in case h is a member of K^*_T. This in turn holds if and only if K ⊢ h. In that case, ∼h is not a serious possibility *unconditionally*.

In a similar vein, h is seriously possible unconditionally if and only if ∼(T > ∼h) is supported by K.

Thus the AGM revision-based Ramsey Test specifies not only when modal judgments conditional on a supposition are supported by K but also when modal judgments are supported by K unconditionally.

It is important that we have the capacity to suppose for the sake of the argument. Supposing for the sake of the argument looms large in practical deliberation where we consider the consequences that would flow from a given policy were we to implement it. It is implicated in considering the testable claims that would be true were a given theoretical conjecture true. Suppositional reason

Supposition and Belief Change

surfaces in explanation of why some event was to have been expected to have happened, how it was possible that a certain event occurred and why it is not surprising that it occurred. In novels and other forms of story telling, authors spell out the premises that serve as suppositions made for the sake of the argument in order to elaborate what must have or might have happened on the suppositions.

But pretending, fantasizing, supposing for the sake of the argument is not coming to believe and, hence, does not require justification. Confusing it with belief is nothing other than confusing fantasy with reality. We should not do that if we are sane.

Because there is no need to justify supposing that h be true as there is for coming to believe that h is true, AGM revision is better suited as a tool for analyzing suppositional reasoning and the acceptability of conditionals than for discussing belief change.

More relevant to current concerns, however, is the circumstance that AGM revision involves an account of contraction that seeks to address the topic of this essay—to wit, how to contract. To the extent that AGM revision is relevant to giving an account of suppositional reasoning, the issue of how to contract ought to be a central concern of students of the logic and interpretation of modal judgments conditional on suppositions.

There is an alternative conception of revision to AGM revision that, in my judgment, is more suitable for the purpose of specifying conditions under which K supports a conditional modal judgment but still emphasizes the importance of determining how to contract:

Ramsey Revision:

> *The belief-contravening case*: If $K \vdash \sim h$, K_h^{*r} is the replacement of $\sim h$ by h in K. $K_h^{*r} = \left[K_{\sim h}^{-}\right]_h^{+}$.
>
> *The belief-conforming case*: If $K \vdash h$, $K_h^{*r} = \left[K_h^{-}\right]_h^{+}$.
>
> *The open case*: If the case is neither belief contravening nor belief conforming, $K_h^{*r} = K_h^{+}$.

Ramsey revision differs from AGM in the belief-conforming case. According to AGM revision, in the belief-conforming, the revision is $K_h^{+} = K$. If the so-called *Recovery* postulate holds for contraction,

$[K_h^-]_h^+ = K$. Removing h from K and then returning it yields K. In that case, there is no difference between AGM and Ramsey revision. If Recovery fails, the difference can be substantial. So the relation between AGM and Ramsey revision pivots on the characterization of contraction, i.e. how to contract.

In any case, Ramsey revision may be succinctly defined in terms of expansion and contraction as follows: $K_h^{*r} = \{[K_{\sim h}^-]_h^-\}_h^+$.

Of course, Ramsey revision of K by T is K just as in the case of AGM revision.

And once more, whether one favors AGM or Ramsey revision depends upon whether the AGM revision-based Ramsey Test for conditionals or the following Ramsey revision-based Ramsey Test for conditionals offers a more adequate account of the conditions under which a state of full belief supports a conditional modal judgment.

Ramsey Revision-based Ramsey Test

(1) h > g is supported by K if and only if the Ramsey revision K_h^{*r} by h has g as a consequence. (Positive)
(2) ~(h>g) is supported by K if and only if the Ramsey revision K_h^{*r} does not have g as a consequence. (Negative)

Thus, the significance of the difference between Ramsey and AGM revision and the importance of the corresponding difference between the corresponding Ramsey Tests pivots on the accounts of how to contract that are developed.

The two types of Ramsey Test considered have some important properties in common:

(1) The revision on which the Ramsey Test is based is *consistency preserving*. If K is consistent and h is consistent, then so is the revision of K by h.
(2) In the open case where neither h nor ~h is a consequence of K, the revision on which the Ramsey Test is based contains the expansion of K by adding h.

Consistency-preserving revisions that satisfy (1) are *consistent expansions in the open case*. In order to guarantee the applicability of a

Supposition and Belief Change

consistency-preserving revision transformation satisfying (2) on any consistent potential corpus, for any supposition h, every potential corpus in the space of potential corpora that contains neither h nor ~h should be *consistently expandable* by adding h.

The two properties are connected in the case of Ramsey Tests based on AGM or Ramsey revision because they both agree that in order to secure consistency preservation in the belief-contravening case, K must be contracted by removing ~h so that the resulting contraction is open with respect to h and ~h. The contraction is then expanded. Because consistent expandability is posited, consistency preservation is assured in the belief-contravening case.

The two types of revision differ in the belief-conforming case where consistency preservation can be secured without contraction as in AGM revision or by first contracting by removing h and then returning h as in Ramsey revision. The contraction removing h in the belief-conforming case is consistently expandable.

The AGM and Ramsey revision are the only types of transformation of K that are successful in the sense that the supposition is in the transformation and in addition satisfy conditions (1) and (2) and, hence, insure consistent expandability.[10]

That conditional modal judgment along the lines I have suggested is intelligible ought not to be a matter of dispute. It is consistency with a potential belief state $T(\mathbf{K}, h)$ that is a definite transformation of X's current belief state **K** or consistency of the potential corpus that expresses $T(\mathbf{K}, h)$ with the corpus expressing **K**.

The thesis that consistency-preserving conditional modal judgments satisfying (1) ought to satisfy (2) is widely ignored or resisted. The majority view among contemporary commentators seems to be that consistency-preserving revisions used in modal judgment conditional on a supposition ought not to be consistently expandable in the

---

[10] Sometimes inquirers may be interested in modal judgment conditional on a supposition where the suppositional corpus or belief-state is extended inductively. Such inductively extended conditionals are discussed in Levi, 1996. Inductively extended versions of AGM revision and Ramsey revision satisfy (1) and (2) and are successful. But in inductively extended expansion, $T(K, T)$, where T is a logical truth, is not identical with K but is a superset of it.

Supposition and Belief Change

open case as condition (2) requires. This is, in particular, the case among champions of closest worlds analysis of so-called counterfactual or subjunctive conditionals.

The main issue that distinguishes closest worlds accounts of supposition from accounts of supposition based on consistency-preserving revisions that are also consistently expandable concerns the manner in which belief states are to be understood.

According to the view I have adopted, X's state of full belief is representable in a regimented language L that contains no modal operators (including conditional modal operators—used to construct sentences expressing modal judgments conditional on suppositions). One can, of course, construct richer regimented languages including L that do provide for sentences that contain modal operators, truth functions of these and sentences in L and, if desired, nesting of such sentences in other sentences using such modal operators. Let L^M be such a language. Given a corpus K in L let K^M be a corpus in L^M consisting of sentences in K, sentences supported by K in some specified sense and all logical consequences of these.

I have adopted the approach of representing the potential state **K** by K in L. But why not represent it by the deductive closure in L^M of K and the judgments of serious possibility and impossibility represented in L^M supported by K?

If we use K as a standard for serious possibility along lines I have suggested and along lines reinforced by the use of positive and negative Ramsey Tests that are based on AGM revision or Ramsey revision, when neither h nor ~h is in K, we can consistently expand K in L but we cannot consistently expand K^M in L^M. The reason is that K^M must imply both that it is possible that h and that it is possible that ~h. Expanding by adding h and taking the deductive closure requires adding also that it is not possible that ~h without removing the claim that it is possible that ~h. Contradiction ensues. In general, potential corpora in L^M do not satisfy consistent expandability. Hence, if the transformations of corpora representing states of full belief in supposition are transformations of corpora in L^M, the transformations cannot satisfy consistent expandability.

Supposition and Belief Change

It is easily seen that contraction cannot be coherently implemented in conformity with the requirements for keeping the belief state as a standard for serious possibility. If K^M entails h it also entails that $\sim$h is not possible. Removing h requires adding that $\sim$h is possible. To avoid contradiction, the claim $\sim$h is not possible must also be removed. The result is not a contraction of K^M since it is not a proper subset of that corpus.

Now on the assumptions about the standard for serious possibility that have been deployed here, X's state of full belief can equally as well be represented by K in L and by K^M in L^M. If one adopts the latter mode of representation, one cannot consistently represent the transformation of the state of full belief used in assessing modal judgment on a supposition as based on AGM revision or Ramsey revision. Whatever the transformation used, clause (2) must be violated in the open case.

This ought to be no cause of concern for those who favor the use of Ramsey Tests. They may insist (as I do insist) that the revision transformations be applied to the deductively closed sets in L. The set corresponding to K_h^* (or K_h^{*r}) in L^M can then be derived. $\left[K_h^*\right]^M$ is supported by K_h^* but is not implied by K_h^* (and the same holds for Ramsey revision *mutatis mutandis*). The belief state can be represented by the set of sentences in L^M supported by the corpus expressible in L but the extra sentences in L^M do not represent additional *full beliefs* to those contained in the corpus expressible in L.

Those who resist the anti-realist view of modal judgment I am urging may insist that when X and Y differ in their judgments of serious possibility, they disagree concerning what is true and false. But according to the anti-realist view advocated here, X and Y may and typically do differ in the states of full belief that support their respective judgments. This difference is a difference in the judgments of truth to which X and Y are committed. Judgments of serious possibility and impossibility may lack truth-values but they are supported by attitudes that do.

Like judgments of serious possibility and impossibility, modal judgments conditional on a supposition that h are supported by a potential state of full belief $T(K, h)$. This potential state of full belief carries a truth value; but the agent X making the supposition is not committed to judging the state $T(K, h)$ true, i.e. free of false consequences. X is committed for the sake of the argument to *supposing* that h is true along with all the contents of $T(K, h)$. But supposing true is a far cry from judging or believing true. Even so the suppositional corpus or belief state $T(K, h)$ is itself supported by X's current state of full belief K to whose truth X is committed. That is to say, the suppositional belief state or corpus is obtained from X's current state of full belief according to some recipe (AGM revision, Ramsey revision or some other alternative). Thus not only do modal judgments conditional on a supposition lack truth values, a feature they share with unconditional modal judgments, but like unconditional modal judgments they are supported by X's commitments to judgments of truth. The support is at one remove transmitted as it is via commitments to suppositions.

This approach can be extended to sentences in richer languages where conditional modal judgments and truth functions of them are embedded in other conditional modal judgments. I omit complications here (see Levi, 1996; Arló Costa and Levi, 1996).

The Ramsey Test based on a consistency-preserving revision transformation satisfying both (1) and (2) on a space of consistently expandable potential corpora can be used to identify conditions under which a corpus in L supports conditional judgments of modality expressible in L^M but not in L without committing the inquirer to belief that such conditional judgments are true or carry truth-values. The inquirer is committed to making the modal judgments conditional on the given supposition supported by the inquirer's corpus. But judgment of possibility whether conditional or unconditional is one thing. Judgment of truth or full belief is quite another. (An immediate corollary is that conditional modal judgments cannot coherently be judged probable to any degree.)

Modal realists disagree. They insist on using transformations of the corpus in L^M that cannot be derived from transformations of the corpus K in L by any transformation satisfying both (1) and (2). From their perspective, there can be no coherent use of revisions that are decomposable into sequences of contractions and expansions.

Supposition and Belief Change

I have been arguing that modal judgment conditional on supposition based on consistency-preserving revision calls for an understanding of how to contract. That is because I expect the space of potential corpora to be consistently expandable. From my perspective, approaches that reject this requirement of consistent expandability saddle us with forms of gratuitous metaphysics that we should not tolerate.[11]

There are transformations of K that may be used to obtain modal judgments conditional on a supposition that are not consistency-preserving. And it is easy to see that it is desirable to have modes of modal appraisal available to us of this variety to deploy when articulating reductio arguments where the supposition made for the sake of the argument is to be refuted by showing that it yields results incompatible with our full beliefs.[12] The most important of these types of transformation is what I have called *consensus revision* (Levi, 1996). In consensus revision adding h, the corpus K expressing the inquirer's state of belief is intersected with another corpus K' expressing perhaps the belief state of some interlocutor or group of interlocutors. The result expresses the shared agreements or common ground between the two belief states expressed by K and K' respectively.

In this case, the contraction of K is determined by the intersection with K'. This contraction is not controlled by the need to transform K into a corpus with which the supposition is consistent. Yet, the consensus is expanded by adding h. The result is a *consensus revision* (Levi, 1996, ch. 2.1). We can introduce a consensus-based pseudo Ramsey Test specifying when K relative to K' supports a modal judgment conditional on a consensus-based revision. If h is inconsistent with the consensus, consistency preservation (1) will be violated. Yet it will not always be violated. h could be inconsistent with K yet consistent with the consensus. Strictly speaking condition (2) will also be violated because when K is open with respect to h and ∼h,

---

[11] For further discussion, see Levi (1996, ch. 3).
[12] Counterlogical supposition and conditional modal judgment is also entertainable when we abandon consistency preservation.

Supposition and Belief Change

one does not expand by adding h to K but to the consensus between K and K'.

Thus, the pure indicative "if Oswald did not kill Kennedy, somebody else did" is appropriately uttered by someone engaged in colloquy with someone who thinks Oswald did not kill Kennedy. The partners in the dispute move to consensus relative to which "Oswald killed Kennedy" is held in suspense. Since the consensus contains "somebody killed Kennedy", it is not a serious possibility according to the expanded consensus that no one different from Oswald killed Kennedy.

Consider another pure indicative "If Her Majesty is present, she is invisible". A consensus view, we may safely think, agrees no one present is invisible. Expanding by adding the supposition is expansion into inconsistency. "If"-sentences in pure indicative form tend to express conditional modal judgments that are not based on consistency-preserving transformations of K but rather on transformations of the consensus revision type I have just briefly sketched. Reductio arguments are often expressed using pure indicatives and never using future indicative or so-called "subjunctive" forms. None of us would judge that if Her Majesty *were* present, she *would be* invisible. To the contrary we would judge that she would be quite visible.

Some variant or other of an account of conditionals proposed by E. Adams (1975) is often endorsed as providing acceptability conditions for "indicative conditionals", i.e. those "if"-sentences that are typically classified as pure indicatives. These cover many of those conditionals I propose to analyze in terms of consensus.

I agree with Adams on one point. Conditional judgments lack truth-values. For that very reason, they cannot coherently be assigned probabilities. Unlike Adams, I deny that such conditional judgments are probability judgments given a supposition. Pure indicative conditionals are, like consistency-preserving conditionals, modal judgments given a supposition.

"If Oswald didn't kill Kennedy, somebody else did" is a pure indicative. "If Oswald didn't kill Kennedy, maybe Ruby did" is the dual of the first. So it too belongs in the same category for the purpose of analysis. Someone uttering the first sentence judges it impossible that no one killed Kennedy on the supposition that Oswald didn't. This suggests that the probability of "no one killed Kennedy" on the given supposition is 0—in the sense of absolute certainty. The second conditional modal judgment is consonant with any probability between 0 and 1 conditional on the supposition.

P. Suppes makes a similar point when he suggests that Adams's approach seems to be insensitive to the distinction between "If Oswald didn't kill Kennedy, somebody else did" and "If Oswald didn't kill Kennedy, it is likely that someone else did" (Suppes, 1994, p. 6 where the example is different but the point seems to be the one I report).

As I noted a few paragraphs ago, reductio arguments are never couched in subjunctive mood in correct grammatical speech. Nor are so called "future indicatives" used. Only pure indicatives are used. But in reductio arguments as those embodied in "if Her Majesty is present she is invisible", what is the unconditional probability assigned "Her Majesty is present"? If it is 0 and not infinitesimal ε, perhaps, reductio arguments can be mounted. If it is positive even if ε, the conditional probability of Her Majesty being invisible is quite likely quite low although this is indeterminate. But there is no reductio. Thus, it is unclear how the probabilistic approach favored by Adams can account for reduction arguments. By way of contrast, with the aid of consensus revision, the cogency of expressing reduction arguments using indicative conditionals is quite straightforward.

In sum, I do not claim that all conditional modal judgments are based on consistency-preserving revisions of the current belief state. Consensus conditionals are a counterexample. However, when such revisions are consistency-preserving they should also satisfy consistent expandability. In those conditional modal judgments (typically expressed in future indicative and subjunctive conditional form), the issue of how to contract becomes an important step in the transformation when the supposition is belief-contravening and, for Ramsey revision, when the supposition is belief-conforming as well.

Supposition and Belief Change

Thus, we have two good reasons to look closely at the question of how to contract. It is relevant to the topic of justified belief change. In particular, it is central to the case I have been promoting for insisting that X can coherently be absolutely certain that h and yet acknowledge that X might have good reason to change X's view in the future. It is also central to accounts of conditional modal judgment that presuppose that such judgments are based on transformations of the inquirer's state of full belief satisfying consistency preservation and consistent expandability in the open case (property (2)).

1.8. Prospectus

Even if we focus attention on consistency-preserving forms of suppositional reasoning, the sort of revision of **K** by adding h suppositionally should not, in general, be an AGM revision but what I call a *Ramsey Revision* (Levi, 1996). The Ramsey revision of **K** by adding h is defined as $[(\mathbf{K}^-_{\sim h})^-_h]^+_h$. As already noted, Ramsey revision coincides with the AGM revision in case the *Recovery Postulate* for contraction holds. The Recovery Postulate stipulates that if h is in **K**, $[\mathbf{K}^-_h]^+_h = \mathbf{K}$. I have argued against Recovery in both Levi, 1991 and 1996 and pointed out that when the Recovery postulate is abandoned, the postulates for Ramsey revision no longer coincide with those of AGM revision. This point is of some importance; for, as Makinson (1987) points out, the AGM revision of **K** by adding h is the same whether the Recovery Postulate holds or not. The Ramsey revision of **K** by adding h, however, can and often will be different.

Although I continue to be skeptical of Recovery and consider Ramsey Revision a better basis for an account of suppositional reasoning than AGM Revision, the positive account I proposed to replace the AGM account of contraction now seems to me to have been defective.

The defect lurks in my account of what I called the problem of how to contract (proposed in Levi, 1991 and reiterated in Levi, 1996). A solution to this problem yields a characterization of $\mathbf{K}^-_h$ and of $\mathbf{K}^-_h$. I have already here sought to explain in summary form why

Supposition and Belief Change

I think the problem of how to contract is important both to an account of justified or legitimate belief change and to modal judgment conditional on a supposition.

In this essay, I shall recapitulate the accounts of how to contract I favored in Levi, 1980, the new one I proposed in Levi, 1991 and reiterated in Levi, 1996, and why now I think these suggestions are defective. I shall offer a new proposal indicating how the defects can be removed. The proposal I would now recommend is the one that Pagnucco and Rott (1999) call "severe withdrawal"[13] and I prefer to call "mild contraction". The difference in terminology reflects a difference in philosophical perspective as I shall try to explain.

This essay, therefore, is focused primarily on rationalizing choices among contraction strategies given that the decision to contract has already been justified or (in the case of supposition) stipulated.

Because the approach to justifying choices among contraction strategies is understood to be a cognitive decision problem, some attention will also be given to the problem of deliberate expansion. In contrast to routine expansion where the testimony of the senses or of other agents is consulted, in inductive generalization, statistical inference, theory choice and cognate modes of reasoning, a choice has to be made between potential answers to a given question. I have long urged choosing among such answers to be a cognitive decision problem (Levi, 1967, 1980, 1984 (ch. 5), 1996 and 2001). Elaborating on the features of cognitive decision problems in this case may be helpful in understanding the respects in which the problem of how to contract can become a cognitive decision problem.

Because even astute authors such as Hans Rott who advocates a decision-theoretic approach to belief revision have not, in my judgment, been sensitive to the demand that choices be justified relative to all the available options, it is important to have an account of what the available cognitive options are in the context of the problem of how to contract removing $\sim h$. Rehearsing the characterization of

---

[13] My information about this joint work was initially based on an oral report delivered by Hans Rott at a Swedish-German Workshop on Belief Revision held in Leipzig early in May 1996 and on some notes Rott kindly sent to me. Rott and Pagnucco have developed their ideas in "Severe Withdrawal (and Recovery)" (Rott and Pagnucco, 1999).

Supposition and Belief Change

cognitive options in the context of expansion should prove a useful preliminary.

One of the "cognitive values" that are central to the account of both contraction and expansion as I conceive of it is maximizing gains in informational value in the case of expansion and minimizing losses of informational value in the case of contraction. In discussing contraction, the emendations I wish to make derive from defects in my previous account of informational value as well as gains and losses in informational value. Discussion of expansion is relevant to this issue as well as to the characterization of cognitive options.

Shackle measures have played an increasingly prominent role in discussions of belief change and supposition thanks to the efforts of Spohn (1988) and Gärdenfors and Makinson (1993). In Levi, 1991 and 1996, I argued that they should play a central role in characterizing how losses of informational value should be evaluated in contraction. I continue to believe that this is so but think I made a crucial mistake in the way I deployed the Shackle measures for this purpose. I aim to correct this mistake here. It is this correction that accounts for the formal similarity between my mild contractions and the severe withdrawals of Rott and Pagnucco.

The use of Shackle measures in evaluating losses of informational value incurred in contraction also explains why I insist that such contractions are mild rather than severe as the withdrawals of Rott and Pagnucco are.

Shackle measures also play a useful role in deliberate expansion (Levi, 1966, 1967 and 1984, ch. 14). This application is quite different than the use of Shackle measures in characterizing losses of informational value in contraction. The difference between the use of Shackle measures in contraction and expansion on my account represents some substantial differences between Spohn's attempt to integrate the two uses of Shackle's idea into a single assessment according to "ordinal conditional functions" (Spohn, 1988). My reasons for resisting Spohn's efforts at integration constitute one source for my resistance to his ingenious efforts to devise an updating rule as a cornerstone of an account of belief change.

Supposition and Belief Change

The significance of the differences between the two intended applications of Shackle measures depends on the similarities and differences between deliberate expansion and contraction. For this reason, a rehearsal of my account of deliberate expansion will be undertaken.

Even so, the primary focus of this essay is on the question of how to contract. I am concerned to correct some mistakes I made in previous publications. I mean to excuse the self-indulgence by explaining why the topic of contraction—including the correction of the mistakes—is important for an epistemology that sees its agenda as being the justification of changes in states of full belief. Even though the formal characterization of mild contraction is indistinguishable from the severe withdrawal of Rott and Pagnucco, I hope to show that there are interesting controversies that are not captured by this similarity.

Appendix to Chapter 1

K is a set of potential states of full belief. Bold face, upper case roman letters will be used to represent members of K. Members of K are states of full belief in the inquiring agent X that should be conceptually accessible to X. In this sense K should be a *conceptual framework*.

K is partially ordered by a relation of *strength*. $\mathbf{K}_1$ in K is at least as strong as $\mathbf{K}_2$ if and only $\mathbf{K}_1$ should relieve doubt as much as (= carries at least as much information as) $\mathbf{K}_2$.

K and the partial order with respect to strength constitute a Boolean algebra closed under meets of subsets of K of the cardinality of K.

Attention shall be concentrated on sets of potential belief states representable in some regimented truth functional or first-order language L through a mapping from sentences in L into K that satisfies a deducibility preservation condition. This condition guarantees that if g in L is deducible from h in L, the potential state of full belief represented by g by the mapping is in the filter generated by the potential state represented by h.

A *potential corpus* in L under the mapping is closed under a Tarskian consequence operation for L so that $K = Cn(K)$. Given any subsets A and B of L, $A \subseteq Cn(A)$, $Cn(Cn(A) \subseteq Cn(A))$ and if $A \subseteq B$, $Cn(A) \subseteq Cn(B)$].

Supposition and Belief Change

Also $Cn(A) = Cn(B)$ for some finite subset B of A. Any such corpus represents a potential belief state by representing all its consequences expressible in L.

Expansions, contractions and revisions of potential belief states are representable by expansions, contractions and revisions of the potential corpora that represent them. A sentence h in L will be equated with the corpus $Cn(\{h\})$ so that the expansion K_h^+ of K by adding h is $Cn[K \cup \{h\}]$. The set K of potential corpora in L is itself partially ordered by set inclusion as a Boolean algebra so that the expansion of a potential corpus K in L by a sentence h in L is well defined.

ML is a language containing all sentences in L and a connective "is possible according to X at t". If p is a sentence in ML, "p is possible according to X at t" is in ML as are all truth functions of sentences in ML

"p is (seriously) possible according to X at t" is in X's corpus MK in language ML at t if and only if $\sim$p is not in X's corpus MK at t and "p is not possible according X at t" is in MK at t if and only if $\sim$p is in MK. In addition to these two conditions on judgments of serious possibility, MK is closed under logical consequence. MK contains K in L. Conversely K uniquely determines MK.

The set of positively valid sentences for X at t in ML, i.e. the sentences present in every potential corpus in ML constitute an S5 doxastic modal system.

Moreover, for every MK and for every sentence p in ML either "p is possible according to X at t" is in MK or its negation is.

Hence, to each potential corpus K in L there corresponds a unique corpus MK in ML. However, the expansion of consistent K in L by adding consistent h in L construed as the logical consequences of K and h in L cannot be represented by the set of logical consequences of MK and h in ML. The result is not a potential corpus in ML. Moreover, supplementing deductive closure with the two conditions on judgments of possibility leads to inconsistency.

The correct representation in ML of expansion of K in L by adding h is to take this expansion in L as the corpus to which the two conditions on judgments of possibility are applied along with deductive closure. If the connective "is possible according to X at t" is replaced by "is possible" ($\Diamond$), the connective in $L^\Diamond$ must be restricted in its application to sentences in L. There can be no iteration of the modal. $K^\Diamond$ is obtained from MK by replacing "it is possible according to X at t" by "$\Diamond$". Unlike the corresponding

Supposition and Belief Change

biographical statements reporting X's modal judgments at t, the judgment $\Diamond$h is neither true nor false.

The sentences in $K^{\Diamond}$ that are not in K do not express beliefs of the agents. "It is possible that h" ($\Diamond$h) expresses a judgment of possibility. A judgment of possibility is not, however, a full belief. Full beliefs are true or false. Conjecturing that *h*—i.e. judging that h might be true—is not judging that it is true and, hence, incurs no risk of error. But from the inquirer's point of view prior to adding h to one's corpus of full beliefs, there is a risk of acquiring a false belief in adding h, i.e. in converting the conjecture into a full belief.

Cognitive Decisions   2

2.1. How to Contract as a Decision Problem

I understand the problem of how to contract by removing h from **K** to be a decision problem. Choosing a contraction removing h from **K** is choosing a change in state of full belief. It may be objected that my understanding of the problem of how to contract is misconceived at the very outset for it presupposes that an inquirer can choose what to cease to believe. Ceasing to believe, it may be claimed, is no more subject to an inquirer's control than coming to believe.

Changes in doxastic *performance* are, indeed, not entirely under an inquirer's control and, when they are subject to control and critical review, modification may be indirect and involve training and the use of various prosthetic devices. The changes under discussion here, however, are changes in doxastic *commitment*. X may not be in a position to have a fit of doxastic conviction that the cat is on the mat at will; but X can undertake to be committed to full belief that the cat is on the mat—at least, that is what I claim.

By the same token X can commit to stop fully believing that the cat is on the mat. The problem of how to contract by removing h from **K** is a problem of how to change a doxastic commitment to fully believing that h to a doxastic commitment not to fully believe h and not to fully believe ~h. Contraction removing h from **K** so understood is a decision problem where one is called upon to choose a

Cognitive Decisions

contraction removing h from **K** *from among all the contraction strategies removing h from* **K** *available from the point of view of the inquirer X.*

The rational decision-maker engaged in contraction chooses the contraction strategy available to him or her that best promotes the goals of the contraction.[1] In this respect, the problem of how to contract is a pragmatic issue just as the problem of how to expand is in the context of deliberate inductive inference as spelled out in Levi, 1967; 1984, ch. 5; 1980 or 1991.

Such a decision-theoretic approach requires that we take two tasks seriously:

1. The specification of the set of contraction strategies that are available options for the agent in the particular setting.
2. The characterization of the goals of contraction in a way that determines how well the available options among the contraction strategies promote these goals.

Let the results of completing these two tasks yield a weak ordering of all of the available options with respect to how well the goals of contraction are promoted so that the decision-maker judges for every pair of options x and y that x is better than y, y is better than x or x and y are equivalued. No pair of options is non-comparable with respect to the extent to which they promote the goals. If the set of available contraction strategies is finite, then the inquirer may be urged to choose a contraction strategy removing h from **K** that is optimal with respect to this ordering. Even if the set of strategies available is infinite, under appropriate conditions a weak ordering of the options can yield an optimum.[2]

---

[1] The focus of this discussion is on giving an account of contraction in decision-theoretic terms. I do not propose a set of axioms for contraction that is complete in some respect. In comparing the views I favor with the AGM theory and other alternatives, however, I make reference to similarities and differences with respect to satisfaction of various postulates that have been considered and take for granted some familiarity on the part of the reader with the AGM axioms for contraction. For me, a condition of adequacy for any axiomatic account of contraction (or revision or expansion) ought to be an account of how the choice of a contraction (revision, expansion) is rationalized with respect to the goals of the inquirer and the options available.

[2] According to the general account of rational decision-making I have proposed elsewhere (Levi, 1986), a rational agent may have value commitments and goals that

Cognitive Decisions

Thus, it is desirable to spell out the conditions a set of available contraction strategies removing h from **K** should meet and the desiderata a weak ordering of these contraction strategies should satisfy to reflect the goals of contraction. Before doing so, however, a review of parallel issues pertaining to inductive expansion might help set the stage.

2.2. Expansion Strategies

In statistical reasoning, theory choice and other types of inductive or ampliative reasoning involving a deliberate expansion of the agent's initial belief state, the inquirer is called upon to choose between alternative expansion strategies or potential answers to the question under investigation. At least so I have argued elsewhere (e.g. in Levi, 1967, and 1984, ch. 5).

Identification of a list of potential answers is the task of *abduction*.[3] The principles of abduction require, for example, that one be in a

are in conflict so that he recognizes more than one evaluation of his options as permissible to use. In such cases, a non-controversial weak ordering of the options may not exist for the agent. Decision-making will have to proceed by identifying which options are optimal according to at least one weak ordering that is consonant with the evaluations the agent can make. Such options are *V-admissible*. Rational agents restrict their choices to V-admissible options.

This idea can be applied to the question of how to contract. I shall postpone discussion of cases where the inquirer's cognitive goals conflict until section 5.12 and focus, instead, on the quite likely unrealistic case where a uniquely permissible weak ordering is available.

[3] The task of abduction as Peirce understood it in 1902 is to formulate conjectures that qualify as potential answers to questions under study. The task of induction is to decide which of the potential answers obtained by abduction at a given stage of inquiry to adopt as the solution to the problem or answer to the question under investigation. Since the aim common to all inquiry is to answer questions, there is no point to abduction unless induction is taken seriously. Moreover, the difference between abduction and induction is not a matter of the degree of confidence or evidential support afforded inductive as compared to abductive conclusions. A conjecture obtained via abduction is then assessed relative to the evidence available before a decision is taken whether to add the conjecture to the full beliefs via induction. Thus, evidential support for a conjecture is assessed relative to the evidence *before* the conjecture is converted to a settled assumption. Conjectures obtained by abduction may differ in the degree to which the evidence supports them; but the difference between the settled conclusions of induction and conjectures is not a matter of degree of support.

Cognitive Decisions

position to regard suspension of judgment between rival potential answers to be a potential answer.

Let belief-states be represented in a regimented first-order language L. Any potential belief-state **K** representable in L is representable by a *corpus* K that is a set of sentences closed under logical consequence in L. Let W be the set of maximally consistent corpora in L and P_K be the set of maximally consistent extensions of K. P_K is, of course, contained in W.

Partition P_K into finitely many cells $c_1, c_2, \ldots, c_n$. Form intersections of members of each cell. Suppose that the set of intersections constitute a set of potential expansions of K representing strongest consistent potential answers of interest to the inquirer in the context of the given inquiry. In general, the language L has means for expressing hypotheses consistent with K that are stronger than the elements of this partition. But someone interested in the value of the GNP for the USA in 1995 will not be thinking of the average rainfall in Iraq as part of the information carried by a strongest consistent potential answer to the question under study.

When L has for each c_i a sentence d_i expressing the "proposition" $|d_i| = c_i$, the strongest consistent potential expansions of interest to the inquirer can be represented as expansions $K_{d_i}^+$ of K by adding d_i and forming the deductive closure.

The inquirer's *ultimate partition* U_K (relative to K and to the inquirer's demands for information) consists of the cells in the partition of P_K into the c_i's or the corresponding set of sentences d_i. Notice that when there is a set of sentences e_i such that for each d_i, K entails the equivalence in truth-value between e_i and d_i the ultimate partition relative to K can be represented by the set of e_i's. Of course, for each d_i, $K_{e_i}^+ = K_{d_i}^+$.

The set of all potential answers (or the potential expansion strategies) of interest to the inquirer in the context of the given inquiry are linguistically representable as expansions of K by adding some sentence h in L equivalent given K to a disjunction of some subset of d_i's in U_K. The disjunction of the empty set is construed as any sentence whose negation is in K.

Cognitive Decisions

It is important to keep in mind the trivial point that the sentences d_i in U_K need not be logically exhaustive but only exhaustive given K. For convenience, the d_i's have been defined so that they must be logically pairwise exclusive. In practice, however, they may be replaced by e_i's that are equivalent to them given K and need not be logically pairwise exclusive but only pairwise exclusive given K.

Moreover, there may be a potential corpus K' that is a proper superset of K such that $U'_K = U_K$. Even though K' carries more information than K, no element of U_K is incompatible with the information in K'. No new information of interest to the inquirer in the context of the particular question under study has been added to K. The set of potential answers remains unaltered. The set of potential expansion strategies relative to K'_- may be representable as expansions by adding disjunctions of the same as the set of cells as the potential expansions relative to K. The difference between the two cases may have an impact on which potential expansion strategy the agent should choose because K' contains information that alters the probabilities of incurring error in adopting one expansion strategy rather than another. But the extra information does not alter the set of available options.

The elements of the ultimate partition U_K are supposed to represent the strongest consistent potential answers to the question under study of relevance to the demands of the question and given the state of full belief U_K.

Consider, for example, the question of predicting who will win a given election relative to initial information that either candidate A, B or C will. X may wonder whether A will win or not in which case, the ultimate partition will consist of the two conjectures "A will win", "A will not win". Or X may be interested in which of the three will win. Or X may ask whether the candidate is from X's hometown or not so that the ultimate partition has six elements. In the first case, the inquirer contemplates only four potential answers. In the second, eight. In the third, sixty-four.

I do not think that there is a standard way of fixing an ultimate partition obligatory on all agents in all settings. There are, to be

Cognitive Decisions

sure, reasonable suggestions available concerning how agents who disagree in their ultimate partitions and have reason to engage in a common inquiry might come to some agreement as to how to proceed together. If they share the same corpus, they can, in particular, adopt the coarsest common refinement of their partitions (see Levi, 1984, ch. 7). Matters become more complex when inquirers differ in their states of full belief. Clearly in such cases, inquirers should seek to identify a *minimal corpus* LK or *minimal belief-state* **LK** such that each party in the dispute can regard their current corpus to be an expansion of LK. That corpus could be the intersection of their respective corpora. This represents the shared agreements of all parties to the dispute. Or it could be a weaker corpus. Each inquirer j may be supposed to have an ultimate partition $^jU_{LK}$ relative to LK. j's current corpus ^jK then determines j's current ultimate partition ^jU_K by eliminating the elements of $^jU_{LK}$ that are inconsistent with ^jK. The parties to the dispute can then identify the coarsest common refinement of their differing basic partitions and adopt it as their common basic partition. The differences in the ultimate partitions of the individual inquirers can then be located in the differences in their states of full belief.

This way of approaching the question of choosing ultimate partitions does not insist that there be a standard ultimate partition relative to U_K for every inquirer in the state expressed in L by K. The inquirers might persist in pursuing their several inquiries relative to their several ultimate partitions relative to K. They may refuse to adopt a common basic partition relative to a common minimal state of full belief LK.

Such refusal might make a great deal of sense for a variety of reasons. The most obvious might be that inquirer 1 is concerned with a question about the genotype of a certain species of worm whereas inquirer 2 is concerned with a question about the climate at the polar regions of Mars. To insist that inquirers 1 and 2 work from a common minimal corpus and basic partition resembles the quixotic notion that the basic partition should consist of the space of maximally consistent potential corpora in a very rich language or maximally consistent belief-states in a rich conceptual framework where the minimal belief-state is the logically weakest potential belief-state (expressible in L by the urcorpus UK).

Nonetheless, there is some advantage to complicating the model of inquiry proposed here by presupposing that the inquirer X engaged in a particular investigation is committed at any given time to a space of potential expansions of a minimal corpus LK and a basic partition U_{LK}.

Inquiries are typically allowed to continue even though inquirers change their minds. I do not pretend to offer a principle for individuating inquiries through all changes of view. Even so the space **K** of potential states of full belief or the potential corpora K expressing them is often a good first approximation to a characterization of an inquiry. K need not represent what is conceptually accessible to inquirer X or what is linguistically expressible in the language L. Rather it represents the space of potential states of information that X could access in the course of sequence of belief changes that would be relevant to the budget of problems that characterize X's inquiry.

LK is minimal for the investigation undertaken in the sense that *at the time* the inquirer regards the contents of LK as fixed for the duration of the inquiry. X might at some stage come to the conclusion that some items in LK need to be removed. In that eventuality, LK may be weakened. Whether the inquiry is taken to have been modified or to have been replaced by a new inquiry will, no doubt, depend upon how radical the contraction of LK is.

The basic partition U_{LK} is the space of maximal potential expansions consistent with LK relevant to the problem of interest to inquirer X. Basic partitions, like minimal corpora, are not written in stone.

As already noted, the ultimate partition U_K—the set of maximally specific potential expansions relevant to that very problem when K is the state of full belief—may be represented as the set theoretic difference between U_{LK} and the elements of U_{LK} incompatible with K. The advantage of introducing the extra bit of complexity is that it enables us to represent aspects of an inquiry that remain constant as X's state of full belief changes. LK represents the minimal presuppositions of the inquiry and U_{LK} represents the maximally specific relevant answers to the problem raised by the inquiry given these presuppositions and regardless of how K changes.

Although LK must be a consequence of the inquirer's K, the choice of that consequence of K and of U_{LK} represents the adoption by the inquirer of certain constraints on the goals of the inquiry undertaken. These constraints are subject to modification. But altering them does not entail altering the inquirer's belief state. Rather it is the inquirer's demands for information, question, or budget of questions that has been changed. Thus, when at time t X holds LK fixed for the duration of the inquiry, X aims to settle certain unsettled questions without modifying LK. When at the same time, X in addition adopts U_{LK}, X is not interested in any information more specific than that conveyed by a member of U_{LK} unless it is shown to contribute to warranting some potential answer generated by U_{LK}.

Nothing said here precludes K from being equated with LK and U_{LK} being equated with U_K. And nothing requires these identifications either. I have already demurred from equating the minimal corpus with the weakest corpus expressible in language L and U_{LK} with W as long is L is a very rich language. But I suppose there is nothing wrong with doing so if L has suitably impoverished means of expression. The advantage of introducing the minimal belief state and the minimal corpus that expresses it is to mark and represent forms of continuity that are sometimes maintained in inquiry in the form of certain fixed problems, potential solutions and presuppositions.

Nonetheless, some substantial requirements have been imposed on proper inquiry. Once an ultimate partition has been adopted, there are some constraints on what can count as potential answers to a question as long as that ultimate partition is endorsed.

1. Given the choice of an ultimate partition, the inquiring agent is obliged to consider as optional expansion strategies all possible forms of suspense between these expansion strategies.
2. The inquiring agent should also take into account the prospect of importing contradiction into the inquirer's beliefs. That is not to

suggest that contradiction is a legitimate mode of expansion; but it is to insist that if it is not, that should be revealed by showing that, given the goals of inductive expansion, contradiction should not be recommended to rational agents.

The choice of an ultimate partition does foreclose consideration of potential expansions of K that are not representable within the framework of the algebra generated by that partition. This choice reflects how fine-grained our interest in new information is.

Making decisions on this point seems unavoidable. One might seek to duck the issue by urging that we should be as fine-grained as the conceptual resources of L or our conceptual framework allow. Each element of the partition in this sense would be a "possible world". But since there are no conceptual limits on how fine-grained discriminations inquirers can make, there are no possible worlds in this sense. Neither a conceptual framework nor a particular language can be used to standardize the choice of an ultimate partition. To be sure, the language L that is to be used allows for the expression of theories that are maximally consistent relative to L. But such theories will fail to be maximal relative to languages with richer expressive resources. If an inquirer chooses as his or her ultimate partition the set of maximally consistent sets of sentences relative to L, that choice is as open to controversy as resting content with an excessively coarse ultimate partition. Relative to L, the elements of that partition are not descriptions of possible worlds. There is no way to escape making a decision as to how fine-grained one's interest in new information is going to be and no reason to insist that it be as specific as a maximally consistent theory in some particular language. To the contrary, the inquirer's interest in new information is going, in general, to be far more coarse-grained than a partition into possible complete histories of the Universe (if this makes sense).

The choice of an ultimate partition can, of course, be a subject of dispute. But as I have suggested, when the choice is challenged, parties to the dispute can reach an agreement as to how to proceed if they care to do so or, at least, articulate the character of their disagreement. To this extent, the choice of an ultimate partition (or a basic partition) can be brought under critical control even though the issues under dispute need not concern a question as to what is true.[4]

I contend that we should not recognize as potential answers to the election question that candidate A will win, that candidate B will win or that candidate C will win without also allowing as potential answers suspension of judgment between any pair or even all three. Philosophers tend to think of suspense or skepticism as an all or nothing affair. Either one suspends judgment between all elements of the ultimate partition or adopts one of them. But the tensions between belief and doubt are more nuanced than the aficionados of the battle between skepticism and opinionation would lead you to think. If someone insists that definite conclusions are to be recommended over suspense, that person should be required to show why suspense is inferior with respect to the goals of the inquiry and, if it is inferior, why some partial skepticism reflecting doubt between elements of some subset of the ultimate partition is not better than opinionation. Ruling out all or merely some forms of suspense as options by stipulation does not meet this demand.

Throughout this discussion, I have assumed that the basic partition U_{LK} and, hence, the ultimate partition U_K are finite. This assumption will continue to hold through Chapter 5. In Chapter 6, a discussion of how to extend the proposals made previously to infinite partitions will be presented.

I understand the choice of an ultimate and basic partition by an inquirer in a given situation as part of the task of abduction in an understanding of abduction that seems to me to conform reasonably well to Peirce's ideas.

---

[4] As I understand Peirce's pragmatism, there is no space of conceptually maximal belief-states unless such states are equated with a budget of problems of interest to an inquirer, i.e. to the inquirer's demands for information. The choice of a set of maximal belief-states, whether these are restricted to maximal extensions of the current belief-state or of some minimal belief-state is, in this respect, a pragmatic issue concerning the inquirer's interests and goals as well as a doxastic one concerning the inquirer's beliefs.

Cognitive Decisions

Many philosophers and computer scientists have understood Peirce's notion of "abduction" differently than I do. Abduction is inference to the best explanation. Peirce's writings from the 1860s, 1970s and 1980s do, indeed, afford textual support for such an interpretation of his conception of hypothetic inference. At the same time, however, he apparently thought of hypothetic inference as engaged in the task of proposing conjectures for testing—a quite different task from testing conjectures and concluding that some are to be eliminated. Drawing inductive inferences fulfills the latter task but not the former.

Around 1902, Peirce explicitly acknowledged that his vision of hypothetic inference (then rebaptized "abduction") should not be "the reasoning by which we are led to adopt a hypothesis". The conclusion of an abductive "inference" is "in the interrogative". It asks whether the conjecture (= the conclusion) is true or false but does not adopt the conclusion as true. Peirce confessed that in his previous work he had confused such conjecturing with adopting a hypothesis as a settled conclusion. He blamed his confusion on his well-known early obsession with trying to provide a formal contrast between hypothesis and induction in terms of different permutations of premisses and conclusions of syllogisms (see Peirce, CP.2.102).

Many contemporary authors have perpetuated the terminological practice that Peirce abandoned without attending to his reasons for doing so. Unlike Peirce, they either explicitly (as in the case of Popper) or tacitly deny the legitimacy of induction as leading to the adoption of a potential answer as the settled answer to a question at the termination of inquiry. Indeed, Popper's anti-inductivism is best understood as recommending conjecturing and testing *without* refutation. Popper's words to the contrary notwithstanding, experiments do not, in general, warrant the rejection of any conjecture. The truth of the reports of outcomes of experiments does not entail the falsity of allegedly refuted conjectures on deductive grounds. Others like Quine and Ullian (1970, pp. 58–9) see induction to be a species of abduction or hypothesis where the latter is the "framing of hypothesis" because if it were true, it would explain some things that the inquirer already believes (p. 43). One cannot be sure whether Quine and Ullian reject induction as a way of fixing new beliefs by construing the term 'induction' as singling out certain ways of forming conjectures or whether they, like Peirce confessed his earlier self to have been, are confusing conjecturing with coming to fully believe and taking to be settled by an ampliative inference. I do not mean to be engaged here in logomachy. The issues under discussion concern the presuppositions of certain terminological practices rather than terminology itself.

2.3. Potential Contractions

The topic of the current essay is not inductive expansion. Deciding how to contract given that we are to remove some specific sentence h from K[5] is another kind of decision problem.

Deciding how to expand and how to contract are not totally disconnected topics. The range of contraction strategies for removing h from K is determined by the agent's problem in a manner dual to the way the range of expansion strategies is determined by the question under study in the case of inductive expansion. Potential contractions are determined by a *dual ultimate partition* in a manner similar to the way potential expansions are generated by the ultimate partition.

Suppose that the potential contraction strategies were constrained only by the inquirer's conceptual framework or, perhaps, by the resources of a language L used to represent potential states of full belief. Consider, in particular, the set $\{W/P_K\} = I_K$. These are maximally consistent potential corpora in L *incompatible* with K. If no restrictions other than linguistic ones are imposed on the potential contractions, the intersection of K with the intersection of any subset of $\{W/P_K\}$ qualifies as a potential contraction.

In particular suspending judgment between all elements of W qualifies as a potential contraction. Let the set S be $\{W/P_K\}$.

---

[5] The question of how to contract by removing h from K is always parasitic on some prior determination that h is to be removed. In 1.6, the considerations relevant to determining whether h is to be removed in belief change were sketched. Section 1.7 addressed the question of removing h in the context of suppositional reasoning.

Cognitive Decisions

Intersecting K with the intersection of an arbitrary subset S of $\{W/P_K\}$ is no more acceptable as a potential contraction than taking the deductive closure of the union of K with the union of an arbitrary subset T of P_K is acceptable as a potential expansion.

Suppose, for example, that in attempting to predict who will win the election discussed in 2.2, X had sufficient warrant to become convinced that A will win. A later poll, however, confounded X's expectations. The poll testified to a last minute decline in A's support and surge in support for B. Such polls are not inconsistent with X's conviction that A will win but they are inexplicable on the assumption that he will. The polls might warrant X's opening up X's mind to give a hearing to the possibility that B might win. X had good reason to open X's mind by giving up B will not win.

What should X's space of potential contractions be in this case? To use the intersection with K of the intersection of S for any $S \subseteq \{W/P_K\}$ where L is a fairly rich language would be absurd. Contracting to maximal ignorance would be a potential contraction. So would suspending judgment between A's running and B's running while El Niño is active and Vesuvius begins erupting again as well as suspending judgment between A's running and B's running while El Niño and Vesuvius remain inactive.

Borrowing a leaf from what has been said about expansion, in contraction the inquirer is seeking to settle some issue. As the inquiry progresses, the agent X's belief-state will be altered. Some part of the information X might consider to be a complete answer will be given and this will change the set of potential answers left as yet unsettled. Nonetheless, the larger question, the problematic or the research program might remain more or less the same. To the extent that the inquirer X has articulated the problem, it may be characterizable by specifying an ultimate partition U_{LK} relative to a minimal corpus LK. In 2.2, this potential corpus was called *basic* in the context of the inquiry being conducted. In that setting, U_{LK} together with K determined the set U_K that constituted the ultimate partition for K and thereby determined the potential expansions of U_k. The same basic partition may likewise determine the potential contractions of K in the context of the given inquiry.

Let $U_K^* = \{U_{LK}/U_K\}$ be *dual ultimate partition* determined by U_{LK} and K.

Let $S \subseteq U_K^*$. The intersection of K with the intersection of the elements of S is a *potential contraction* of K.

In the election example, the corpus from which contraction is undertaken is K_1. LK could be identified with K and U_{LK} could be equated with U_K. The significance of this stance would be that the inquirer X understands his investigation as having identified as strongest consistent potential answers to the question under study the elements of the ultimate partition relative to U_K. In K_1, however, the question raised has been answered by ruling out all but one element of U_K. That element is the claim that A will win the election. It is the sole member of U_{K1}. If X judges that X must remove the claim that B will lose from K_1 while remaining engaged with the question characterized by U_K, X will rule out in advance any contraction of K_1 that requires giving up information in K and will regard strongest potential contractions to be intersections of K_1 with $\{U_K/U_{K1}\}$.

K entails that exactly one element of U_K is true. This consequence is the *presupposition* of the question for which the members of U_K are the strongest consistent potential answers. Thus, the minimal belief state **LK** or minimal corpus LK represents the minimal presuppositions that are held fixed as long as the question is being investigated. This does not mean that LK is immune to modification. But to contract LK is one way to change the question under investigation—the other being to refine or coarsen the elements of U_{LK}. One can alter LK as would often be done in inquiry. But doing so will entail modifying the class of relevant answers including those that remain a serious possibility at the current stage of inquiry and those that have been ruled out.

Among the potential contractions of K_1 are the following:

1. Suspense as to whether A or B will win.
2. Suspense as to whether A or C will win.
3. Suspense as to whether A or B or C will win.

Because the minimal corpus is K, contracting to suspense between the contents of 3 and its negation is not a potential contraction. It is a presupposition of the inquiry that one of these three candidates will win. That presupposition can be revised (without changing the state of full belief K_1). This could be done in any number of ways. Suppose it is done, for the sake of illustration, by suspending judgment between 3 and its negation. The minimal corpus could then be the truths of logic, mathematics and whatever conceptual necessities are countenanced. The basic partition could then be A will win, B will win, C will win, none of the above. "None of the above" might be refined in many ways. How all of this is sorted out will determine the potential contractions of K pertinent to the inquiry being undertaken.

Potential contractions of K_1 are one thing. Potential contractions removing the claim that B will not win are another. In our example where $K = LK$, the potential contractions removing B will not win are suspending judgment between A and B and suspending judgment between A, B and C. Suspense between A and C will not do the trick.

It should now be clear that whatever slack there may be in the inquirer's choice of a basic partition or ultimate partition, thinking of the basic partition as the set of possible worlds could be very misleading.

X might conceivably move to a position of suspense as to whether A will win or B will win. Perhaps, X might move to a position of suspense as to whether A will win, B will win or C will win. X may regard suspension of judgment between the prospect of A winning, B winning and C winning and none of them winning as a potential contraction. He could do so by equating the minimal corpus LK with the urcorpus UK of logical, mathematical, and conceptual truths. This is what I tended to do in Levi, 1980, p. 7. But X need not be obliged to do this. Indeed, the presuppositions of an inquiry tend to be far more substantial than truths of logic, mathematics or conceptual necessity.[6]

---

[6] One setting in which minimal contractions seem useful is in the analysis of future-indicative "if" sentences. In such cases, it seems that the suppositional reasoning expressed is prohibited from removing any belief about events occurring at the time of utterance or previous to that time. If this view (suggested by V. Dudman, 1984) is an accurate reflection of English usage, then in those settings where future indicatives are used in this way LK includes the convictions about events occurring in the past and present (as well as theories and generalizations) that remain in the suppositional corpus. Notice

Nor is X required to recognize as a potential contraction relevant to his problem, suspending judgment between A's winning and B's winning while El Niño is active and a volcano erupts in Hawaii. The potential contractions are restricted to matters that are relevant to the inquiry. Taking W to be the ultimate partition seems absurd.

In the general case, consider the cells in $U_K^* = \{U_{LK}/U_K\}$. These are represented by sentences in U_{LK}^* incompatible with K. Moreover, these cells represent the strongest hypotheses given the demands of the inquirer's problem incompatible with K. U_K^* is the *dual ultimate partition* relative to K and U_{LK}. The set of potential contractions of K under consideration may now be represented in the following way.

A *potential contraction of* K *relative to* U_K^* is representable by the corpus that is the intersection of K with the intersection of some subset of U_K^*. Potential contractions that replace U_K^* by $\{W/P_K\}$ in the definitions that follow constitute a special case of the proposal made here when $U_K^* = \{W/P_K\}$.

A *potential contraction of* K *removing h relative to* U_K^* is a potential contraction of K that is obtained by intersecting K with a subset of U_K^* containing at least one element of U_K^* that implies $\sim$h if such exists. Otherwise it is K.

Clearly contraction of K removing h will be successful (i.e. non-degenerate) only if U_K^* is sufficiently fine-grained to contain at least one cell implying $\sim$h. This is not a serious restriction, however, since we may expect that no one would contemplate removing h from K in earnest unless he was using a dual ultimate partition that was sufficiently fine-grained to have this effect.

---

that sentences in LK are immune to removal by contraction as long as LK remains fixed. In this sense, the deliberating agent is prohibited from supposing that LK contains error. But I am not suggesting that the deliberating agent misunderstands or fails to entertain the conjectures to that effect. LK does not demarcate a realm of conceptual possibility from items that are not entertainable. In a given context, the interests of an agent engaged in supposition are focused in certain directions and not others. Because of those interests, the agent *refuses* to entertain removal of certain convictions from the belief-state even though such removal is conceptually entertainable. LK serves to fix the boundary between those items that are entertainably removable from K given the inquirer's interests and those that are not. Of course, if my interlocutor insists on entertaining a claim I do not wish to entertain and I wish to engage in joint deliberation with him, I may have to "contract" my LK so as to render his claim entertainable by my lights.

Cognitive Decisions

We may go even further and assume that a dual ultimate partition U_K^* is *suppositionally decisive* with respect to sentences eligible for removal from K if and only if the following holds:

> Given any sentence h in L eligible for consideration as an item to be removed from K, all cells in U_K^* either entail h or entail $\sim$h.

In general, the domain of inputs for contraction and the dual ultimate partition will be assumed to satisfy the condition of suppositional decisiveness. All definitions used subsequently will be based on this assumption whether the contraction removing h is for the sake of the argument or constitutes a genuine belief change.

> A *maxichoice contraction of* K *relative to* U_K^* is the intersection (or meet) of K with a single element of U_K^*.

In the election example where LK is K and K is K_1, intersecting K_1 with "B will win" or with "C will win" is a maxichoice contraction.

> A *maxichoice contraction of* K *removing* h *relative to* U_K^* is the intersection of K with a single element of U_K^* that entails $\sim$h.

Using the same notational shifts as before, intersecting K_1 with "B will win" is a maxichoice contraction removing "B will not win". Intersecting K with "C will win" is not.

> A *saturatable contraction of* K *removing* h *relative to* U_K^* is the intersection of a maxichoice contraction of K removing h relative to U_K^* with the intersection of a set of elements of U_K^* none of which entail $\sim$h.

Intersecting K_1 with "either B will win or C will win" is a saturatable contraction removing "A will win" that is not maxichoice.

Unlike the case with maxichoice contraction, saturatable contraction is defined only for contractions removing some specific sentence from K. However, that is sufficient to provide us with a means for characterizing all potential contractions that should be optional for the inquirer concerned to remove h from K relative to U_K^*, i.e. relative to K and U_{LK}.

Cognitive Decisions

Potential contraction condition: Every potential contraction of K removing h relative to U_K^* is the intersection of a subset of saturatable contractions of K removing h relative to U_K^*.

I take the position that no potential contraction removing h relative to U_K^* should be eliminated as a candidate for choice as the recommended contraction removing h unless it is shown to be inadmissible or suboptimal for choice among all potential contractions removing h relative to the goals of the inquiring agent. Thus, intersecting K_1 with B will win or C will win ought not to be ruled out in advance of showing that contraction of this sort is suboptimal with respect to the goals of contraction. This substantive prescription is advanced in the same spirit as is the requirement that if h is a potential expansion of K qualifying as a potential answer and f is another, adding h or f is a third.

2.4. Partial Meet Contractions

The set of *partial meet contractions* of K removing h relative to U_K^* is, in general, a proper subset of the potential contractions of K removing h relative to U_K^*. Such partial meet contractions are intersections of subsets of maxichoice contractions removing h from K relative to U_K^*. In the AGM account of contraction, the only potential contractions countenanced are the partial meet contractions. This stands in violation of the potential contraction condition.[7]

Ruling out contractions that are not partial meet contractions has been defended on the grounds that it guarantees satisfaction of the Recovery Postulate for contraction. This strategy may appear very attractive at first glance. But the appeal to postulates that seem intuitively compelling at first blush is a risky business. In the case of Recovery, the plausibility of the postulate is highly doubtful as many proffered counter-instances suggest.

Consider, for example, a situation where it is believed that Jones tested HIV positive, received a drug treatment and subsequently

---

[7] Makinson (1987) calls contractions that are not partial meet contractions *withdrawals*.

Cognitive Decisions

showed HIV negative. It is also believed that a very high percentage just short of 100 per cent of those who initially test positive, receive drug treatment and are tested again show HIV negative. Contract the corpus by giving up "Jones received the drug treatment." Casting doubt on Jones's receipt of the treatment would not cast doubt on his having tested HIV positive unless it is initially believed that almost everyone in Jones's circumstances as known to the inquirer receives treatment for Aids upon testing positive. Nor will it cast doubt on the claim that nearly everyone who receives the treatment tests negative the second time. But the judgment that Jones showed HIV negative later on would be abandoned because the conviction that Jones was tested would be given up.

Restoring the judgment that Jones received the drug treatment would not deductively entail that Jones subsequently showed HIV negative. It would have done so had the inquirer believed initially that the drug treatment has a surefire disposition to eliminate the HIV virus. According to the example, however, all that is believed is that the drug treatment is followed by cure in the sense of showing negative on the test in some percentage of cases less than 100 per cent. The expansion of the contraction does not then logically entail that the test shows negative. The Recovery Condition is, therefore, violated (see Levi, 1991, pp. 134–5 for a related illustration). According to the expansion of the contraction, it is seriously possible though improbable that Jones would have a positive reaction to the second HIV test.

On a more theoretical level, the merits of postulates for contraction ought to be scrutinized from a decision-theoretic viewpoint. If a decision-maker faces a set **O** of available options and *all* of the options in **O** are weakly ordered with respect to how well they promote the agent's goals and values, the agent is obliged to restrict choice to one of the optimal options according to that weak ordering. (An option is optimal if it is weakly preferred to every other option in **O**.) If more than one option is optimal, the decision-maker *may* invoke a secondary criterion to decide between the optimal options.

Contraction removing h from K is a decision problem. No potential contraction available as an option to the inquirer should be ruled

Cognitive Decisions

out until it has been shown to be inferior given the goals of efforts to remove h from K.

Such an approach takes a dim view of stipulating that certain available options (potential contraction strategies) be ruled out of court without showing that they are suboptimal means for promoting the goals of contraction.

It may, perhaps, be countered that relativizing contraction to dual ultimate partitions (that is to say, minimal belief-states, basic partitions and current belief-states) is itself a way of restricting the set of potential contraction strategies. The point is well taken. The appeal to a minimal belief-state LK stipulates that in the setting of the inquiry or problematic under consideration, no doubt will be registered concerning any consequence of LK. And the basic partition U_{LK} stipulates that discriminations that cannot be captured within the framework of that partition are not relevant to the inquiry.

Such relativization is unavoidable as long as we are prepared to characterize a space of potential states of full belief K that are representable by deductively closed sets of sentences in a given regimented propositional or first-order language L. According to this approach, the logical truths will be included in every potential corpus (deductively closed set) and, hence, will be immune to contraction. Someone might wish to adopt as LK the smallest deductively closed set in L. And the elements of U_{LK} might be the maximally consistent expansions of LK, i.e. the elements of W.

Even so, it may be complained that the view I have advanced here allows stronger restrictions on the potential contractions than that they be potential states of full belief. LK may be stronger than UK and the elements of U_{LK} may be more coarse-grained than elements of W.

The requirement that a contraction removing h should be a partial meet contraction is more restrictive than this. As I have just pointed out, advocates of partial meet contraction and recovery take for granted that we are given a minimal belief-state and a framework identifying most fine-grained discriminations. They presuppose, after all the availability of maxichoice contractions. Whether they insist that LK and U_{LK} represent the features of some conceptual

63

Cognitive Decisions

framework or whether they think, as I do, that they represent features of the demands for information of the inquirer or inquirers engaged in the given deliberation—demands that may be altered in the course of inquiry itself, advocates of partial meet contraction and Recovery must say that regardless of the LK and U_{LK} that are adopted, the potential contractions removing h from K cannot consist of all contractions removing h from K generated by U_K^*. No matter what results ensue Recovery must be satisfied.

This restriction is far more rigid than relativization to LK and U_{LK}. The latter factors can be modified when justifiably challenged. Champions of Recovery insist that no matter how LK and U_{LK} are chosen, the potential contractions determined by these factors and K must be partial meet contractions. There is no challenge that will lead them to reconsider the requirement.

As in the case of expansion, failure to consider all potential contractions amounts to failure to entertain certain types of skeptical responses that might be appropriate in the context. In particular, failure of Recovery, which is a species of partial skepticism, is ruled out. The appropriate level of opinionation ought not to be legislated by stipulating which of the meets of saturatable contractions are optional and which are not.

The Recovery Condition might, perhaps, be defended by argument rather than stipulation. One might show that contraction strategies violating Recovery are less efficient means for realizing the goals of contraction (whatever these are taken to be) than contraction strategies that satisfy Recovery. This approach concedes, however, that contractions that are not partial meets are genuinely options available for choice when deliberating concerning how to contract so as to remove h from K. It seeks to show that there are always better options that obey Recovery. To stipulate that the options must be partial meet contractions at the very outset is to stipulate without argument that options that do not meet this requirement are non-starters.

I do not claim thus far to have refuted the Recovery Condition. Reasons for rejecting it as untenable will be offered subsequently. My point right now is to rebut a misguided vision of what constitutes a

Cognitive Decisions

potential contraction removing h from K that mandates conformity with Recovery Condition.

To illustrate the use of dual ultimate partitions, consider a corpus K that contains the claim E that a coin is tossed near the surface at time t and the claim H that the coin lands heads at that time. K contains two general claims: C asserts that the coin lands on the surface when and only when it is tossed near the surface. C′ asserts that the coin lands on the surface if and only if it lands heads or lands tails but not both. Let LK imply the "modeling assumptions" C and C′. K also contains the claim O that the coin lands on the surface at time t. The contraction of K contemplated is removing E.

Consider the following dual ultimate partition:

U_K^*: E&T = the coin is tossed at t and lands tails but not heads.
∼E&∼O = the coin is not tossed at t and does not land on the surface = ∼E&∼H&∼T.[8]

Relative to the modeling assumptions in LK, these items are pairwise incompatible and together with E&H are exhaustive.

Relative to U_K^*, the intersection of K with the deductive consequences of {∼E&∼O} is the only maxichoice contraction removing E from K.

U_K^* is quite coarse-grained. One way to fine-grain is to refine ∼O into, say, O_1 = the coin melts, O_2 = the coin is exchanged for a chocolate candy, and O_3 = fails to land on the surface in some other way. Such refinement need not call for modifying LK. But it would allow for more maxichoice contractions removing E.

A banal but more interesting possibility is that LK is weakened by replacing C′ with C″ = the coin lands on the surface if and only if it lands heads, tails or on its edge. If the dual ultimate partition is then refined to allow for the claim G = that the coin lands on its edge at t, we can obtain three saturatable contractions that are not maxichoice.

---

[8] (Notice that the modeling assumptions C and C′ entailed by LK imply that E&∼H&∼T is false. E&∼ H&∼T is equivalent to the claim that the coin is tossed at t, and lands neither tails nor heads (i.e. does not land on the surface) or E&∼O. So E&∼O is not a member of the basic partition relative to LK and, hence, cannot be part of the ultimate partition relative to LK and K.)

65

Cognitive Decisions

Observe, however, that K still is assumed to entail C' so that adopting a saturatable contraction allowing for the possibility that the coin lands on its edge would call for questioning C' even if C and C" remain secure. Such a contraction could not then be ruled out in virtue of the stipulated constraints on LK due to modeling assumptions. It might be ruled out, however, on the grounds that the loss of informational value incurred would be too great to be borne. Or the loss of informational value incurred by countenancing the possibility may be regarded as sufficiently small to warrant contracting in a way that gives up C'.

It is arguable that intersections of sets of saturatable but not maxichoice contractions removing h are presystematically recommended over intersections of some sets of maxichoice contractions removing h. Consider, for example, the coin-tossing example as initially specified. The only maxichoice contraction removing E is the intersection of K with {~E&~O}. This contraction suspends judgment between "the coin was not tossed and did not land" and "the coin was tossed and landed heads."

Recommending this contraction goes against the grain and decisively so. Let the inquirer move to a position of suspense as to whether the coin was tossed. From that agnostic perspective, it is a serious possibility that the coin was not tossed and did not land. It is also a serious possibility that the coin was tossed and landed heads. Finally, knowing the behavior of normal coins, the inquirer will recognize as a serious possibility that the coin was tossed and landed tails. The inquirer could, of course, rule out that latter hypothesis if he or she initially was convinced that the coin was two-headed. Being certain that the coin is fair and normal, the sensible inquirer would suspend judgment between the coin was not tossed and did not land, the coin was tossed and landed heads and the coin was tossed and landed tails. This contraction is saturatable but not maxichoice. Good sense thus leads to violating the dictates of Recovery.

This counter-instance to the Recovery Postulate is by no means exceptional. Any belief state relative to which the outcome of an experiment is known but where general experiments of the given

Cognitive Decisions

kind can yield one of several different types of outcome may serve to undermine confidence in the Recovery Postulate.

I concede that the appeal to presystematic judgment or intuition I have invoked here ought not to be the sole basis for abandoning Recovery. In spite of the fact that the intuition is as robust as they come, no intuition should suffice as proof. But I think it is fair to appeal to the intuition to call into question the insistence on Recovery and the rejection of contractions that are not partial meet contractions as candidates for consideration. The rest of the case against Recovery will then be grounded on an examination of the way contraction strategies ought to be evaluated in a problem where K is to be contracted by removing h relative to U_K^* with respect to the goals of contraction.

I have been arguing that the set of available strategies for contracting K by removing h relative to U_K^* should consist of all potential contractions removing h from K satisfying the Potential Contraction Condition relative to U_K^* and LK as defined in section 2.3. Apologists for the Recovery Postulate have followed Alchourrón, Gärdenfors and Makinson (1985) in restricting the options for contraction to a proper subset of such potential contractions—namely, the partial meet contractions (relative to U_K^*) and proceeding to evaluate the surviving partial meet contractions. This procedure is unacceptable from a decision-theoretic point of view because it does not establish the suboptimality of the potential contractions that are not partial meet contractions among *all* potential contractions with respect to the goals of contraction.

The same complaint should be directed against other approaches to evaluating contraction strategies. In Chapter 7, base contraction will be discussed from this point of view. Even though base contraction can provide for failures of Recovery, it often does so by restricting the options for contraction to a proper subset of the potential contractions as defined here. This practice is just as objectionable as restricting the options for contraction to partial meet contractions.

Thus, we return to the thesis advanced at the end of 2.3. The options for contraction available to the inquirer relative to K and U_K^* constitute the set characterized by the Potential Contraction Condition.

2.5. The Commensuration Requirement

In Levi, 1991, p. 65 (see also Levi, 1980, chs. 2–3), I took the position that every *legitimate* change of belief state from initial state K_1 to K_2 should be decomposable into a sequence of contractions and expansions each of which is *legitimate*. This *commensuration requirement* implies that every justification of a change in state of full belief should be a justification of an expansion or of a contraction. The only kind of changes that are not expansions or contractions are *replacements* where K_1 entails that h and K_2 entails that $\sim$ h and *residual shifts* where K_1 entails that h but leaves the issue of the truth of g open while K_2 leaves h open while entailing that g. Both of these transformations are decomposable into sequences of contractions and expansions. That is the content of the (almost trivial) *commensurability thesis* (Levi, 1991, p. 65).[9] The (non-trivial) commensuration requirement holds that no residual shift or replacement is justifiable unless it is decomposable into a sequence of contractions and expansions (in some order or other) each step of which is legitimate.

Why should the commensuration requirement be respected? I claim that an answer is to be found in referring to the *common* features of the goals that *ought* to be pursued in justifying changes in full belief.

The commensuration requirement, therefore, is not dictated by principles of rational decision-making alone. It presupposes endorsement of a substantive view of what the common features of the aims of inquiries concerned to justify changes in belief ought to be.

There is no doubt that scientists and other inquirers seek to solve different kinds of problems and settle different kinds of issues. The goals of inquiry are in this sense as diverse as the problems that occasion inquiry. There is no single aim that all inquirers strive to realize in justifying changes in their views. This must be so if for no other reason than the subject matter of inquiries are so diverse.

---

[9] The commensurability thesis is satisfied as long as the conceptual framework K is a Boolean algebra as I am supposing here.

Cognitive Decisions

Even so, there may be some common features that the goals of all properly conducted inquiries share in common. It may be the case that rational pursuit of goals sharing such features entails endorsement of methodologies for fixing beliefs of certain kinds rather than others.

Most authors who agree that beliefs are to be justified by showing how well they satisfy certain goals are skeptical of there being any common features that could serve as the basis for a sensible methodology for fixing beliefs as contrasted with engaging in other practical deliberation. According to such thinkers, inquirers seek to justify their beliefs by way of reference to goals that focus on moral, political, theoretical, economic, prudential and aesthetic considerations. Agents sometimes fix their beliefs in certain ways because doing so will promote their personal interests or the interests of the group they serve. Relative to the goals they seek to promote, such agents may sometimes succeed in justifying their beliefs in a rationally coherent fashion. In this respect, inquiry displays the same kind of rationality as practical deliberation. According to this view, there are no distinctively cognitive values to pursue and even if there were, there is no basis for recommending them over other kinds of values.

I contend that inquirers engaged in inquiries that issue in change of view ought to be concerned with seeking new important, error-free information. The quest for such replacement of doubt by true belief is the common feature that I claim ought to be a feature of every serious effort to change beliefs. To endorse this view of the kinds of goals that inquiries aimed at fixing beliefs ought to pursue is to advocate the *autonomy* of inquiry. Efforts to fix belief ought not to be subordinated to the moral, political, economic, aesthetic or prudential interests of "use and enjoyment" as Dewey insisted. Seeking new, important, error-free information is a *cognitive* goal.

I cannot and shall not pretend to be able to demonstrate that one should pursue autonomous cognitive goals in fixing belief. The best defense that can be offered is an exploration of the ramifications of taking the pursuit seriously. And one of the ramifications is endorsement of the commensuration requirement.

Cognitive Decisions

How might one violate the commensuration requirement? By justifying a change in state of full belief that is neither an expansion nor a contraction relative to one's goals.

Replacement is one such kind of violation. In replacement, the inquirer shifts from K_1 to K_2 where K_1 contains h and K_2 contains $\sim$h for some sentence in L. According to the view I favor, such a replacement is never justifiable. By hypothesis, the inquirer is committed initially to the truth of every claim in K_1. To shift to K_2 is to deliberately change one's commitments so that one comes to fully believe what one initially judged to be false. From the prior point of view relative to which the inquirer justifies the change, such a shift cannot be justified *if the inquirer is concerned to avoid error*. Such a shift deliberately replaces sure truth with certain error. I claim that such a shift is illegitimate because inquirers should seek to avoid error in justifying changes in full belief (Levi, 1980, ch. 3; 1991, ch. 4).

There are a great many authors who clearly wish to discount a concern to avoid error as a goal of inquiry. My objection to the legitimacy of replacement will not count with them. All I am claiming now is that those who share the view that one ought to avoid error in changing one's full beliefs will have good reason to deny that replacement is ever justifiable.

The other way to violate the commensurability requirement is by changing from K_1 to K_2 where the latter is a *residual shift* from the former. From the initial point of view relative to K_1 no hypothesis is imported that is certainly false. But hypotheses that might from that point of view be false are imported while *at the same time* hypotheses that are certainly true from that point of view are relinquished.

Now an inquiring agent, so I claim, can be justified from the agent's initial point of view in adding some hypothesis that might be false provided that the agent has an incentive for incurring the risk of error. I contend that the incentive is to be found in the *addition in valuable new information* promised by adding the new hypothesis. In a residual shift, however, such an addition in new information is accompanied by a *loss* of information that, from the initial point of view, is certainly true. There is no logical obstacle to adding the new information without incurring the loss of old information as in an expansion. But the incentive to risk error would be greater if one added the new information without giving up information as well.

Perhaps, the promise of valuable new information compensates for the risk of error incurred in adding the new information. This would justify an expansion—not a residual shift. Perhaps, also, there is a way to justify surrendering the information to be given up in a contraction. If so, that would be a good reason for implementing a contraction. Thus, justifying a residual shift appears to decompose into a justification for an expansion and a justification for a contraction.

To sum up, the commensuration requirement implies that neither replacement nor residual shift can be justified unless decomposed into a sequence of justified contractions and expansions. I have just argued that if inquirers should be concerned with justifying changes in belief aimed at acquiring new error-free information, neither replacement nor residual shift is directly justifiable. Thus, the commensuration requirement is supported by the vision of inquiry as being aimed at obtaining new error-free information.

This argument for the commensuration requirement might seem to support the conclusion that contraction is also never to be justified. To be sure, contraction never incurs a risk of error from the point of view of the agent prior to contraction. Every item in K_1 is judged true. As long as no new item is added to K_1 there is no risk of error from that quarter. And removing sentences from K_1 cannot incur error from the inquirer's point of view. What such removal does is reduce the information judged to be true with certainty. Insofar as part of the aim is to add new information, contraction appears to be counterproductive.

I have argued elsewhere (Levi, 1980a, ch. 3 and 1991, ch. 4. See also Chapter 1.) that sometimes inquirers do legitimately contract. There are two contexts in which this is so.

Sometimes an inquirer inadvertently expands into inconsistency and is compelled to contract because his or her belief-state can no longer serve to distinguish between what is possibly true and not possibly true. This can happen when the inquirer legitimately relies on the testimony of experts or reliable witnesses or trusts the testimony of his or her senses aided by reliable instruments of observation and measurement. Yet, the results of relying on such trustworthy oracles contradict what the inquirer initially takes for granted.

In such cases, there is no need to justify incurring a loss of information. Contraction is coerced if one is to avoid what Gärdenfors (1988) called "epistemic hell". In my previous discussions I took the challenge to be whether to give up the new information h that injected inconsistency, the information ~h in the initial corpus, or both. I described the problem as one of deciding what to remove in order to escape from inconsistency.

In taking the task to be to decide what to remove, I appreciated that the inquirer could not appeal to the total information available to him in epistemic hell. Yet, I took the challenge to be to decide how to retreat from epistemic hell. In Levi, 1980a ch. 3 and 1991, ch. 4, I explored various stratagems for bypassing this problem.

Erik Olsson (2003) has rightly chided me for the inadequacy of the maneuvers I deployed. I now think that the inquirer should be regarded as committed beforehand to contingency plans for addressing inadvertent expansion into inconsistency so that the retreat from inconsistency should be regarded as a product of choices made (commitments undertaken) prior to such expansion (Levi, 2003). I continue to think that the account of what to remove to retreat from inconsistency that I offered before may remain substantially the same. The issue is whether to remove the oracular testimony, the background information that conflicts with it, or both. That answer is found in evaluations of relative losses of valuable information incurred. The only difference is that these evaluations are of contingency plans drawn up before making observations or consulting experts when the inquirer is not in epistemic hell. Consequently, inadvertent expansion into inconsistency and subsequent contraction remain transformations that are legitimated by the adoption of legitimate programs for routine decision-making. The commensuration requirement is, in this sense, obeyed.

On other occasions, agents may deliberately contract K_1 and incur the loss of information because doing so allows them to give a serious hearing to some important conjecture without begging the question either in favor of or against the conjecture or current doctrine. Such deliberate contraction offers some prospect that through further inquiry new information will be added (and added legitimately) that will yield more valuable information than is available in K_1 (Levi, 1991, ch. 4). Deliberate contraction, like coerced contraction, is consonant with the commensuration requirement.

To sum this up, the importance of the commensuration requirement from my point of view derives from its connection to the thesis that the common features of the aims of inquiry relevant to the justification of changes in states of full belief ought to be to seek error-free and valuable information. If one eschews a concern with providing an account of how changes in states of full belief are to be justified or if one thinks that such changes are justified relative to goals that do not involve a concern to avoid error, the commensuration requirement may not be convincing. The conception of the aims of inquiry and its ramifications for a normative methodology to which I am gesturing is one I have been elaborating starting in the 1960s. Those who do not endorse this conception may agree with the construal of the "Levi Identity" as the nearly trivial commensurability thesis but reject the "Levi Identity" construed as the substantive commensuration requirement.

2.6. Options in Cognitive Decision-Making

Not all expansion is deliberate. Acquiring new information by consulting witnesses or through observation may be deliberate in the sense that the inquirer may deliberately decide to consult the witness or expert or to take a look. But the formation of a new belief is a response to the testimony whether it is from the senses or witnesses. It is not inference and it is not by choice.

Nonetheless, some expansion is deliberate. Inquirers weigh evidence when choosing between conjectures whether these conjectures are grand theories, estimates of parameters of interest, predictions of some future event and the like. In many such cases, inquirers weigh

Cognitive Decisions

all the evidence and make a decision on the evidence as to which of rival conjectures to endorse. Such deliberate or inductive expansion is quite different from following a program that commits the inquirer before initiating the program to respond to inputs by forming new beliefs. In the latter case, there is no reasoning from premises to a conclusion. Deliberate expansion requires choosing the best between rival potential answers to a question, solutions to a problem and the like with respect to the goals of the inquiry in the light of these goals and the information available to the inquirer. A deliberate expansion is justified, from the inquirer's point of view, if the recommendation of the expansion is warranted by showing that it is optimal or at least admissible given the aims and goals and the information available to the agent in that context.

Determining which of rival potential contractions removing h from K also involves a choice among rival cognitive policies with respect to cognitive goals. Here the options are choosing which of rival potential contractions to adopt.

Potential expansions of K to be considered as options should take into account the adoption of any expansion that rejects some subset or other of members of the ultimate partition U_K. Potential contractions of K removing h to be considered as options should take into account the adoption of any contraction removing h from K that is the intersection of a set of saturatable contractions removing h relative to the dual ultimate partition U_K^*. In this way, all eligible potential contractions will be considered.

Thus, no deliberate expansion may be justified unless recommended over all potential expansions in the largest domain of potential expansions recognized as relevant according to the ultimate partition and no contraction may be justified unless it is recommended over all potential contractions in the largest domain of potential contractions recognized as relevant according to the dual ultimate partition. If options are to be eliminated, this had better be so because the eliminated options are clearly inferior given the goals of the inquiry.

Both in the context of deliberate expansion and deliberate contraction, a minimal belief state spelling assumptions that in the context are not to be given up and a basic partition specifying how fine-grained the potential answers in the inquiry are allowed to be determines the space of potential expansions and potential contractions relative to the state of full belief. That this is so is not controversial. Controversy arises when one asks whether there is a rationally obligatory standard for determining the minimal belief-state and basic partition or whether features of the context control the choice of these factors.

In my judgment, the inquirer's interests or demands for information control the choice. If controversy or doubt erupts, the inquirers can always modify their views of how fine-grained their discriminations and how rigid their presuppositions should be.

Before turning to an examination of contraction, which is the main topic of this essay, a brief summary of how I think deliberate expansions should be justified will be presented.

Deliberate Expansion 3

3.1. Seek Valuable Information! Shun Error!

In deciding how to expand his or her belief-state, an inquirer ought to seek to obtain new error-free information (Levi, 1967; 1984, ch. 5; 1980a, ch. 2; 1991, ch. 3; 1996). That is to say, all *proximate goals* of specific attempts to justify changes in state of full belief by adopting one of the available expansion strategies generated by an ultimate partition U_K relative to corpus K should share in common a concern to avoid error and to increase valuable information. Of course, the proximate aims of different efforts to expand differ in the kind of information being sought. They may differ with respect to how the importance of different types of information is assessed. And inquirers can disagree about the risks of error that are to be incurred by instituting different changes in point of view. But there are certain features that the proximate goals of all properly conducted inquiries seeking to expand share in common.

By the proximate goals of a decision problem, I mean those value considerations that are relevant to assessing the currently available options as better or worse in reaching a decision as to what to do. The proximate goal of any effort at deliberate expansion should assess each potential expansion strategy with respect to two desiderata:

1. *Avoidance of error.* On the assumption that every consequence of the inquirer's belief-state is true (or that all sentences in K are

Deliberate Expansion

true), the inquirer should be concerned to avoid adding new information that is false. From the point of view of the agent endorsing K, adopting K_h^+ avoids error if and only if h is true. That agent takes for granted that all sentences in K are true so that all sentences in K_h^+ are true if h is true and some are false if h is false.

2. *New valuable information*: The inquirer is concerned to eliminate elements of U_K and to add the result to his state of full belief in order to produce new information of value with respect to the question under investigation.

I claim that the proximate aims of efforts at expansion of states of full belief *should* be to avoid error and to acquire new, valuable information. I do not claim that agents including scientific inquirers always do focus on these two desiderata. Perhaps Peirce is right in claiming that removing doubt is the only common feature of the aims with which agents in general engage in inquiry. Nor do I contend that it would be irrational to pursue different goals in expanding one's state of full belief. Even if everyone seeks to relieve doubt in expansion, the information they seek may be frivolous or unimportant from their point of view; and many agents do not seem to put any priority on avoiding the importation of false belief into their belief-state.

I preach a sermon on epistemology. I advocate a view of what the common features of the aims of inquiry ought to be and explore the methodological ramifications of such a view if these aims are pursued. But I do not claim that the prescriptions I advocate are derived from minimal principles of rational consistency or coherence. Fixing belief in some alternative way need not be irrational even though the goals promoted may be epistemically deplorable.

The concern to avoid error is manifested in an evaluation of the potential answers generated by U_K with respect to the risk of error incurred. Recall that a potential expansion strategy is represented by a corpus K_h^+ where h is a disjunction of a subset of members of U_K. Such an expansion incurs error *from the point of view of the inquiring agent whose state of full belief is represented by* K—i.e. on the assumption

Deliberate Expansion

that the consequences of K are all true—if and only if h is false.[1] As a consequence, the risk or probability of error incurred by adopting that expansion strategy is equal to the degree of credal or belief probability the agent assigns to ∼h relative to the state of full belief represented by K. Let that probability function be $Q_K(.)$.

Another way to understand Q_K is as the value of a function (the inquirer's *confirmational commitment*) from potential corpora to credal probability functions (Levi, 1974, 1980). Confirmational commitments characterize how the inquirer judges potential answers to be probabilistically supported relative to various bodies of information K.

In Levi, 1974, 1980 and 1986, I take the position that judgments of credal probability or probabilistic support are better represented by convex sets of Q-functions. Such convex sets then become values of the functions representing confirmational commitments. For the time being I shall simplify the discussion by assuming that the convex sets are singletons.

Obviously if an inquirer were concerned exclusively with avoiding error, the inquirer would refuse to expand except in the degenerate sense that the agent would expand by adopting the disjunction of all elements of U_K. Relative to K the risk or probability of error then incurred would be set at 0. The inquirer judges this strategy without risk of error on the assumption that every consequence of the inquirer's state of full belief is true. Claims that are not items of the agent's belief-state but are consistent with it are possibly true and possibly false.

If an inquirer is going to expand his or her state of full belief in an ampliative fashion, some risk of error is going to be incurred. To

---

[1] The inquiring agent judges truth "as earnestly and as seriously as can be relative to his evolving doctrine". That is to say, the inquiring agent is committed to the truth of all of his or her current full beliefs and to ruling out as impossible that any one of them is false. This does not preclude others from disagreeing. And it does not preclude the inquiring agent from acknowledging that he or she might have good reason to contract K subsequently by dropping some of his or her current beliefs and after that might acquire reason to replace the dropped beliefs by others incompatible with them. But such revisability or corrigibility in no way undermines the inquirer's assessment of risk of error in the manner sketched in the text. See Levi, 1980a and 1983.

Deliberate Expansion

justify taking on such a risk, the inquirer must have some incentive. According to the conception of the common features of inquiry I am propounding, incentive is to be found in the new information that is to be obtained. Inquiry aims to relieve doubt as Peirce rightly observed. In deciding whether to expand his state of full belief by adding such a claim to the initial state, the agent acquires new information but incurs a risk of error and must balance the benefit of the new information against the risk of error.[2]

Adopting an expansion strategy K_h^+ is a choice that has one of two possible consequences of relevance to the concern to obtain new error-free information:

(a) If h is true, the inquirer has increased the value of the information of the state of full belief K to the value of the information carried by K_h^+ and has done so (on the assumption that no item in K is false) without error.
(b) If h is false, the inquirer has increased the value of the information obtained but has incurred an error in doing so.

Thus, each of the consequences is represented by a two-dimensional vector. The first component $T(h, x)$ specifies whether error was avoided ($x = t$) or incurred ($x = f$) and the second spells out the increment $C(h, x)$ in informational value obtained (which shall be assumed to be the same whether $x = t$ or $x = f$). To evaluate the expansion strategy as compared to others generated by the ultimate

---

[2] Throughout this discussion, I am supposing that the justification of a change in belief-state is to be based on the information available to the inquirer and the goals the inquirer is seeking to promote. From the inquirer's point of view, all propositions that the inquirer fully believes are true are true. It would be incoherent for the inquirer to acknowledge that any one of them is false. The inquirer may coherently acknowledge that he or she might change his or her mind in the future; but from the inquirer's current point of view, such a change of mind will involve an exchange of true information for false. If the inquirer seeks to avoid error in changing his or her state of full belief, he will do so on the assumption that replacing his current belief that h by belief that $\sim$h is to incur an error. If the concern to avoid error is to be consistent with an acknowledgement that it is sometimes legitimate to cease to be certain that h, the concern to avoid error should be restricted to avoiding error at the next change of state. Avoidance of error in subsequent changes should be ignored. (See the discussion of Messianic and secular realism in Levi, 1991, ch. 4.)

Deliberate Expansion

partition U_K, the values of the two components need to be aggregated into a single value $V(h, x)$.

A common approach to addressing the aggregation of several dimensions of value is to identify some quantitative method of evaluating components in each dimension and then taking some weighted average of the values of the components. In our case, we need to assign utilities to avoiding error and incurring it and to obtaining information carrying certain kind of value.

$V(h, x)$ then equals $\alpha T(h, x) + (1 - \alpha)C(h, x)$.

Rehearsing this somewhat more carefully, given the inquirer's initial corpus K and ultimate partition U_K, a potential expansion strategy K_h^+ is restricted to cases where h is a disjunction of some subset of elements of U_K.

Let $x = t$ if and only if all items in K and h are true and $x = f$ if and only if all items in K are true and h is false.

Let $T(h, t) = a$ and $T(h, f) = b$ where $a > b$. $T(h.x)[x = t$ or $x = f]$ is the utility of K_h^+ on the assumption that avoidance of error is the sole concern of the inquirer in expansion.

Let $C(h, t) = C(h, f) =$ the utility of K_h^+ on the assumption that the sole concern of the inquirer in expansion is to maximize informational value.

Let $V(h, x) = \alpha T(h, x) + (1 - \alpha)C(h, x) =$ the utility of K_h^+ on the assumption that the aim of the inquirer in expansion is to obtain new valuable error-free information.

3.2. Undamped Informational Value in Expansion

Assigning utilities to the first component $T(h,x)$ is easy enough. One can assign an arbitrary value a to avoiding error and a value $b < a$ to incurring it. Let $a = 1$ and $b = 0$. In that way, we can represent an inquirer concerned only with avoiding error as evaluating expansion strategies in terms of expected utility by equating expected utility with the probability that h is true. Maximizing expected utility is maximizing $Q_K(h)$ or minimizing the risk of error $Q_K(\sim h)$ as noted before. An inquirer maximizing expected utility where the utility

Deliberate Expansion

function is sensitive to the concern to avoid error alone will fail to reject any item in U_K and as a consequence the expansion strategy to adopt will be to refuse to expand at all. So now we have:

$$T(h, t) = 1 \text{ and } T(h, f) = 0.$$

The problem we need to face concerns the second component. How is the value or utility of information (informational value) to be assessed? The current temporary focus is on the value of information in the context of expansion. But the ultimate target is the value of information in the context of contraction.

The information carried by K_h^+ can be represented by the set of elements of U_K that are *rejected* in expanding K by adding h.

One expansion strategy K_h^+ *carries more information* than another K_g^+ (where g and h represent joins of subsets of U_K) if and only if the set of elements of U_K rejected by expanding by g is a proper subset of the rejection set for the expansion by h.

K_h^+ carries more information than K_g^+ if and only if $K_g^+ \subset K_h^+$. Thus, the concept of one expansion strategy carrying more information than another partially orders the potential expansion strategies generated by U_K.

The *information* carried by a potential expansion strategy is one thing. The *informational value* carried by such a strategy is another. Information carried by potential answers partially orders these answers relative to K. An assessment of informational *value* could (but need not) yield a weak ordering of the potential expansion strategies. If a weak ordering is achieved, all potential expansions are comparable with respect to informational value. Potential expansions that are non-comparable with respect to the information they carry are evaluated with respect to other considerations to achieve such comparability. Considerations of simplicity or explanatory power may be invoked. Sometimes an appeal may be made to conformity to some moral, political or aesthetic requirement. I propose to call the resulting assessment an assessment of *informational value* as long as it extends the partial order with respect to information. Assessments of informational value should be grounded in

Deliberate Expansion

judgments of the information carried. This grounding should satisfy the following condition:

> *Weak Positive Monotonicity*: If K_h^+ carries more information than K_g^+ it carries at least as much informational value.

This condition may be strengthened as follows:

> *Strong Positive Monotonicity*: If K_h^+ carries more information than K_g^+ it carries more informational value.

Advocates of strong positive monotonicity insist that positive increments of information always should yield a positive gain in informational value. Strictly speaking the partial ordering with respect to information is extended or completed only when strong positive monotonicity is satisfied.

Advocates of weak positive monotonicity insist that additional information is sometimes worthless. As just noted, assessments of informational value take into account not only how much information potential expansion strategies carry but also such considerations as the explanatory power, simplicity or other attractive (or unattractive) features of potential expansions.

It is entertainable that a potential expansion that carries more information than another is no improvement with respect to the other desiderata that characterize informational value. In such a case, the stronger, more informative expansion fails to increase informational value.

By way of contrast, suppose that a stronger and, hence, more informative expansion is less attractive with respect to the additional desiderata. For example, stronger potential answers may be complex in ways that deter explanation. Even so, if the inquirer is concerned with obtaining potential answers carrying valuable information and not merely in optimizing with respect to the other desiderata, stronger potential answers should not be ranked inferior to weaker ones with respect to informational value.

The *C*-function should induce a weak ordering of the potential expansion strategies that satisfies weak monotonicity. But it should be more than a weak ordering. I am supposing here that seeking new

Deliberate Expansion

error-free information requires taking risk of error into account. Maximizing expected utility requires, therefore, that the balance between probability of avoiding error and the informational value that compensates for the risk of error incurred can be given in quantitative terms. This calls for a quantitative representation of informational value. This representation should be a real valued function satisfying the weak ordering that is unique up to a positive affine transformation. That is to say, it should be a utility function.

Moreover, the utility function should be bounded from above and from below. Indeed, if the utility representation for avoidance of error takes two values, a and b, such that a > b, it is useful (but not mandatory) to restrict the values for the C-function to the interval from a to b. By adopting this convention, the numerical weight α assigned the T-function attaches the same relative importance to the concern to avoid error as compared to the concern to maximize informational value represented by the C-function regardless of the values assigned to a and b.

Rejecting an element d_i of U_K does not decrease and may increase the informational value of an inquirer's state of information or full belief. Is the increment in informational value obtained the same no matter how many or which other elements of U_K are rejected? Or is there some other relation between the increment and the set of elements of U_K that are also rejected? The issue here concerns the sense in which an inquirer is or should be concerned to obtain new information. The only way to settle this question would be to explore the implications of different proposals. The following assumption (proposed in 1967 in Levi, 1984, ch. 5) works very well in the context of expansion:

> *Constant marginal returns in informational value of rejection*: Let the set of elements S of U_K that are rejected in expanding K be $R \cup \{d_i\}$. The difference between the informational value obtained by rejecting the elements of S and the elements of R is the same no matter which subset of U_K R happens to be as long as it does not contain d_i.

This increment can be characterized by introducing a measure M_K that assigns non-negative values to the elements of U_K summing up

83

Deliberate Expansion

to 1 and such that the M_K-value of a disjunction of elements of U_K is equal to the sum of their M_K-values. The increment in informational value in expanding by adding h to K is the sum of the M_K-values of elements of U_K that are rejected when the expansion by adding h is implemented. That is to say, it is equal to $M_K(\sim h) = 1 - M_K(h) = Cont_K(h)$. I shall call this evaluation of the increment in informational value obtained in expansion an assessment of *increment in undamped informational value*.

In Levi, 1967 I proposed a model of deliberate inductive expansion that was a special instance of one where $C(h, x) = Cont(h)$. In that special case, I required all elements of U_K to be assigned equal M_K-values.

In Levi, 1984, ch. 5 [also first published in 1967], I proposed the condition that $C(h, x) = Cont(h)$. I took note of the fact that the M_K-function has the formal properties of a probability function. However, I explicitly denied that the M_K-function represents the inquirer's degree of belief function or assessment of how well potential expansions are probabilified by the initial corpus K (i.e. by the evidence). The M_K-function is *informational value determining*. Credal probability or degree of belief is *expectation determining*. Many authors have assumed without argument that the two kinds of probability should be equal. As shall become apparent shortly, they should not.

The C-function is supposed to evaluate the increase in informational value afforded by a deliberate or inductive expansion of corpus K as compared to other potential expansions of K allowed by the ultimate partition U_K.

In the contexts both of expansion and of contraction, it is sometimes worthwhile considering the increase in informational value yielded by an expansion of a minimal corpus LK relative to the partition U_{LK}. This permits us to assign informational value $C^*(K)$ to the current corpus K. It may be equated with $Cont^*(K) = 1 - M^*(K)$ where the function $M^* = M_{LK}$ is simply the M-function determining increments in informational value from rejecting elements of U_{LK} when expanding to K.

Let h be equivalent given K to a disjunction of some subset of U_K. The difference between the informational value of the result

Deliberate Expansion

K_h^+ of expanding K by adding h and forming the deductive closure and the informational value of K could be represented using the function M^*:

(i) $[1 - M^*(K_h^+)] - [1 - M^*(K)] = M^*(K) - M^*(K_h^+) = M^*(h)$

In general, U_K is a proper subset of U_{LK} so that the maximum new informational value to be added to K cannot be greater than $M^*(K)$. Since it is convenient to let the maximum be equal to 1, divide $M^*(h)$ by $M^*(K)$ to form the measure of increment of informational value obtained by adding h to K.

(ii) $M_K(h)$ where $M_K(h) = M^*(h)/M^*(K)$ for h that are disjunctions of elements of U_K.

Represented in this way, the assessment of informational value relative to K and U_K is derived from an assessment of informational value relative to LK and U_{LK}. The advantage of this representation is that it allows for tracing assessment of informational value over a sequence of changes in state of belief where each change brings a state representable as an expansion of LK relative to U_{LK} and M^*. As long as these three factors, the minimal contraction LK, the basic partition $V_{LK,K} = U_{LK}$ and the informational value determining M-function, M^*, relative to U_{LK} are held fixed, for any potential expansion K of LK, both the ultimate partition U_K and the assessment of increments in informational value by adding information to any expansion K allowed by U_K can be determined.

A given inquiry may involve several different expansions in state of full belief. There is no requirement of rationality insisting that evaluations of increments in informational value should be relative to the same LK, U_{LK} and M^*. On the other hand, there is no general dictate of reason that precludes keeping these factors constant over a given range of belief changes. Such constancy in evaluations of increments in undamped informational value is to be expected when (a) the inquirer does not change the range of hypotheses regarded as relevantly entertainable in the given inquiry as defined by LK and U_{LK} and (b) holds the M-function relative to LK and U_{LK} fixed. In such a case, the inquirer has not altered his or her *demands for information*.

Deliberate Expansion

3.3. Epistemic Utility as the Utility of New Error-Free Information

The utility function V representing the utility of new error-free information satisfies the following condition:

$$V(h, x) = \alpha T(h, x) + (1 - \alpha)Cont(h)$$
$$= \alpha T(h, x) + (1 - \alpha - (1 - \alpha)M(h).^3$$

If we divide the right-hand side by α and subtract $q = [1 - \alpha]/\alpha$ we obtain the following positive affine transformation of V.

$$V^*(h, x) = T(h, x) - qM(h).$$

Since the ordering of expected utilities of options is not altered by transforming utility functions by a positive affine transformation, we can treat V^* as equivalent to V.

3.4. Maximizing Expected Epistemic Utility

Both the V-function and the V^*-function are *epistemic utility functions* representing the cognitive goal of acquiring new error-free informational value.

The *expected epistemic utility function* becomes the following:

$$EV^*(h) = Q_K(h)(1 - qM_K(h)) - Q_K(\sim h)qM_K(h)$$
$$= Q_K(h) - qM_K(h).$$
$$= \sum [Q_K(d_i) - qM_K(d_i)].$$

The d_i's are the elements of U_K that are disjuncts in h.

In addition to the assumptions made thus far, a special constraint needs to be imposed on the range of q. I assume that an inquirer seeking new error-free information should never prefer to add false hypotheses no matter how informationally valuable rather than avoid error even if doing so adds no new informational value. This

---

[3] Where there is no threat of confusion, I drop the subscript for the belief-state or corpus from the Q-function and the M-function.

Deliberate Expansion

condition implies that $\alpha \geq 0.5$ and $0 \leq q \leq 1$. q is called the *index of boldness*.

Assuming that q is restricted to the unit interval in the manner indicated, if there are d_i's for which $Q(d_i) - qM(d_i) > 0$, then every potential expansion strategy carrying maximum expected utility is a disjunction of all such d_i's together with some subset of the d_j's such that $Q(d_j) - qM(d_j) = 0$.

An inquirer concerned to obtain new error-free information of value in expansion should, therefore, reject an element d_i of U_K if $Q_K(d_i) - qM_K(d_i)$ is negative, refuse to reject it if this difference is positive and may or may not reject it if the difference is 0.

When maximizing expected utility leads to a tie in optimality, a decision-maker is free to choose any one of the optimal options. The decision-maker may, however, undertake to adopt some rule for breaking ties for optimality.

In inductive expansion, it makes sense to adopt a *Rule for Ties* recommending the *weakest* of the optimal expansions if there is one. As long as the expectation determining probability Q_K and the informational value determining probability M_K are determinate, there will be a uniquely weakest option and it can serve as the tiebreaker.[4]

Maximizing expected utility and the Rule for Ties then leads to the following *rule for inductive expansion*:

Relative to K, U_K, Q_K, M_K, and q,

(1) Reject all and only those elements of U_K such that $Q_K(d_i) - qM_K(d_i) < 0$.

---

[4] Maurice Pagnucco (1996) has introduced a conception of *abductive expansion* according to which all elements of U_K are evaluated according to some index of explanatory merit. The recommended expansion is the meet of those expansions by adding elements of U_K that rank best. There is no effort to show that the meet or intersection is also optimal since the evaluation of expansion strategies is only of elements of U_K or maximally consistent extensions of K. Not only is the proposal I am making one that insists on the optimality of such tie-breaking recommendations but, setting this to one side, it is not true that according to my proposal the recommendation is to take the intersection of all expansions by adding elements of U_K carrying maximum EV^*-value. The recommendation is to take the intersection of all such expansions carrying non-negative EV^*-value.

Deliberate Expansion

(2) Expand K by adding the assertion that one of the unrejected elements of U_K is true.

As already noted, this rule was presented for the special case where $M_K(d_i) = 1/n$ for all n elements of U_K in Levi, 1967 and was generalized in Levi, 1984, ch. 5. Further elaborations are found in Levi, 1980 some of which are further discussed in Levi, 1991 and 1996.

Notice that if the expectation determining probability Q_K and the informational value determining probability M_K are the same for all members of U_K, no element of U_K can be rejected for any allowed value of q. Hence, if it is *required* that $Q_K = M_K$ in all contexts, there can be no non-trivial inductive expansion according to the rule for inductive expansion. That is an excellent reason for not requiring Q_K to equal M_K.

3.5. Stable Inductive Expansion

Given the expansion yielded at a level of boldness q, the rule may be reapplied over and over again with the same q until no further elements of U_K can be rejected. The result is the *stable inductive expansion* of the initial K at the given level of caution. When $q = 1$, the result of stable inductive expansion is the addition to K of the proposition represented by the set of elements of U_K for which $Q_K(d_i)/M_K(d_i)$ is a maximum. Stable inductive expansion or acceptance is discussed in Levi, 1980, 1996 and 2001.[5]

Notice that stable inductive expansion is defined on the assumption that we may hold U_K fixed and derive the ultimate partitions relative to inductive expansions of K as truncations of this one. Not only is this assumed but it is also taken for granted that the assessments of undamped informational value for the iterated expansions are normalizations of the initial *M*-value. Successive iterated expansions are

---

[5] In Levi, 1996 and 2001, the notions of an inductively extended expansion and revision of K by adding h are introduced and employed in order to construct Ramsey Test conditions for the acceptability of conditionals and corresponding non-monotonic consequence relations. The non-monotonic consequence relations obtained by Gärdenfors and Makinson (1993) and Reiter (1980) are explored in the context of these ideas.

Deliberate Expansion

supposed to cohere in assessments of undamped informational value relative to K, U_K and M_K. Such assumptions seem entirely appropriate to make. Inquirers should not alter demands for information without good reason in the context of a given inquiry.

3.6. Degrees of Surprise and Belief (Plausibility)

Both inductive expansion and stable inductive expansion are heavily context-dependent. The legitimacy of an inductive expansion depends on the following contextual parameters:

(i) The information already available in the state of full belief as represented by the corpus K.
(ii) The ultimate partition U_K and the set of potential answers (potential expansion strategies) generated by U_K.
(iii) The credal probability function Q_K defined over the Boolean algebra defined by U_K.
(iv) The informational value determining M-function M_K defined over the same domain.
(v) The index of boldness q (or caution) representing the relative importance attached to the concern to avoid error and to acquire new information of value.

An inquirer who has commitments with respect to K, U_K, Q_K and M_K may wish to appraise the potential answers relative to the various values of q from 0 to 1. The values of q have been allowed to take any real value between 0 and 1. For any potential answer h that fails to be rejected for some value q, there is a maximum value for the index of boldness q such that h fails to be rejected relative to that value for q. The function $q(h|K, U_K, Q_K, M_K)$ = the degree of unrejectability of the conjecture h relative to K, $U_k..Q_K$, and M_K may, therefore, be defined as follows:

Definition of the degree of unrejectability of $h = q(h|K, U_K, Q_K, M_K)$:

$q(h|K, U_K, Q_K, M_K) = \max_q$ (h is not rejected at K, U_K, Q_K, M_K, q) if h is rejected at K, U_K, Q_K, M_K, q for some value of q.

Deliberate Expansion

$q(h|K, U_K, Q_K, M_K) = 1$ otherwise.

In the following, degree of unrejectability or $q(h|K, U_K, Q_K, M_K)$ is abbreviated as $q(h)$ where the context is clear.

The degrees of unrejectability satisfy the following formal conditions:

(1q) If $K \vdash g \equiv g'$, $q(h) = q(h')$.
(2q) $K \vdash \sim g$ only if $q(g) = 0$.
(3q) $q(g) = 1$ or $q(\sim g) = 1$
(4q) $q(h \vee g) = \max(q(h), q(g))$.

We may then offer the following definitions of *degrees of potential surprise* (= degrees of disbelief = degrees of implausibility) and *degrees of belief* (= degrees of plausibility).

The degree of potential surprise that h relative to K, U_K, Q_K, and M_K

$= d(h|K, U_K, Q_K, M_K) = 1 - q(h)$.

The degree of belief that h relative to K, U_K, Q, and M

$= b(h|K, U_K, Q_K, M_K) = d(\sim h|K, U_K, Q_K, M_K)$.

Suppressing the contextual parameters, we can show that potential surprise and degree of belief satisfy the following axioms:

(1d) If $K \vdash g \equiv g'$, $d(g) = d(g')$.
(1b) If $K \vdash g \equiv g'$, $b(g) = b(g')$.
(2d) $K \vdash \sim g$ only if $d(\sim g) = 1$.
(2b) $K \vdash g$ only if $b(g) = 1$.
(3d) $d(g)$ or $d(\sim g) = 0$.
(3b) $b(g)$ or $b(\sim g) = 0$.
(4d) $d(h \vee g) = \min(d(h), d(g))$.
(4b) $b(h \wedge g) = \min(d(h), d(g))$.

These axioms for potential surprise (the d-function) were proposed informally in Shackle (1949) and more formally in the second edition of 1952. (Shackle also offered a definition of degrees of belief (the b-function) as the dual of d.) Shackle understood these measures to be measures of uncertainty but gave them nothing more than an intuitive

Deliberate Expansion

interpretation. I proposed the interpretation of them in terms of the boldness dependent criterion for deliberate expansion just explained in Levi, 1966 and 1967. (I originally called the rules or criteria "caution dependent". R. C. Jeffrey suggested the terminological improvement.) The interpretation was elaborated further in Levi, 1984, ch.14.

Subsequently, Lotfi Zadeh (1978) introduced the notion of a possibility measure that appears to have the properties of the q-function that indexes unrejectability of conjectures. This becomes quite clear in the publications of Dubois and Prade (such as 1978). Other authors have reinvented Shackle's formal measures as measures of degree of belief, support, plausibility or as the dual. Most recently, Gärdenfors and Makinson (1993) have done so. However, none of these authors has seriously improved on Shackle's intuitive interpretation of this kind of measure.

The definitions of degrees of potential surprise and belief introduced in Levi, 1966 and 1967 establish a clear link between potential surprise or degree of belief and deliberate expansion of full belief. The higher X's degree of belief that h, the higher X's degree of disbelief that ∼h and the lower the degree of unrejectability of ∼h. X does not have to be very bold to reject ∼h. Given the account of inductive expansion I have sketched here, a threshold for rejecting the least surprising element of the ultimate partition that is a disjunct in ∼h is determined. That threshold is a function of the credal probability of the least surprising element of the ultimate partition and the informational value determining probability. Potential surprise and degree of belief or plausibility has an identifiable use in evaluating deliberate expansions of states of full belief. Zadeh, Dubois and Prade (1992), Gärdenfors and Makinson and many others who have reinvented Shackle's ideas do not go beyond Shackle when it comes to providing an interpretation for their measures.

L. J. Cohen (1977) presented a serious alternative to my own proposal for explicating Shackle measures as degrees of belief. He sought to derive them from measures of inductive support he had previously constructed predicated on his vision of how "Baconian" methodology would severely test conjectures. I have discussed Cohen's views in Levi, 1984, ch. 14.

Deliberate Expansion

Many authors think of degrees of belief as subjective probabilities. Like full belief or absolute certainty, subjective probability indexes the risks a rational agent should be prepared to take. Unlike full belief, however, subjective probability fares poorly in capturing doxastic commitment to deductive closure. The set of sentences carrying subjective probability above a threshold k is not closed under deductive consequence.

The reverse applies to Shackle measures. X is committed at a given time to full belief in the deductive consequences of what X fully believes. So too, X is committed to believing to a degree above threshold k all deductive consequences of what X believes to degree greater than k. But Shackle measures fare poorly as means of assessing risk or expectation in the guidance of conduct.

Credal probability is relevant to the determination of expected value in decision-making. Shackle measures are a convenient way to represent assessments of conjectures with respect to their eligibility for addition to the current state of full belief through expansion.

Thus, whether credal probability or the b-function can make a better claim for being an index of degree of belief is an idle terminological issue. Both ways of characterizing belief as a matter of degree capture some aspects of full belief. If X does not fully believe that h, X is not certain that h. Credal probability measures that degree of uncertainty. But credal probability does not in itself determine how bold X should be to reject h (i.e. to come to full belief that $\sim$h) or to reject $\sim$h. The former is represented by q(h) or $1-$ d(h) or $1-$b($\sim$h). The latter by q($\sim$h) $= 1 -$ d($\sim$h) $= 1-$ b(h).

Degrees of belief as credal probability and as Shackle measure have useful conceptual roles to play. Credal probability is expectation-determining. b-functions are useful as satisficing measures of degree of belief or evidential support.

Spohn (1988) introduces a measure of degrees of disbelief that satisfies (3d) and (4d). Where Shackle would allow extralogical propositions to be assigned maximum degrees of disbelief, Spohn disallows this and does not allow for a finite maximum degree of belief even for logical falsehoods. Spohn puts his theory of ordinal conditional or ranking functions to work in giving an account of how

Deliberate Expansion

states of belief representable by deductively closed sets of sentences are changed via contraction or revision after the fashion of AGM, an account of relevance and irrelevance and causality. So Spohn's proposal, like Cohen's, is an exception to the prevailing practice of relying on presystematic intuitions exclusively in providing an interpretation of Shackle-type measures. Spohn undertakes to integrate his idea with other concepts in an interesting manner.

According to Spohn, agent X's epistemic state at a time is characterized by a function κ defined over a suitable algebra of propositions taking ordinal numbers as values or at entities in some well-ordered set. This ordinal conditional function, ranking function or measure of degrees of disbelief κ satisfies postulates (3d) and (4d) for d-functions. If K is stronger than the set of logical truths, (1d) and (2d) fail. In any case, (2d) must fail because there is no maximum value for degree of disbelief in extralogical propositions. (And there is no maximum value for the b-function for degree of belief.)

According to Spohn, X's state of "plain belief" consists of all propositions carrying positive degrees of belief (i.e. whose negations carry positive degrees of disbelief or κ-value). Plain beliefs are thus different from propositions believed to a degree greater than some specific positive degree or to a maximum degree (that Spohn does not allow).

I agree with Spohn that plain belief makes good sense. X plainly believes that h if and only if X believes that h to some positive degree. I take this to mean that X would be justified in expanding X's current state of full belief represented in L by corpus K to one that contained h if X were maximally bold.

Spohn cannot endorse this interpretation without betraying his own philosophical project. The interpretation presupposes that degrees of disbelief (and degrees of belief) constitute a satisficing measure of evidential support useful in deliberate expansion where expansion is understood to be a change in state of *full belief*, i.e. the state characterizable by those propositions X is absolutely certain are true and whose negations X is absolutely certain are false. To change the state of full belief by deliberate expansion is to add propositions whose negations are surprising to a sufficiently

Deliberate Expansion

high degree, i.e. to convert these degrees of surprise to the maximal degree.

Spohn explicitly and correctly acknowledges that there can be no legitimate changes in states of full belief according to his account of changes in κ-functions and states of plain belief. As a consequence, X's current κ-function is of no use in determining how X's current state of full belief ought to be changed. X's current state of plain belief cannot be understood as the state of full belief to which the current state of full belief ought to be changed were X to be maximally bold.

Spohn is a Parmenidean epistemologist of the sort I discussed in Chapter 1. I do not want to repeat my complaints against this view here. My concern here is with the specific variant of Parmenideanism embraced by Spohn. This approach is based on an understanding of the κ-function as a primitive notion of disbelief. Spohn skillfully deploys this notion to construct the concept of plain belief, of change in the κ-function by updating, a characterization of AGM contraction and revision of *plain* belief (without change in full belief), of irrelevance and causal dependency notions. But the understanding of all these reconstructions depends critically on understanding Spohn's conception of degrees of disbelief. This understanding is left in the hands of presystematic intuition.

Shackle-type measures have application, so it seems to me, in the context of efforts to add new information to a state of full belief—an effort Spohn cannot condone. At some initial stage t when X's corpus is K, X might identify those sentences that represent X's corpus of plain beliefs at t, i.e. those sentences whose degrees of belief as defined in terms of κ-functions are positive. That corpus should include all sentences in the current state of full belief K. These should have b-value of 1. But it should include any sentence in L carrying positive b-value less than 1 as well even though they are not in K. If X then determines how bold to be in the context, X can then determine the expansion to adopt via deliberate expansion.

Plain belief is a useful notion ancillary to full belief. However, X's corpus PLK of plain beliefs has no use in inquiry unless X contemplates adding those items in PLK to K with b-value above some threshold k that are not already in K to yield a corpus representing an

Deliberate Expansion

expanded state of full belief. If X were not entitled to come to full belief (as Spohn contends), there would be no point in considering a corpus of plain beliefs before expansion. Spohn's insistence on plain belief without full belief deprives plain belief of any interesting application.[6]

3.7. Context Dependence

According to the decision-theoretic account of deliberate or inductive or ampliative expansion just presented, the justifiability of a deliberate expansion is heavily context-dependent. Recognizing the sensitivity of ampliative reasoning to context is just the beginning of wisdom. In a discussion of the conditions under which deliberate expansion is justified, it is desirable to identify the relevant contextual factors that are relevant and to indicate how the values of such parameters determine which expansions if any are legitimate.

I have identified five factors that are relevant to the legitimacy of a deliberate expansion. I am not prepared to claim that these factors exhaust the list. No doubt there will be complaints that the number of contextual parameters is excessive. I can understand this kind of objection coming from someone suffering from the Curse of Frege (Levi, 1980)—that is, the excessive fear that taking into account context threatens importation of unwanted psychologism, sociologism and historicism into an account of justifiable change of view. Even if those recovering from the Curse acknowledge that a few contextual parameters may be brought under critical control, the

---

[6] In Levi (1967, ch. IX), I drew a distinction between "acceptance" and "acceptance as evidence" that comes close to the contrast between "plain acceptance" and "full belief". I was at that time still unclear as to the relation between revisability and absolute certainty and, hence, was still reluctant to equate "acceptance as evidence" with full belief or absolute certainty. The objection I level against Spohn in the text is one I would address to my former self as well. When I became clearer on this score to my own satisfaction, it also became clear to me that plain belief in the sense of belief to a positive degree is but a special case of belief to a degree greater than k for some non-negative value k. For any fixed value of k, the set of propositions believed to a greater degree than k is deductively closed. No one of them is of conceptually greater interest than any other.

Deliberate Expansion

fear remains that the more parameters, the more difficult it will be to maintain a properly objective stance.

But it is not the number of such parameters that creates an obstacle to critical control. It is the absence of a conception of how values of these parameters determine the legitimacy of changes in belief. According to the approach I have adopted, one feature of the context is the initial state of full belief **K** or the corpus K representing it. The second is the ultimate partition U_K. These two contextual features determine the relevant cognitive options. A third is the credal probability distribution Q_K over U_K. The fourth is the informational value determining probability distribution M_K over U_K and the fifth is the index of boldness. The last three parameters determine the values of the cognitive options. The need for three parameters derives from the two-dimensional aspect of the goals of inductive expansion: The aim is at once to avoid error or minimize risk of error and to obtain valuable information. Q_K and M_K represent these two dimensions respectively. The index of boldness reflects the relative importance attached by the inquirer to these two dimensions of value.

One could reduce the last three parameters to one by summarizing them all by the *EV*-function. To my way of thinking, this approach masks the contributions of the assessment of risk of error, the assessment of informational value and the relative importance attached to the two desiderata. These three factors can vary independently of one another so that it is desirable to keep each one of them subject to some sort of critical scrutiny.

One might go in the other direction. Perhaps, the *M*-function itself may be further decomposed into several desiderata. I do not want to rule this out or put any upper bound on how fine-grained the analysis could, in principle, be. I rest content here with the level of generality and refinement that the five-parameter approach can bring.

Other contextual parameters have been introduced to link the evaluations of expansion strategies relative to one state of full belief with evaluations of expansion strategies relative to another state of full belief. To achieve this, the notions of a minimal state of full belief and a basic partition have been introduced. Given a potential expansion K of minimal corpus LK and the basic partition U_{LK}, the

Deliberate Expansion

ultimate partition U_K is uniquely determined. And given a credal probability distribution over U_{LK} and an informational value determining probability distribution over the same basic partition, credal probability and informational value probability distributions over U_K can be derived from K (see 4.1). Thus, if certain features of context at one time are held fixed while others are allowed to vary, the impact on the legitimacy of inferences can be explored in a systematic manner.

If contextual factors are introduced unnecessarily, I can see reason for complaint at their multiplicity. But if the factors are identified as relevant to the legitimacy of decisions or inferences, the complaint that there are too many parameters does seem to be symptomatic of suffering from the Curse of Frege. We should inoculate ourselves against that disability.

Informational Value in Contraction 4

4.1. Probability Measures as Determiners of Informational and of Expected Value

The idea of using probability-based notions of informational value is an old one. Authors like Popper, Carnap and Bar Hillel explored measures of information as decreasing functions of probability. Given a probability measure $M(x), 1 - M(x), 1/M(x), -\log M(x)$ have been suggested as measures of information.

These authors and their epigones equated the probability measure $M(x)$ determining the measure of informational value with $Q(x)$—the credal or expectation determining probability or with the degree of confirmation on the basis of which such credal probabilities are to be derived. The proposal I made in the 1960s departed from this approach by distinguishing between expectation and informational value determining probability (Levi, 1984, ch. 5). Informational value is *probability-based* in the sense that it can be represented as a function of informational value determining probability. The informational value determining probability measure satisfies structural requirements of the calculus of probability, just as credal or subjective or expectation determining probability does. This common structural feature of $M(x)$ and $Q(x)$ does not imply that they have the same intended domain of application.

Informational Value in Contraction

Of course, the two measures could have the same intended domain of application. For authors (like Carnap and Bar Hillel) who had no intention to use quantitative measures of information or informational value as utility functions representing values of payoffs in cognitive decision problems, the considerations I deploy to argue for the distinction will not seem relevant. In the context of modeling deliberate inductive expansion as a cognitive decision problem, the motive for using a quantitative assessment of informational value derives from the view that the value of a consequence of a potential inductive expansion is determined by its truth-value and the value of the information acquired. In decision-making under risk, the aggregate value of these components should be quantitive suggesting that we evaluate the components quantitatively. Probability-based assessments of informational value are eminently suited as candidates for use in this setting.

This argument does not require that the informational value determining probability should be the same as the credal or expectation determining probability. To support such a claim, some additional consideration would need to be invoked. The account of expected epistemic utility given in Ch. 3.4, in point of fact, points in the opposite direction. The proposals made there form the basis for a strong argument in favor of distinguishing the M-function from the Q-function.

According to Ch. 3.4, in deliberate expansion the measure $Q(h) - qM(h)$ is to be maximized where K_h^+ is a potential answer to the question under investigation according to U_K. If $Q(h) = M(h)$ and $0 \leq q \leq 1, 0 \leq Q(h) - qM(h)$. This is true, in particular, of all h's in U_K. Hence, the weakest potential expansion that maximizes expected epistemic utility is complete suspension of judgment. Hence, the recommended expansion would be no expansion at all even if the inquirer is maximally bold, i.e. uses $q = 1$. Unless the values of Q and M are sometimes allowed to differ, the proposed account of expected epistemic utility becomes untenable.

This result could have been avoided by taking informational value to be a decreasing function of probability alternative to $Cont(x) = 1 - M(x)$. The most familiar candidates are $1/M(x)$ and $-\log[M(x)]$.

Informational Value in Contraction

Both of these measures satisfy the requirement of weak positive monotonicity endorsed in Ch. 3.2:

Weak Positive Monotonicity: If K_h^+ carries more information than K_g^+ it carries at least as much informational value.

$Cont(x) = 1 - M(x)$ differs from alternative measures of informational value such as $1/M(x)$ or $-\log[M(x)]$ in two important respects:

(1) $Cont(x)$ satisfies the assumption of constant returns in informational value of rejection. Take any element x of U_K. Consider the increment in informational value afforded by rejecting it alone and rejecting it in addition to rejecting elements of some subset S of other elements of U_K. According to the measure $Cont$, the increment is the same in both settings. If one uses $1/M(x)$ or $-\log[M(x)]$, the increment increases with the informational value of rejecting the other values of S.

(2) $Cont(x)$ has a finite upper and lower bound. Because informational value is to be balanced with the utility of avoiding error in a way that never tips the scales in favor of informational value so much so that importing false belief is ranked above avoiding error and because the utility of avoiding error takes on two finite values, the utility of information in the relevant sense should be bounded both above and below. The other two measures range between 1 and ∞.

The second objection could be obviated by replacing $1/M(x)$ by $1/[M(x) + \delta]$ and $-\log[M(x)]$ by $-\log[M(x) + \delta]$ for some small positive δ. But since the attractiveness of these measures seems largely to derive from their formal features, much of this attractiveness would be lost. In any case, this response would not avoid the first difficulty. These alternative measures violate the requirement of constant marginal returns in informational value of rejection formulated in Ch. 3.2.

Relative to a given belief-state **K** (as represented by corpus K), the inquirer's assessment of the increment in valuable information to be obtained by rejecting an element of U_K should not depend on whether any other elements of U_K are to be rejected as well and, if

Informational Value in Contraction

so, which are, how many are, how valuable the information they carry is, etc.

According to the terminology I deploy, all evaluations of potential expansions of K relative to U_K are evaluations of informational value if and only if they satisfy weak positive monotonicity. These evaluations are assessments of increments of *undamped informational value* if and only if, in addition to satisfying weak positive monotonicity, constant marginal returns in informational value of rejection is satisfied. Any positive affine transformation of *Cont*(x) is a measure of increments of undamped informational value accruing from expansion of U_K relative to K that satisfies constant marginal returns in informational value from rejection.

In the subsequent discussion, we shall have occasion to consider the role of appraisals of undamped informational value in connection with the evaluation of contraction strategies. In contraction, information is lost and it is desirable to minimize loss of valuable information. The question arises as to whether loss of informational value should be assessed using $Cont(x) = 1 - M(x)$ as a measure of informational value.

As we shall see, there are reasons in favor of the idea and stronger reasons against. Consequently, we shall want to explore ways of evaluating information alternative to undamped assessments.

The most promising approach uses measures formally similar to Shackle measures. However, just as informational value determining probability ought not to be confused with expectation determining probability so too the use of Shackle measures to represent assessments of losses of *damped informational value* should not be confused with their use in representing degrees of belief and potential surprise. Shackle measures, like probability measures, have many different uses.

This matter will be examined more closely in connection with contraction. In the context of deliberate expansion, I have suggested adopting the undamped measure of increments in informational value that presupposes constant marginal in undamped informational value from rejecting elements of the ultimate partition.

4.2. Indeterminacy in Probability and Utility

I do not mean to insist that evaluations of consequences of options and of probabilities must be assessed numerically in order to evaluate options in decision problems in general or in assessing deliberate, inductive expansions strategies in particular. For a variety of reasons (Levi, 1974, 1980, 1986, 1999, 2000), rational agents may very well not have and often should not have evaluations of consequences representable by utility functions, quantitative assessments of the probabilities of hypotheses or numerically determinate assignments of expected utility to the options from which they choose.

Perfectly rational agents need not, as a consequence, be expected utility maximizers. The injunction to maximize expected utility should be seen as a special case of a more general account of rational choice. The problem is how to generalize appropriately. I shall briefly summarize in somewhat truncated form the proposals I have made.

Let $\mathbf{A}$ be a finite set of propositions the decision-maker judges to be optional for him or her. Let U_K be a partition relative to K as before where each element is consistent with K. Assume also that each element of U_K is consistent with K_a^+ for every a in $\mathbf{A}$. Since the elements of $\mathbf{A}$ are the propositions whose truth-values are, from the decision-maker's point of view, under the decision-maker's control, any element of U_K may be true from that agent's perspective no matter which option the agent chooses. In that sense, which element of U_K is true is not under the decision-maker's control. Finally, let O be a set of "consequence" descriptions such that for each a in $\mathbf{A}$ and each h in U_K, $K_{a \wedge h}^+$ entails the truth of exactly one o in O.

The *value structure* $V(\mathbf{A})$ for the set of options is representable by a convex set of *permissible* utility functions defined over $\mathbf{A}$. Let M[$\mathbf{A}$] be the set of all "mixtures" or "roulette lotteries" on elements of $\mathbf{A}$. Each permissible utility function in $V(\mathbf{A})$ extends to a permissible utility function in $V(\text{M}[\mathbf{A}])$ that represents a weak ordering of M[$\mathbf{A}$] satisfying the requirements for being a Von Neumann–Morgenstern utility function. So $V(\text{M}[\mathbf{A}])$ can be taken to be a set of weak orderings of M[$\mathbf{A}$] obeying Von Neumann–Morgenstern utility

Informational Value in Contraction

requirements. The convexity condition is guaranteed in the following way. Let a and b be members of M[**A**]. a is *categorically weakly (strictly, equi) preferred to* b if and only if a is weakly (strictly, equi) preferred to b according to every permissible weak ordering in $V(M[\mathbf{A}])$. If decision-maker X weakly prefers a to b, X rules out any ranking that places b above a as permissible to use in making decisions. If X categorically strictly prefers a to b, X rules out any ranking that rates b at least as good as a as permissible. And if X categorically equiprefers a to b, X rules out any ranking that rates a and b differently.

The categorical weak preference induces a quasi ordering over $V(M[\mathbf{A}])$. The set of permissible utility functions according to $V(M[\mathbf{A}])$ is convex if and only if every extension of the categorical quasi ordering over $V(M[\mathbf{A}])$ to a weak ordering satisfying Von Neumann–Morgenstern utility requirements is a permissible weak ordering in $V(M[\mathbf{A}])$.

The *credal state* $B(U_K)$ is a set of permissible probability functions over Boolean combinations of U_K conditional on each element of **A**. It is convex in the following sense. Take any pair of such conditional probability functions $Q_K^1(h/a)$ and $Q_K^2(h/a)$ in the credal state. Let $Q_K^\alpha(h/a)$ equal $\alpha Q_K^1(h/a) + (1-\alpha)Q_K^2(h/a)$ for any value of α between 0 and 1. $Q_K^\alpha(h/a)$ is also in $B(U_K)$. *The extended value structure $EV(O)$ is a convex set of permissible utility functions defined over O.*[1]

The following rules constrain the value structure, extended value structure and credal state.

Cross Product Rule: The set of *permissible probability-utility pairs* is the set of pairs in $B(U_K) \times EV(O)$.

Expected Utility Rule: Let S be any non-empty finite subset of M[**A**]. $Exp(S)$ is the set of expected utility functions defined over members of S by using the permissible probability-utility pairs in $B(U_K) \times EV(O)$.

The Principle of Expected Utility: $V(S) = Exp(S)$.

---

[1] I require that the consequence set O be *basic* in the sense of Levi (1999).

Informational Value in Contraction

An option is V-admissible in S if and only if it is optimal according to some permissible utility in the value structure $V(S)$. If the expected utility principle is imposed, a V-admissible option is said to be E-admissible. Of course, when **A** is the set of options, V-admissibility and E-admissibility are evaluated relative to $V(\mathbf{A})$.

One may then supplement V-admissibility with secondary, tertiary, etc. criteria of admissibility. In deliberate expansion, for example, we may have a convex set of epistemic utility functions defined over the consequences in O and two or more options may be V-admissible. We can urge suspension of judgment provided that suspension of judgment is V-admissible. In the special case, where the credal state is determinate as is the extended epistemic utility function over O, the secondary criterion becomes the rule for breaking ties.

Many authors who seek ways to relax the requirements for quantitative probabilities and utilities seek to do so by an appeal to partial or quasi-orderings of the option set, the consequence set and ultimate partition. I contend that the use of convex sets of numerical functions permits recognition of a wider variety of different modes of evaluating options to be rational than approaches that are based on using binary relations alone can distinguish.

This technique allows for a wider variety of relevant modes of evaluating consequences and probabilities than can be achieved by exclusive focus on *either* cardinal assessments *or* on ordinal assessments. If one considers value structures over "mixture sets" of **A** and extended value structures over mixture sets of O, these structures can be replaced by *sets* of weak orderings with respect to "preference" over the appropriate mixture sets where each permissible weak ordering satisfies Von Neumann–Morgenstern type requirements. Each of the two sets of weak orderings will consist of all extensions of the categorical quasi-ordering of the given domain obtained by focusing on the preferences that are the same according to every (extended) utility function. Of course, proceeding in this way is going well beyond comparisons among the available options and consequences as is the more explicitly quantitative mode of representation I propose to deploy.

Informational Value in Contraction

Ordinalists refuse to recognize any difference between two distinct value structures for the available options when the quasi-ordering that the two value structures induce on the options is the same (even if there are differences in the respective value structures for the mixture set). Far from being a more modest and less dogmatic approach to rational choice than the approach I am advocating here, such an approach refuses to recognize that certain types of differences might be relevant to the decisions taken by rational agents.

In some contexts, of course, there may not be much difference. In contraction, unlike expansion, there is no risk of error from the inquiring agent's point of view. Hence, at least one consideration arguing for the relevance of anything other than ordinal comparisons is undermined. But if it can be argued that the evaluations of informational value relevant to deliberate expansion have some bearing on contraction, the use of the quantitative representations may prove helpful nonetheless.

Expansion or contraction in cases where epistemic utility goes indeterminate (as will be common in real life) will not be the focus of attention in this essay although some issues bearing on this matter will be discussed in 5.12. The cardinal representability case may often (but not always) be unrealistic. It is relevant to real life cases, however, because the general constraints proposed for cardinal epistemic utility functions can be construed (legitimately I believe) as constraints on the utility functions that are eligible for membership in a convex set of permissible epistemic utility functions.

In the context of inductive expansion aimed at seeking new error-free information, every permissible epistemic utility function should be (a positive affine transformation of) a weighted average of the T-function representing the utility of avoiding error and one of a convex set of permissible utility of information or *cont*-functions. Every permissible expected epistemic utility function should be the weighted average of some permissible credal or expectation determining probability Q and a permissible *cont*-function.

The situation is quite different in the context of choosing among potential contraction strategies relative to K and U_K^*.

Informational Value in Contraction

4.3. Undamped Informational Value in Contraction

At the end of section 2.5, I suggested that inquirers contract either because they are compelled to do so to remove a conflict in a state of full belief or to give a hearing to some interesting conjecture. And in suppositional reasoning, one may seek to contract for the sake of the argument in order to allow for consistent expansion by adding the supposition. In all of these contexts, we need to consider the following problem. Given that contraction by removing ~h from K is contemplated, what is the best contraction meeting this constraint to adopt?

In coerced contraction inquirer X faces the need to contract from inconsistency. When an inquirer X is in the inconsistent belief-state, X lacks a coherent perspective from which X can deliberate between rival contraction strategies—as Erik Olsson (2003) rightly insists.

X may not be in a position to anticipate in advance precisely where and when inadvertent expansion into inconsistency will occur. But X can devise a general criterion in advance for coping with such an eventuality. X can anticipate that three strategies for retreating from inconsistency should be available: (a) retreating from inconsistency by returning to the state **K** entailing ~h prior to expansion into inconsistency so that the testimony h of witnesses or the senses is ignored, (b) retreating from inconsistency by shifting to the result of first contracting **K** by removing ~h and then expanding by adding h and (c) adopting the belief-state that is the join of these two belief states.

If K is the corpus representing the outcome of (a), $[K^{-}_{\sim h}]^{+}_{h} = K^{*}_{h}$ represents (b) and the intersection of these corpora (i.e. $K^{-}_{\sim h}$) represents (c).

The criterion will need to compare the merits of adopting any one of these alternatives as a retreat from inconsistency. And doing so will require identification of the best way to remove ~h from K required for determining both K^{*}_{h} (option b) and $K^{-}_{\sim h}$ (option c).

When someone has proposed a hypothesis h to account for some anomaly where X is convinced that h is false, X may have good reason to open X's mind to give h a hearing. The identification of a contraction removing ~h from K once more becomes urgent.

Informational Value in Contraction

In the context of suppositional reasoning, X hypothesizes that h is true, for the sake of the argument, in those contexts where K entails ∼h. This requires that one remove ∼h from K and then expand by adding h. But in removing ∼h, one must decide among many potential contraction strategies.[2]

No matter which of the motives for removing ∼h from K listed above is relevant, avoiding error cannot be a concern in choosing among contractions removing ∼h from K.

In suppositional reasoning X is committed to judging all consequences of K true both before and after contraction since X does not change beliefs. In opening up X's mind to give a hearing to h, X is committed to judging all consequences of K true before contraction. Whether removing ∼h for the sake of the argument or to give h a hearing, nothing is added to K. No error can be imported because no information is added to K and everything in K is error-free.[3] So there is no risk of adding erroneous information to what X judges to be true.

If X has inadvertently expanded into inconsistency by adding h to K, the question of how to contract from K by removing ∼h arises in the evaluation of options (b) and (c). In these evaluations, X does not take for granted that K is free of falsehood. But given that the evaluations arise only in determining relevant options for retreating

---

[2] According to the view of consistency-preserving supposition I favor, this is true also when the supposition is belief conforming where K entails h. In that case, the supposition that h must be removed from K just as in the belief-contravening case.

[3] Since every item in the initial corpus is judged to be true by the inquirer prior to contraction, removing an item from the corpus cannot, from the inquirer's point of view, incur error. As noted in 1.5, rationalization of a change of belief should be based on the inquirer's point of view prior to the change whether the change is an expansion or a contraction. Moreover, according to the view expressed in 1.5, the concern to avoid error is focused on avoiding error at the next step (i.e. contraction or expansion). It could happen in genuine belief change, contraction removing h might lead in subsequent inquiry to coming to full belief that h is false. In rationalizing contraction, such a long-term concern to avoid error should not be present—counter to the messianic realism of Peirce and Popper. A secular realism that insists on a concern to avoid error at the next change but not two or more changes down the sequence of belief changes can consistently endorse the legitimacy of fully believing that h at time t while at the same time recognizing the possibility that h will be given up legitimately at some subsequent stage in inquiry (Levi, 1991).

Informational Value in Contraction

from inconsistency, there is no basis for distinguishing elements of K that are certainly true from those that might be false. Even if the choice of ways to retreat from inconsistency is planned as part of a precommitment strategy prior to implementation of a program for routine expansion, consideration of risk of error is irrelevant.

Thus, whether contraction is part of a genuine change in view or is merely suppositional, desiderata other than avoidance of error are invoked in determining how to proceed. For those who think, as I do, that the two chief cognitive desiderata in belief change are avoidance of error and acquisition of valuable information, when avoidance of error ceases to be relevant, the first order of business is to offer an account of informational value and loss of informational value in a sense elaborating the idea that informational value is to be maximized and loss of informational value is to be minimized.

According to the proposal in section 2.6, the set of potential contractions that constitute the set of options available in contraction from K is determined by the demands for information expressed by LK, and U_{LK}, and by the inquirer's current state of full belief **K** or the corpus K that represents it.

If U_{LK} has n members, there are 2^n potential expansions of LK relative to U_{LK}. An informational value determining M-function M^* can be defined for these potential expansions such that for any disjunction x of elements of U_{LK}, $M^*(LK_x^+)$ is well defined. $Cont^*(x) = 1 - M^*(x)$ satisfies weak positive monotonicity. Hence $M^*(x)$ is an evaluation of the increment in undamped informational value accruing from expansion from the minimal state LK by adding x. If K is any corpus in L that expands LK, for some disjunction x of elements of U_{LK}, $K = LK_x^+$. So $M^*(K)$ is well defined. Hence, M^* can be used to define the undamped increment in informational value by adding h to K_x^+ when assessing potential expansions of K as determined by the ultimate partition U_K. In that case, however, it is useful to normalize the measure by letting $M_K(h) = M^*(h)/M^*(LK_x^+)$. And it follows immediately that $Cont_K(x) = (1 - M_K(x))$ is an assessment of undamped informational value for expansions of K. Assessments of undamped informational value for potential expansions from K relative to U_K can be derived from

Informational Value in Contraction

the assessments of undamped informational value for potential expansions of LK, U_{LK} using M^* and then appealing to K. LK, U_{LK} and K determine U_K. These three factors and M^* determine M_K (or $Cont_K$).

Both $Cont^*$ and $Cont_K$ so conceived also satisfy in their respective domains the requirement of constant marginal returns of rejection. This distinguishes them from other measures of informational value.

Potential contractions of K are generated from the dual ultimate partition $U_K^* = \{U_{LK}/U_K\}$. Each potential contraction can be evaluated with respect to the undamped informational value relative to U_{LK} with the aid of M^* just as potential expansions of K can. Hence, if there is no change in the demands for information in successive expansions and contractions, a fixed M^* will be used to evaluate both *gains* in undamped informational value and *losses* in undamped informational value.

To be sure, there is no special need to normalize the M^*-values of potential contractions to values between 0 and 1. Indeed, if we wish to compare potential contractions of K with potential expansions, it is useful to utilize the function M^* rather than a normalization for the purpose of evaluating gains in undamped informational value.

Although each potential contraction of K has an informational value equal to its undamped informational value relative to LK and U_{LK} and this is equal to $Cont^*(x)$ where the contraction is the expansion of LK by adding x, the *loss of undamped informational value* incurred by shifting from K to a potential contraction K' of it is equal to $Cont^*(K) - Cont^*(K') = M^*(K') - M^*(K)$. This difference is equal to the sum of the M^*-values of the cells in U_{LK} that are eliminated in expanding from K' to K.

The assessment of losses in informational value incurred in potential contractions of K like assessments of gains in informational values yielded by potential expansions of K are derived from an evaluation of content or undamped informational values of potential expansions of LK generated relative to U_{LK}. Both the assessments of losses in contraction and of gains in expansions have been represented quantitatively.

Informational Value in Contraction

Quantitative assessments in evaluating expansion strategies are needed because possibility of error has to be taken into account so that the problem of deciding how to expand becomes a problem of decision-making under risk.

The problem of contraction differs in this respect. In choosing among potential contractions, there is no risk of error to be incurred. The relevant consequences of a contraction strategy (the information given up) are known with certainty. In such a setting, quantitative assessment appears to be gratuitous. We could rest content with an ordinal evaluation of losses of informational value.

Nonetheless, as long as the demands for information remain constant, we should expect that the evaluation of losses in undamped informational value incurred in contraction from K should be derived from the same LK, U_{LK} and M^* as is the M-function relative to K in the context of expansion. It is true that the inquirer needs to take into account only the weak ordering of contraction strategies determined by the quantitative assessment of losses in undamped informational value. But the weak ordering should cohere with the demands for information by being derivable from LK, U_{LK}, M^* and K.

I take for granted that this feature of evaluations of undamped losses and gains of undamped informational value holds even when evaluations of losses of informational value are not undamped. Such modes of evaluation shall be examined later. But I shall formulate a constraint that is neutral with respect to whether losses or, for that matter gains, are undamped or not.

Common Basis for Determining Gains and Losses of Informational Value:

> Losses in informational value by removing h from K and gains in informational value by adding g to K are uniquely determined by LK, U_{LK}, M^* (defined over U_{LK}) and K.

In Levi, 1980, pp. 61–2, I asserted that the aim of contraction should be "to minimize the loss of informational value resulting from contraction subject to the constraint that the need occasioning the demand for contraction be satisfied." In particular, the constraint can be that h should be removed from K.

Informational Value in Contraction

In Levi, 1980, the understanding of informational value used was that explained in section 2.4 of that essay. Informational value for contraction paralleled the conception I had already adopted for expansion in 1967b. Relative to an ultimate partition, a probability measure M_K is defined over the cells and their Boolean compounds. The informational value of expanding K by adding h where h is a disjunction of elements of U_K is $Cont_K(h) = 1 - M_K(h)$ or $M_K(\sim h)$ which, given the truth of K is equal to the total informational value determining probability (M-value) of the rejected elements of U_K.

This is the understanding of informational value I deployed in Levi, 1980.[4] I called the 1980 conception "probability based" informational value in Levi, 1991, 4.3 and "undamped informational value" in Levi, 1996. In Levi, 1991, I first introduced the idea of using basic partitions and assessments of the informational values of potential belief states and corpora relative to such partitions for the purpose of evaluating gains of probability based or undamped informational value in expansion from K and loss of probability based or undamped informational value in contraction from K.

I did not endorse minimizing loss of undamped informational value in contraction in Levi, 1991. But I did insist that the assessments of losses of damped informational value I proposed as an alternative be determined by the same M^*-function over the basic partition U_{LK} as the one that generates the assessment of undamped informational value for the purpose of expansion. In effect, I was recommending conformity with the Common Basis principle formulated above.

I did not then and do not now mean to deny that an inquirer X is prohibited from changing the M^*-function. X may for good reason alter X's demands for information. X can alter the minimal corpus, the basic partition and the M^*-function. My contention is, however,

---

[4] To my own recollection, I introduced informational value in the context of contraction for the first time in a paper that I began reading to various audiences starting in 1970. (It is in this paper that I first introduced the classification of changes in state of full belief in terms of expansions, contractions, replacements and residual shifts.) Although this essay was accepted for publication in 1975 after five years of public exposure, it was not published until 1983—three years after Levi, 1980. It was reprinted as Chapter 8 of Levi, 1984.

Informational Value in Contraction

that given a commitment to an M^*-function (or convex set of such functions) in a given context, as long as it remains fixed, it determines the informational values of expansions from K and contractions from K.

4.4. Weak and Strong Positive Monotonicity

Levi, 1991 proposed to understand the extension of the partial ordering with respect to information to a weak ordering of the potential expansions (potential contractions) from K to be an assessment of gains (losses) of informational value provided it satisfies the Weak Positive Monotonicity Condition.[5] I did not require that K_1 carry more undamped informational value than K_2 if K_1 is stronger than K_2 as the Strong Positive Monotonicity Condition requires. I allowed for the possibility that the increments in informational value 0 obtained by rejecting some cell in U_{LK} may be null even though there is an increase in information. This can happen when, according to the inquirer's demands for information, the increment in information is of no value (and, hence, the cell in question carries 0 M-value).

Allowing for this possibility is surely coherent; but it is subject to an important caveat.

Suppose that d is a cell in finite U_{LK} such that $M^*(d) = 0$. (I have assumed that U_{LK} is finite throughout thus far in this essay.) This implies that for any expansion K of LK relative to which the truncation U_K of U_{LK} contains d, it is not possible to reject d via inductive expansion no matter what $Q(d)$ might be. An inquirer who endorsed assessments of informational value of this kind would have rendered d immune to rejection relative to all credal probability distributions over U_K and would in this sense have rendered the testing of d

---

[5] The weak positive monotonicity condition is introduced as a constraint on assessments of informational value in Levi, 1991, 122. The germ of this idea is already present in Levi, 1984, 69, n. 31 (originally published in 1967) where I proposed aggregating desiderata such as simplicity, explanatory power and other such theoretical virtues into the assessment of informational value in an important departure from the idea in Levi, 1967.

Informational Value in Contraction

pointless. This is so even though d is a serious possibility relative to both LK and K.

Thus, there is an interesting argument against allowing $M^*(d) = 0$ for cells in a finite basic partition and, hence, for $M_K(d) = 0$ in a finite ultimate partition U_K. But there are considerations that appear to point in the other direction.

For example, if $\theta = r$ were a seriously possible hypothesis specifying the precise real value of some parameter θ, an inquirer might be interested in whether $\theta = r$ is true or false. The inquirer might be taken as adopting a two-element ultimate partition consisting of $\theta = r$ and $\theta \neq r$. $M(\theta = r)$ could plausibly be assigned the value 0 and $M(\theta \neq r)$ the value 1. These assignments are not rationally mandatory but they often appear compelling.

It would be unwise to prohibit the use of finite basic partitions assigning 0 M^*-value to some cells in U_{LK} or 0 M_K = value to the cells in U_K unless the questions for which such partitions represent spaces of potential answers can be addressed using other basic and ultimate partitions. In the case of estimation of a real valued parameter, there are such alternatives.

$\theta \neq r$ may be equivalent given X's belief-state to the claim that θ is equal to some unique real value distinct from r in a specified interval from l_* to l^*. Suppose the ultimate partition is not finite but is the noncountably infinite set of hypotheses consisting of all real point estimates of values from l_* to l^*. Although it is not mandatory to assign probability 0 (in this case M-value) to each point value (one might assign positive probability to countably many points), in general it would make sense to do so. In that case, $M(\theta = r)$ would equal 0 and $M(\theta \neq r) = 1$. But in this case, $\theta \neq r$ is not an element of the ultimate partition that is noncountably infinite although it is a potential answer.

For the sake of the argument, let X adopt as ultimate partition the twofold partition consisting of $\theta = r$ and $\theta \neq r$ while using the restriction of the M-function from the noncountably infinite partition to this case. To do so while using the approach to inductive or deliberate expansion I am proposing would have the untoward consequence that $\theta = r$ cannot be rejected in deliberate inductive

Informational Value in Contraction

expansion. X should either suspend judgment or add $\theta = r$ to X's full beliefs depending on the credal probabilities for these alternatives.

There are two related ways for X to address the question as to whether r is the true value of θ without embracing this consequence. One is to adopt the noncountably infinite ultimate partition for use in deliberate expansion. Chapter 6 discusses suggestions as to how the account of inductive expansion proposed here may be extended to that case.

Closely related is the adoption of an ultimate partition consisting of $\theta = r \pm \varepsilon$ and $\theta \neq r \pm \varepsilon$ for some suitably small ε. Both alternatives carry positive M-values. The inquirer X may, depending on credal probability judgment, reject one alternative or the other or reject neither.

$\theta = r$ will be rejected according to the methods of 6.1 if and only $\theta = r \pm \varepsilon$ is rejected in the binary ultimate partition for all such partitions with ε smaller than some specific positive value.

Other types of cases can arise where X might adopt a finite basic or ultimate partition with 0 M^* or M_K value assigned to some elements. In these cases, the partition is replaceable by a countably infinite number of cells. Methods proposed in 6.2 might be used in those cases.

Why worry about finite basic (and ultimate) partitions with M^*-functions assigning 0 values to some cells? Using the approach to deliberate expansion I am proposing, adopting such basic partitions with such M^*-values throws up roadblocks in the path of inquiry by rendering some answers to questions immune to rejection. Let us call such basic partitions cum M^*-functions *roadblockers*.

The untoward results of using such roadblockers may be avoided by replacing the partitions U_{LK} and U_K by infinite ones and proceeding according to the approach proposed in Chapter 6. Nothing is lost and something is gained. In infinite ultimate partitions, there is every reason to insist on weak rather than strong monotonicity.

When finite U_{LK} cum M^* is not a roadblocker, as is frequently the case, all M^*-values assigned elements of the perforce finite dual ultimate partition U_K^* will be positive.

Informational Value in Contraction

When finite U_{LK} cum M^* is a roadblocker replaced by an infinite U_{LK} cum M^*, U_K^* could be finite or infinite and some cells could be assigned 0 M^*-value. According to the Common Basis Constraint that was already tacitly endorsed in Levi, 1991 and 1996, elements of U_K^* could be assigned 0 M^*-value even when roadblockers are replaced.

Those who insist that all cells carry positive M-value and use an undamped measure of informational value adopt a *hyper-undamped* assessment of informational value. Undamped informational value whether hyper-undamped or not preserves the partial ordering with respect to information in the weak sense just stated. In this weak sense the conception of undamped informational value is a conception of the value of information in the entailment or set inclusion sense.

I continue to endorse the position I took in Levi, 1991 and 1996, where hyper-undamped assessments of informational value are not mandated. In the many applications where finite basic partitions cum M^* are not roadblockers, if assessment of informational value is undamped, it should be hyper-undamped.

In cases where roadblocking threatens, such finite basic partitions should be replaced by infinite basic partitions and methods appropriate to such problems (such as those proposed in Chapter 6) should be applied. In those cases, if assessment of informational value is undamped, it need not and often should not be hyper-undamped. When this is the case, then whether the dual ultimate partition U_K^* is finite or infinite, situations can arise where some or all cells carry 0 M-value.

4.5. Why Losses in Undamped Informational Value ought not to be Minimized

As already stated, in Levi, 1980, I adopted an evaluation of undamped informational value for the purpose of assessing contraction strategies.

In the later essays, I *abandoned* my endorsement of undamped informational value on the grounds that minimizing loss of

Informational Value in Contraction

undamped informational value leads to recommending a saturatable contraction removing h from K.

The objection to doing so is that if one subsequently expands by adding ~h to the contraction, the result is going to be expanding to a cell in the dual ultimate partition U_K^*. Mandating this kind of result in every case is clearly absurd. According to those who regard this result to be unacceptable (and this includes Alchourrón, Gärdenfors and Makinson), minimizing loss of informational value in contraction cannot be minimizing loss of probability based or undamped informational value.[6]

Since the issue is relevant to interpreting the injunction to minimize loss of informational value, it will be well to elaborate on details somewhat more explicitly.

Consider the minimal corpus LK and the ultimate partition U_{LK} relative to LK. I shall assume that U_{LK} is finite here. Let us be given an M-function, M^*, defined for Boolean combinations of elements of U_{LK}. The corpus K is an expansion of LK that, as noted before, may contain sentences additional to those in LK that are not expressible as Boolean combinations of elements of U_{LK}. However, in the context in which contraction of K by removing h is being assessed, the probability based or undamped informational value of K is equal to the M value of the *disjunction* of those elements of U_{LK} that are *rejected* when K is endorsed. That is to say, it is the undamped informational value of the disjunction of all elements of the dual ultimate partition U_K^*. Any potential contraction strategy removing h from K will be tantamount to shifting to a corpus K' whose ultimate partition $U_{K'}$ is a superset of the ultimate partition U_K for K and where at least one element of $U_{K'}$ implies ~h.

The loss of undamped informational value incurred by contracting from K to K' is $Cont^*(K) - Cont^*(K') = 1 - \Sigma_{d \in U_K} M^*(d) - 1 + \Sigma_{d \in U_{K'}} M^*(d)$. This loss is equal to the sum of the M-values of those

---

[6] I had not thought through the implications of my 1980 proposal at that time and was only prompted to do so when I saw a prepublication version of the classical AGM paper of 1985 and the several papers of Alchourrón and Makinson of that period. My objection to the 1980 proposal has nothing to do with its being a quantitative notion of informational value but rather with the structural properties of that measure.

Informational Value in Contraction

elements of the dual ultimate partition U_K^* for K that are shifted to the ultimate partition U_K' for K'. The greater this sum, the greater the loss incurred.

Let us now consider the ramifications of seeking to minimize losses of undamped informational value when contracting by removing h from K. I shall examine a series of special cases first.

Special Assumption 1 about M^*: All elements of U_K^* carry positive M-value.

An immediate corollary is that no more than one element of U_K^* should be shifted to U_K' if shifting from K to K' minimizes loss of informational value among contraction strategies. Moreover, the element shifted must be one entailing h. Hence we have the following:

Observation 1: If we are to minimize loss of undamped informational value in removing h from K and if the special assumption 1 about M^* is applicable, all optimal contractions removing h from K must be maxichoice and, hence, saturatable.

If two or more maxichoice contractions are optimal as is possible, under special assumption 1 we cannot recommend using the meet of these maxichoice contractions. The M^*-value of the meet must be greater than any of the maxichoice contractions and, hence, incur a greater loss of informational value. *Hence, the meet (intersection) of the optimal maxichoice contractions must be suboptimal.* Given the goals of contraction as stated, partial meet contractions in the sense of AGM are *forbidden*.

Special Assumption 2 about M^*: All elements of U_K^* entailing ~h carry positive M-value. Some elements of U_K^* that entail h receive 0 M-value.

Observation 2: If special assumption 2 about M holds, then all optimal contractions removing h are either maxichoice or intersections of a single optimal maxichoice contractions with elements of U_K^* that entail h and carry 0 M-value. The latter type of contraction is saturatable but not maxichoice.

Informational Value in Contraction

Special Assumption 3 about M^*: Some elements of U_K^* entailing $\sim$h carry 0 M-value and some entailing h do so as well.

Observation 3: If special assumption 3 about M^* holds, the optimal maxichoice contractions are precisely those shifting single cells entailing $\sim$h and carrying 0 M-value from U_K^* to U_K'. Optimal saturatable contractions exist consisting of the intersections of K and such singletons and intersections of cells from U_K^* entailing h and carrying 0 M-value. Any intersection of K with a subset of such optimal saturatable contractions is also optimal.

Special Assumption 4 about M^*: Some elements of U_K^* entailing $\sim$h but none entailing h carry 0 M-value.

Observation 4: Under special assumption 4, all optimal contractions are either maxichoice or intersections of sets of optimal maxichoice contractions (that is to say, partial meet contractions).

In previous discussion (Levi, 1991, 124–5), I restricted attention to cases characterized by special assumptions 1 and 2 about M^*. For those cases, I concluded correctly that minimizing probability-based informational value requires choosing a saturatable contraction while forbidding intersections of optimal saturatable contractions. This seems as absurd as mandating maxichoice contractions as special assumption 1 alone does.

I neglected special assumptions 3 and 4 where, indeed, intersections of optimal saturatable contractions can be optimal and in the case of 4, partial meets of optimal maxichoice contractions can. At the time, it seemed to me that the only interesting cases of contraction from K removing h would be those where removing h incurred a positive loss of undamped informational value as under special assumptions 1 and 2. And so it seems to me now. But strictly speaking, the implications of assumptions 3 and 4 ought to be taken into account. (Of course, if we require assessments of informational value that are hyper-undamped, only special assumption 1 need be considered.)

Long before 1991, I had argued that if two or more contraction strategies are optimal, they should "if feasible" be implemented

Informational Value in Contraction

jointly (Levi, 1980, p. 62). The qualification "if feasible" should have been if the "joint implementation" is optimal relative to the goals of the decision problem. The recommendation is to adopt the contraction that is the intersection of all optimal contractions, i.e. those minimizing undamped informational value.

When two or more options are tied for optimality with respect to the goals of the decision-maker, the decision-maker can, *without betraying his primary aims*, invoke a secondary standard of evaluation to "break ties". Some think of principles recommending giving preferential treatment to minorities in hiring for jobs in just these terms. If two candidates for a job are equally qualified but one comes from a disadvantaged group, the principle recommends breaking ties in favor of the disadvantaged.

The adoption of such secondary-value commitments (there could be tertiary, etc. principles) is not required by standards of rationality. The agent's primary-value commitments are reflections of the agent's personal, political, moral and aesthetic goals and values. Rationality requires that these commitments meet minimal standards of consistency or coherence. The same is true of secondary-value commitments. However, rationality does not require that the decision-maker have secondary-value commitments.

The recommendation that the intersection of optimal contraction strategies ought to be implemented is an expression of a secondary cognitive value commitment.

In inductive expansion, the primary-value commitment I advocate is to obtaining new error-free information. I introduced a "Rule for Ties" urging suspension of judgment between optimal expansion strategies at the same time that I proposed this view of the cognitive aims of expansion (Levi, 1967).

I have advocated minimizing loss of informational value in contraction since 1980 and there also recommended breaking ties by urging suspension between optimal contractions (Levi, 1980, p. 62).

Rule for Ties:

> Given a set of optimal expansion (contraction) strategies, one should always choose the weakest of them if it exists.

Informational Value in Contraction

Such a Rule for Ties does not evaluate the weakest expansion (contraction) strategy as better than the others. And it does not evaluate this strategy as inferior to the others. In inductive expansion, the aim ought to be to obtain new, valuable error-free information. When several answers do equally well in this respect, the Rule for Ties urges the inquirer to choose the weakest among the optimal answers.[7]

In contraction, the inquirer should seek to minimize loss of informational value. If two or more potential contractions are optimal in this respect, the Rule for Ties recommends choosing the weakest or least informative of these.

Because the weakest expansion (contraction) is tied for optimality with the other optimal strategies, it is equipreferred to them. The Rule for Ties assesses the optimal strategies for some property other than the loss of informational value it incurs. When two or more expansion (contraction) strategies are optimal, we should choose an optimal strategy in a manner that minimizes controversy. We should choose the weakest among the optimal.

Minimizing controversy is not a primary aim of expansion (contraction). But when the primary aim fails to render a verdict, we are free to choose among the optimal options according to some other standard. I am urging adoption of a secondary tie-breaking standard that minimizes controversy. The Rule for Ties captures that idea.

In the case of contraction, the Rule for Ties recommends choosing the weakest potential contraction minimizing loss of informational value (in the sense as yet to be explained). Given that assessments of

---

[7] In Levi, 1980, I sought to extend the Rule for Ties to cases where there are no optimal expansion strategies because of indeterminacies in probability judgment or in evaluations of informational value. The obvious generalization is to insist that the intersection of all E-admissible expansion strategies be adopted. In keeping with my principles, I should have restricted this requirement to cases where the intersection of E-admissible expansion strategies is also E-admissible. As it turns out, there are cases where the intersection of E-admissible expansions is not E-admissible. In Levi, 1980, I retained the requirement that the intersection be chosen and abandoned the requirement that admissible options be E-admissible. That is to say, I gave up the requirement that admissible options should maximize expected utility relative to at least one permissible pair of probabilities and utilities. Thanks to the entirely just admonitions of Teddy Seidenfeld, I subsequently (Levi, 1986) came to insist that tie breaking criteria must recommend optimal or, more generally, E-admissible options. Even so, I continue to urge the Rule for Ties in cases where the option of suspending judgment is E-admissible.

Informational Value in Contraction

informational value must satisfy the condition of weak positive monotonicity, we know that the weakest potential answer in this sense cannot carry more informational value than other potential contractions minimizing loss of informational value unless there are no others.

AGM agrees with the idea that one should adopt a "skeptical" stance vis-à-vis potential maxichoice contractions that tie for optimality. And Gärdenfors (1988) registers some sympathy for the idea that the value of maxichoice contractions resides in its informational value. But AGM fails to offer an account of how intersections of maxichoice contractions are to be evaluated and registers no concern to insure that the intersection or "meet" of optimal contractions that they recommend is itself optimal. To secure such optimality, it is necessary to extend the "preference" over potential maximal contractions to intersections of such contractions. AGM fails to do this. In this respect, AGM is not sufficiently committed to a decision-theoretic approach to contraction.

Lindström (1990) and Rott (1993) show how "preferences" over maxichoice contractions that are candidates for being ingredients in partial meet contractions can be characterized within the framework of revealed preference theory. However, they do not include intersections of maxichoice contractions among the options in the domain over which choice functions are defined. Yet, both Lindström and Rott claim that according to the versions of AGM they are exploring, partial meet contractions are recommended. As a consequence, partial meet contractions ought to be considered options in AGM theory. If that is so, the preference relation ought to be defined for partial meet contractions. Lindström and Rott fail to extend their choice function-based notion of preference to the domain of partial meet contractions. As I have argued, the option set should be extended even further so that intersections of saturatable contractions are included in the preference ranking. (I elaborate further on Rott's use of choice functions in 5.1.)

The same neglect is revealed in the use of Grove models that do well in representing a weak ordering of states or worlds and representing various types of contractions in a geometric picture

Informational Value in Contraction

but fail totally to incorporate sets of points, states or worlds into the preference ranking.

The idea of using a probability-based measure of undamped informational value to achieve this end is the first that comes to mind. If we understand attempts to minimize loss of informational value as attempts to minimize loss of probability-based or undamped informational value and combine this recommendation with Rule of Ties, we get the following:

> *Main Thesis A*: Attempts to minimize loss of undamped informational value in contraction of K by removing h supplemented by the Rule for Ties have the following consequences:
>
> Under special assumption 1, the contraction *must be* a maxichoice contraction even if there are several optimal maxichoice contractions. Recovery is *mandated*. Violation of Recovery is *forbidden*.
>
> Under special assumption 2, the contraction *must be* a saturatable contraction even if there are several optimal saturatable contractions. Recovery must be violated.
>
> Under special assumption 3, the contraction *must be* the intersection of all optimal saturatable contractions and must incur 0 loss of undamped informational value. Recovery must be violated.
>
> Under special assumption 4, the contraction *must be* the partial meet contraction that is the intersection of all maxichoice contractions carrying minimum (hence, 0) loss of undamped informational value and must itself incur such 0 loss. Recovery is mandated.

In sum, if a positive loss of undamped informational value is incurred by an optimal contraction removing h from K (so that either special assumption 1 or 2 obtains), minimizing loss of undamped informational value combined with the Rule for Ties entails choosing an optimal saturatable contraction. The Rule for Ties is vacuously satisfied because the intersection of a set of two or more optimal saturatable contractions removing h is not itself an optimal contraction removing h.

Informational Value in Contraction

If a 0 loss of undamped informational value is incurred (so that special assumptions 3 or 4 obtain), intersections of all saturatable contractions incurring 0 loss in undamped informational value is mandated.

So it turns out that the only way we can require conformity with the Recovery Condition without recommending maxichoice or saturatable contractions is by enforcing special assumption 4 even when two or more maxichoice contractions minimize loss of undamped informational value. But given that the loss of informational value is loss of undamped informational value derivable from LK, U_{LK} and M^*, special assumption 4 cannot hold for all K that are expansions of LK. Some such K, K_1, is the intersection of all elements of U_{LK} that entail h. Let K_2 be the intersection of all elements of U_{LK} that entail $\sim$h. $U_{K1} = U_{K2}^*$ and $U_{K2} = U_{K1}^*$. Special assumption 4 cannot apply both to removing h from K_1 and to removing $\sim$h from K_2.

This means that the AGM recommendation that the intersection of all maxichoice contractions removing h from K that incur minimum loss of undamped informational value relative to LK, U_{LK} and M^* fails to minimize loss of undamped informational value in every case. We must either give up the AGM recommendation that contractions should be partial meet contractions or reject the attempt to minimize loss of undamped informational value.

Gärdenfors (1988) has advocated a *principle of informational economy* as a "heuristic" principle urging that loss of information (or informational value) in some sense or other be kept at a minimum. Gärdenfors invoked the principle in the context of contraction to defend the Principle of Recovery or (K$^-$5) (1988, 62). Makinson (1987) introduces a similar observation. The "heuristic" argument is that the recommended contraction removing h should be "large enough" to guarantee that if h is added back to the contraction, K will be returned. It is clear that Makinson and Gärdenfors intended to invoke a standard of loss that appealed to a subset inclusion or entailment notion of *information* just as I have done. However, unlike the approach I favor, Makinson and Gärdenfors assumed that if one potential contraction of K removing h is a proper subset of another such contraction, the first contraction incurs a strictly greater loss of *informational value*.

Informational Value in Contraction

If such a standard of loss is extended to a complete ordering of the space of potential states of full belief, it becomes not only an assessment of undamped informational value but one that obeys the strong positive monotony condition. That implies that assessments of informational value are hyper-undamped. All maxichoice contractions incur a positive loss of informational value as assumption 1 requires. So the principle of informational economy deployed by Gärdenfors and Makinson to argue for partial meet contractions *mandates* maxichoice contractions. This is a result that neither Gärdenfors nor Makinson want. Yet, abandoning the use of a hyper-undamped assessment of informational value undermines the argument for restricting contractions to partial meet contractions of optimal maxichoice contractions.[8]

Shifting to undamped informational value that is not hyper-undamped does not help much. According to the argument I have just offered, Gärdenfors's appeal to the principle of informational economy to defend (K^-5) can succeed only under assumptions 1 and 4. Under assumption 1, maxichoice contraction is recommended counter to Gärdenfors's (and AGM's) intentions. And as we have seen, assumption 4 cannot be enforced relative to all potential states of full belief that are representable as expansions of LK.[9]

Main Claim A shows that minimizing loss of undamped informational value is unacceptable as a goal for contraction whether or not contraction is to satisfy AGM requirements. So the failure of AGM contraction to be rationalizable on that basis should not count against AGM theory.

---

[8] This point is made in Levi, 1991, 130.

[9] There is another more direct way to reach the conclusion that enforcing partial meet contractions is untenable given the injunction to minimize undamped informational value. For any expansion K of LK, U_K^* is a subset of $U_{LK} = V_{LK,K}$. It is the part of U_{LK} consisting of elements inconsistent with K. Relative to LK, at least some elements of U_{LK} must carry positive M-value when U_{LK} is finite. Hence, there must be an expansion of LK, K″, such that all elements of $U_{K''}^*$ carry positive M-value. For such cases, contractions removing any extralogical sentence from K″ whose negation is entailed by at least one element of $U_{K''}^*$ must incur positive loss of undamped informational value and, indeed, must do so under the conditions of special assumption 1. In those cases, any such contraction must be maxichoice even if several maxichoice contractions are optimal with respect to undamped informational value. The AGM recommended partial meet contraction cannot be endorsed.

Informational Value in Contraction

4.6. The Damping Constraint

The AGM restriction of legitimate contractions to partial meet contractions can be rationalized according to a conception of loss of informational value alternative to loss of undamped informational value. This alternative approach is also supported by a principle of informational economy.

In contrast to Hans Rott (2000) I continue to adhere to the "dogma" that in contraction one should aim at minimizing loss of informational value in a sense satisfying weak positive monotonicity. The contraction recommended for removing h from K should be optimal (or at least E-admissible) among the potential contractions removing h generated by U_K^* with respect to this goal.

Minimizing loss of undamped informational value is unsatisfactory. When two or more saturatable contractions removing h minimize loss of informational value, we want to be in a position to recommend adopting the "skeptical" contraction that is the intersection of these optimal contractions. And we want to be in a position to do so while still claiming that informational value is being minimized. The Rule for Ties recommends taking the intersection of all optimal saturatable contractions removing h. This rule may be invoked provided this intersection is optimal in the sense that it minimizes loss of informational value.

The question, therefore, is whether there is a way of assessing informational value that obeys weak positive monotonicity and satisfies the following condition:

Intersection Equality:

> *Strong Version*: If members of a set S of contractions from K are equal in informational value, their intersection is equal in informational value to the informational value of any element of S.
>
> *Weak Version*: If members of a set S of saturatable contractions removing h from K are equal in informational value, their intersection is equal in informational value to the informational value of each element of S.

Informational Value in Contraction

The strong version imposes a constraint on all potential contractions from K. The weak version imposes a constraint on potential contractions from K removing a specific h.

Weak positive monotonicity requires assessments of informational value to be weakly faithful to the partial order of potential states with respect to strength or information. But let K_1 be stronger than K_2. By positive monotonicity, it should carry at least as much informational value as K_2. Let K_3 be a consistent corpus incompatible with K_1 and with K_2. $K_3 \cap K_1$ is stronger than $K_3 \cap K_2$. Positive monotonicity requires that $K_3 \cap K_1$ must carry at least as much informational value as $K_3 \cap K_2$.

Let K_4 carry at least as much informational value as K_2. The two corpora can be noncomparable with respect to strength. Comparable or not, weak monotonicity precludes K_4 from being weaker than K_2. Let K_3 be incompatible with K_4 as well as K_2. Positive monotonicity should be extended to require that $K_3 \cap K_4$ carry at least as much informational value as $K_3 \cap K_2$. Guaranteeing this calls for supplementing the weak positive monotonicity requirement.

Extended weak positive monotonicity:

> Consider potential expansions K_1, K_2 and K_3 of LK allowed by U_{LK}. Let $IV(K_j)$ be the informational value of K_j. and let K_3 be incompatible with both K_2 and K_3. $IV(K_1) \leq IV(K_2)$ if and only if $IV(K_3 \cap K_1) \leq IV(K_3 \cap K_2)$.

Every potential contraction of K is the intersection of K with the intersection of some subset P of U_K^*. By extended weak positive monotonicity, the ordering of potential contractions of K with respect to informational value is isomorphic with the ordering of the corresponding intersections of subsets of U_K^* with respect to informational value. In particular, the ordering of saturatable contractions removing h from K is isomorphic with the ordering of intersections of subsets of U_K^* each of which contains exactly one element u_h entailing $\sim h$. The ordering of maxichoice contractions from K is isomorphic with the ordering of elements of U_K^*. We can, therefore, focus on the evaluation of informational value of subsets of U_K^* and

Informational Value in Contraction

draw conclusions about contractions from K using extended weak positive monotonicity.

Let $S(\sim h)$ be the subset of U_K^* each element of which entails $\sim h$. $S(h)$ is the set of elements of U_K^* each of which entails h. Each potential contraction removing h from K is the intersection with K of the intersection of some nonempty subset R of $S(\sim h)$ with the intersection of some subset of $S(h)$. If R is a unit set, the contraction is saturatable removing h. If the contraction is saturatable removing h and $S(h)$ is empty, the contraction is a maxichoice contraction removing h. The intersection of R and a subset of $S(h)$ corresponds to a contraction removing $\sim h$ from K in the sense that its intersection with K is the corresponding contraction. The intersection of saturatable contractions corresponds to the intersection of the nonempty subset R of $S(\sim h)$ with a subset of $S(h)$. By weak positive monotonicity, the intersection of R with a subset of $S(h)$ can carry no more informational value than the intersection of R. Consequently, a best contraction removing h corresponds to an intersection of some nonempty subset R^* of $S(\sim h)$ with a subset of $S(h)$ where the intersection of R^* carries maximum informational value among all intersections of nonempty subsets of $S(\sim h)$.

Extended weak positive monotonicity and the weak intersection equality condition imply that if members of a subset R of $S(\sim h)$ all carry equal informational value x, the intersection of R carries informational value x as well. If the strong intersection equality condition is adopted, then if all members of the subset P of U_K^* carry equal informational value y, the intersection of P also carries informational value y.

Weak positive monotonicity, extended weak positive monotonicity and the (weak and, hence, strong) intersection condition imply the following condition:

> *Weak min*: For any nonempty subset R of $S(\sim h)$, the informational value of the intersection of R is the smallest informational value carried by an element of R.

Weak positive monotonicity, extended weak positive monotonicity, and the strong intersection condition imply the following:

Informational Value in Contraction

Strong min: For any nonempty subset P of U_K^*, the informational value of the intersection of P is the smallest informational value carried by an element of P.

Weak min and extended weak positive monotonicity establish the following:

Damping Constraint:

The intersection of contractions in a finite subset T of the set Ω of saturatable contractions removing h from K is a contraction from K removing h incurring a loss of informational value equal to the greatest loss in informational value yielded by a saturatable contraction in T.

Here is a sketch of the argument for weak min.

The argument proceeds by an induction on the number of elements of R. Assume that the *min*-rule for elements of U_K^* that imply $\sim$h holds for n. Let R be a subset of n elements and let the minimum informational value be carried by member A of T. Let B be an element of U_h^* entailing $\sim$h that does not belong to R.

Case 1: $IV(B) \leq IV(A) = IV(\cap R)$.

Let C be another element of U_K^* implying $\sim$h that does not belong to R such that $IV(C) = IV(B)$. On the assumption that elements of the basic partition (and, hence, the dual ultimate partition) are indefinitely refinable), we can always guarantee the availability of such a "copy" of B by splitting B into two equivalued parts, replacing B by one part and the copy by another.

1. $IV(\cap R \cap B) \leq IV(B)$ by weak positive monotonicity.
2. $IV(B \cap C) \leq IV(\cap R \cap C)$ by the supposition and extended weak positive monotonicity.
3. $IV(\cap R \cap B) = IV(\cap R \cap C)$ by extended weak positive monotonicity.
4. $IV(B \cap C) \leq IV(\cap R \cap B)$ by lines 2 and 3.
5. $IV(B \cap C) = IV(B)$ by the weak intersection equality condition and $IV(C) = IV(B)$.

Informational Value in Contraction

6. IV(B) ≤ IV(∩ R ∩ B) by lines 4 and 5.
7. IV(B) = IV(∩ R ∩ B) by lines 1 and 6.

This proves that the min-rule holds for n + 1 in case 1.

Case 2: IV(∩ T) < IV(B).

Replace A in R by B to form the set R^*. Since R^* contains n elements, the min rule holds by assumption. IV(∩ R^*) = IV(D) for some element D of R^* and IV(A) ≤ IV(∩ R^*) = IV(D). Case 2 is reduced to R^*. This proves weak min for n + 1. When n = 1, weak min is trivial.

One important question remains open: how to evaluate the informational values of saturatable contractions removing h from K or the losses incurred by such contractions while observing weak positive monotonicity, extended weak positive monotonicity, and the intersection condition? There are two ways to meet these demands that merit consideration as long as informational value assessments are determinate so that there are optimal contractions.

According to version 1 undamped informational value, the informational values of saturatable contractions removing h and maxichoice contractions that do not remove h from K are equal to their undamped informational values

According to version 2, the informational values of maxichoice contractions from K—whether they remove h from K or not—are equated with their undamped informational values. The informational values of intersections of maxichoice contractions including saturatable contractions removing h that are not maxichoice are determined by strong min. This, in turn, is derived using strong intersection equality by an argument that parallels the one provided above for weak min. A strengthened damping constraint can be formulated for maxichoice contractions from K rather than for saturatable contractions removing h from K.

It is also possible to consider partitioning the saturatable but not maxichoice contractions removing h into two subsets: one where informational value is undamped and the other where the damping condition prevails. There does not seem to be much advantage to considering the many possible varieties of this third alternative.

Informational Value in Contraction

Under special assumption 1, AGM or partial meet contraction can be rationalized as minimizing loss of version 1 damped informational value. A decision theoretic rationale for AGM may thus be adopted in conformity with the principle of informational economy. Without special assumption 1, partial meet contraction fails as I reported in Levi, 1991 and as Hansson and Olsson (1995) confirm. I realized that the statistical counterexamples to Recovery and partial meet contraction are applicable under special assumption 1 only after I finished Levi, 1996.

Minimizing loss of version 2 damped informational value gives relief from commitment to Recovery as an obligatory requirement under special assumption 1. Sections 4.7 and 4.8 elaborate.

4.7. Damped Informational Value: Version 1

In Levi, 1991, I proposed a method of evaluating loss of informational value that I called loss of *damped informational value*. I reaffirmed my endorsement of its use in Levi, 1996 as well. In this essay, I mean to *disown* my endorsement and to explain my change of view. Before identifying the method of evaluating such loss that seems adequate, however, I shall first explain the properties of this one. I shall now call the view I mean to reject *version 1 damped informational value*.

Version 1 damped informational value satisfies the following requirement:

Damping, version 1:

> The intersection of contractions in a finite subset T of the set Ω of saturatable contractions removing h from K is a contraction from K removing h incurring a loss of informational value equal to the greatest loss in *undamped* informational value yielded by a saturatable contraction in T. Equivalently stated, the informational value of the intersection of a set of saturatable contractions removing h from K in the finite subset T is equal to smallest *undamped* informational value belonging to a saturatable contraction in T.

Version 1 Damping Thesis:

> If Weak Positive Monotonicity and Damping version 1 are satisfied by a weak ordering over the set Ω' of potential contractions from K and S' is the set of saturatable contractions removing h that are at least as good as the best saturatable contraction removing h from K, the intersection of S' is *an* optimal contraction removing h from K.

The Version 1 Damping Thesis guarantees that if an agent contracts by removing h from K with the aim of minimizing loss of version 1 damped informational value and more than one saturatable contraction is tied for optimality among the set of all potential contractions removing h from K, the intersection of all optimal saturatable contractions removing h from K is included among the options tied for optimality. As a consequence, the Rule for Ties can be invoked as a secondary criterion to recommend choosing the intersection of all optimal contractions removing h without contradicting the injunction to minimize loss of version 1 damped informational value.

In keeping with the Common Basis Condition of 4.3, damped informational value as defined in Levi, 1991, ch. 4.4 and in Levi, 1996, 263 is represented by a numerical measure derived from the M^*-function for elements of the basic partition U_{LK} restricted to the dual ultimate partition U_K^* that satisfies weak positive monotonicity and damping version 1. It is characterized as follows:

Damped Informational Value - Version 1:

> Consider all potential contractions of K removing h as defined relative to LK, $V_{LK,K} = U_{LK}$ and M^*.

(1) The version 1 loss in damped informational value incurred by shifting from K to a saturatable contraction removing h from K is equal to the loss in undamped informational value thereby incurred as represented by M^*.

(2) The version 1 loss in undamped informational value incurred by shifting from K to an intersection of saturatable contractions removing h from K is the largest loss incurred by any saturatable contraction in the set.

Informational Value in Contraction

Thus, loss in version 1 damped informational value is derived from losses in undamped informational value derived from LK, U_{LK} and M^* according to the following recipe. Given the dual ultimate partition U_K^*, the first clause of the definition combined with the injunction to minimize loss of informational value tells us to consider those maxichoice contractions that minimize loss of undamped informational value in removing h from K. They consist of intersections of U_K with each of those d_i's in U_K^* entailing $\sim$h for which the M^*-value is a minimum. For each such maxichoice contraction, we can construct the saturatable contraction obtained by intersection with all d_j's entailing h that carry 0 M^*-value. The resulting saturatable contraction will carry the same undamped informational value as the maxichoice contraction corresponding to it. Thus, the first clause determines the weakest saturatable contractions removing h that carry minimum version 1 damped informational value (i.e. minimum undamped informational value).

The second clause stipulates that preference between intersections of sets of optimal saturatable contractions removing h from K should satisfy the damping condition. That is to say, the informational value of a set S of such saturatable contractions removing h should equal the informational value of a saturatable contraction in S incurring greatest loss of undamped informational value.

We are thus not concerned to minimize loss of undamped informational value any longer. What we wish to minimize is greatest loss in undamped informational value found in a set of saturatable contractions representing a potential contraction.

Maximizing version 1 damped informational value avoids some of the grosser deviations from common sense that are thrust on us by the injunction to maximize undamped informational value—to wit, requiring maxichoice contraction under special assumption 1 even when two or more maxichoice contractions are optimal and saturatable contraction under special assumption 2 even though two or more saturatable contractions are optimal.

Main Thesis B:

> If the contraction recommended for removing h from K is the result of minimizing loss of damped informational value

Informational Value in Contraction

according to version 1 and the Rule of Ties, the contraction is the intersection of K with those saturatable contractions removing h from K that carry maximum undamped informational value among saturatable contractions removing h from K.

Observation 1': Under special assumption 1, minimizing loss of version 1 of damped informational value and using the rule for ties requires choice of a partial meet contraction—to wit, using the intersection of all maxichoice contractions removing h from K carrying minimum M^*-value. Recovery is mandated.

Observation 2': Under special assumption 2, minimizing loss of version 1 of damped informational value and using the Rule for Ties recommends choosing the intersection of all saturatable contractions removing h from K where each saturatable contraction is produced by forming the intersection of a maxichoice contraction incurring minimum (but positive) loss of informational value with the intersection of all those cells of U_K^* that carry 0 M^*-value and entail h. Recovery fails.

Observation 3': Under special assumption 3, minimizing loss of version 1 of damped informational value and using the Rule for Ties recommends the intersection of all saturatable contractions removing h from K incurring 0 loss of undamped informational value. Recovery fails.

Observation 4': Under special assumption 4, minimizing loss of version 1 of damped informational value and using the Rule for Ties recommends the intersection of all maxichoice contractions incurring 0 loss of undamped informational value. Recovery is satisfied.

Under none of the special assumptions does minimizing loss of version 1 damped informational value require choice of a maxichoice or even a saturatable contraction (although such choices may be permitted sometimes). Under special assumption 1, however, the recommended contraction removing h from K must be a partial meet contraction.

Informational Value in Contraction

I have argued previously (4.4) that special assumption 1 ought to be mandated in cases where the dual ultimate partition is derived from K and a finite U_{LK} that is a component of a non-road-blocking partition cum M^* pair. This type of case will surface in many common applications. In such cases, minimizing version 1 damped informational value supplemented by the Rule for Ties does justify partial meet contractions and, hence, conformity to AGM contraction as best suited to achieve minimization under ordinary conditions. Moreover, this is shown *without* imposing unargued for restrictions on the domain of available contraction strategies after the fashion of AGM or with arguments urging minimizing loss of information or of *undamped* informational value as Makinson has sometimes done.

Counter to what I claimed in 1991 and 1996, AGM is vindicated in a qualified but important way by the decision-theoretic approach I took according to which minimizing losses in version 1 damped informational value is advocated. The proposal can be seen as an improvement on AGM precisely because it offers a decision-theoretic rationale for AGM that—*pace* Lindström (1990) and Rott (1993)—is the only one that shows that when choosing between *all* potential contractions removing h, choosing a partial meet contraction of the best maxichoice contractions removing h is an optimal choice.

But the vindication is qualified. When dual ultimate partitions are derived from infinite basic partitions, special assumption 1 can fail.

In Levi, 1991 and 1996, I sought to show how Recovery might fail. And under special assumptions 2 and 3 it does indeed fail. So strictly speaking, minimizing loss of damped informational value version 1 can lead to violations of Recovery.

In Levi, 1991, I had in effect conceded that if special assumption 1 were made, partial meet contractions would be optimal.[10] I had appealed to illustrations of violation of Recovery to support the thesis that special assumption 1 must be violated.

---

[10] On 134 (Levi, 1991), I considered the possibility of a "strong monotonicity condition restricted to saturatable contractions". I silently conceded that in that case using the damping condition on the saturatable contractions would yield partial meet contractions. Such a restricted strong monotonicity condition presupposes special assumption 1 and that the damped informational value of a saturatable contraction removing h is its undamped informational value. That is to say version 1 damped informational value is

Informational Value in Contraction

The counterinstances to Recovery cited are genuine. I did not realize, however, that such counterinstances apply in the presence of special assumption 1. I was mistaken to think that the presence of counterinstances to Recovery warrants the failure of special assumption 1 when version 1 damped informational value is minimized.

Recall that requiring that loss of undamped informational value is to be minimized leads to maxichoice contraction in the face of special assumption 1. That fact was not the basis for rejecting special assumption 1. In order to avoid maxichoice contraction, minimizing loss of undamped informational value was abandoned instead.

By the same token, once it is recognized that requiring loss of damped informational value to be minimized leads to partial meet contraction and Recovery in the face of special assumption 1 ought not to be the basis for rejecting special assumption 1. In order to avoid mandating Recovery—as presystematic precedent clearly indicates we should—we should abandon minimization of type 1 damped informational value.

There is another version of damped informational value to consider that avoids the implication of Recovery under special assumption 1. Minimizing loss of damped informational value version 2 is, for that reason, a better recommendation as to how to contract than minimizing loss of informational value version 1.

It is important to appreciate that some types of violation of Recovery are compelling presystematically. Accounts of contraction that mandate Recovery in such cases are unacceptable.

Let X be convinced that a coin was tossed and landed heads. If asked whether the coin might just as well have landed tails on that toss, should X deny it? Clearly not! But to say this is to violate Recovery!

To say that the coin might have landed tails on that toss even though it is not a serious possibility that the coin landed tails according to X's corpus K is to make a modal judgment conditional

being minimized. I explicitly complained that there is no reason for such a procedure. Having endorsed damping, I could not have been objecting to the second requirement. So I was (confusedly and obscurely) complaining about special assumption 1. I denied that we could require that the special assumption 1 hold.

Informational Value in Contraction

on the supposition that the coin is tossed. Transforming K by supposing something already believed (the belief conforming case) involves revising K by removing the claim that the coin was tossed and then returning that claim. The result is a Ramsey revision $K^{*r}_{\text{the coin is tossed}}$ of K.

Neither "the coin landed heads" and "the coin landed tails" are in $K^{*r}_{\text{the coin is tossed}}$ although "the coin landed heads" is in K. On the other hand, "the coin landed on the surface" is both in K and $K^{*r}_{\text{the coin is tossed}}$. So Recovery is violated but its dictates are observed for those issues where common sense expects them to be.

Consider now the ramifications of this illustration for the idea that in contraction version 1 damped informational value is minimized.

X is convinced that E (coin a was tossed) and H (coin a landed heads) are both true. Let X contract by removing E. This could be a genuine change of belief or it may be "for the sake of the argument". Either way the resulting contraction is one according to which both E and ~E are serious possibilities. Tossing the coin is a type of statistical experiment. It is predictable by lawful regularity that on any such experiment near the earth, the outcome will be describable as the coin's landing on the surface. It will also be describable in accordance with lawful regularity as landing either heads up or tails up. There is another lawful regularity licensing the prediction that the landing will not be describable both as a landing heads and a landing tails. There is no lawful regularity licensing prediction of the landing being a landing heads (landing tails). In other words, relative to trials that are tossings there is a sample space of possible outcomes (in this case landing heads and landing tails). When in suspense between E and ~E, X should judge it a serious possibility that the coin is tossed and lands heads up and that it is tossed and lands tails up (perhaps also that it is tossed and lands on its edge although I shall mention this alternative no more). If the contraction step leads to this result, expansion by adding E will not return H and Recovery will be violated.

Whether a claim G is or is not returned when E is returned depends upon whether ~E ∨ G is retained when E is removed. In the example, that depended upon whether ~E ∨ G instantiated a regularity X judges explanatory. But that is not crucial. What is

Informational Value in Contraction

critical is the informational value of $\sim E \vee G$. That value may depend upon whether $\sim E \vee G$ is or is not an instance of an explanatorily important principle. But, perhaps, explanation may not be the factor that is controlling informational value. I wish to leave that open. It is enough for the example that explanatory value can be a determinant of informational value and that when it is, examples where the outcome of experiment is representable by a "point" in a sample space represent clear counterinstances to Recovery.[11]

Minimizing losses of version 1 damped informational value under special assumption 1 does not provide room for assessments of informational value that are sensitive to differences in explanatory significance that can lead to violations of Recovery. To my way of thinking, this renders this conception of loss of informational value unacceptable in an account of how to contract.

At the cost of some repetition, the coin example will be examined a little more closely.

The Open Case: X is contemplating tossing coin a. X does not as yet know whether X will do it. X is sure that either the coin will not be tossed or it will land on the surface. However, as far as X is concerned, the two claims (E&H) the coin will be tossed and land heads and (E&T) the coin will be tossed and land tails are both serious possibilities. So is the claim $\sim E$ that the coin will not be tossed. X is certain that $\sim E$ is true if and only if the coin does not land heads and does not land tails. Indeed, it does not land at all. So relative to X's corpus K, U_K could be E&H, E&T (or E&$\sim$H) and $\sim$E.

X then expands corpus K by adding E asserting that the coin will be tossed. X becomes certain that the coin will land on the surface. But pending witnessing or obtaining a report of the outcome of the toss, it is a serious possibility that the coin will land heads and also that the coin will land tails. If K' is the expansion of K by adding E, $U_{K'}$ is H and T.

According to the Ramsey Test, X should say if the coin is tossed it may land heads and it may land tails. Or if the tossing occurred in the

---

[11] Perhaps the circumstance that, in many contexts, interest in explanatory power controls assessments of losses of informational value misleads so many authors into thinking that conditional claims are truth-value bearing assertions of causal dependency of some kind.

Informational Value in Contraction

past, X should say that if the coin had been tossed, it might have landed heads and it might have landed tails.

The Belief-Contravening Case: X is convinced that the coin has not been tossed. $\sim$E is in X's corpus K^*. So X removes $\sim$E for the sake of the argument.

In this setting it is not unreasonable to think of K described for the open case as the minimal corpus LK and U_K of the open case as the basic partition U_{LK}. The dual ultimate partition then becomes EH and ET.

One could, of course, use a weaker minimal corpus. LK could be a contraction of K that calls into question various items that are taken for granted according to K that are relevant to the behavior of the coin. For example, relative to LK, E$\sim$H$\sim$T could be a serious possibility. (The coin might land on its edge.) More interestingly, EHT, $\sim$EH and $\sim$ET could be serious possibilities. The latter three are counterinstances to universal regularities that are judged important for purposes of explanation. One could construct a basic partition relative to such a minimal belief-state.

But given that K rules out the above-mentioned items as serious possibilities and given that contractions that recognize them as serious possibilities would incur losses of information much greater than the alternative contraction strategies available relative to K^* regardless of whether undamped informational value or damped informational value of one of the varieties under consideration is used, no maxichoice contraction that is not in $\{U_K/U_{K^*}\}$ is a serious candidate maxichoice contraction. For this reason, we can simplify and take K to be the minimal corpus LK.

I contend that the contraction from K^* should be the same as the corpus K for the open case. That is to say, X should be the intersection of the deductive closure of $\sim$E $\vee$ EH and the deductive closure of $\sim$E $\vee$ ET both of which are maxichoice and, hence, saturatable contractions removing $\sim$E from K^*. On the assumption that loss of version 1 damped informational value is being minimized, the intersection is recommended provided the two saturatable contractions both minimize this loss.

The upshot is that if X then expands by adding E, it should remain a serious possibility that the coin landed heads and that it landed

Informational Value in Contraction

tails. X should say as before: if the coin had been tossed it might have landed heads and it might have landed tails.

This brings us to the case of concern here.

The Belief-Conforming Case: X is convinced that the coin has been tossed and landed heads. The corpus is then K^{**} X contracts for the sake of the argument by removing E. *I contend that in this case too X should revert to the open case.* Imagine that X initially had been in the open case, had expanded by adding E and had then observed the coin landing heads. In contracting by removing E, X is obliged also to remove the claim that the coin landed heads. For X will want to preserve the little lore from physics X knows that suggests that in the absence of being tossed, the coin did not land on the surface and that landing on the surface is a necessary condition for landing heads. *Just as in the belief contravening case*, X normally would be returned to the open case. And once more, expanding by adding E will lead to the judgment that the coin might have landed heads and might have landed tails on the toss that took place. Recovery has failed.

This procedure must fail to minimize loss of version 1 damped informational value. If we assume that the basic partition remains U_K, the dual ultimate partition should be $\sim$E and ET. Intersecting K^{**} with the deductive consequences of ET is a maxichoice contraction from K but is not one removing E from K. Intersecting K^{**} with the deductive consequences of $\sim$E is a maxichoice and, hence, a saturatable contraction removing E from K^{**}. The intersection of K^{**} with $\sim$E $\vee$ ET is not maxichoice but it is a saturatable contraction removing $\sim$E from K^{**}. But according to version 1 damped informational value, the second saturatable contraction carries less informational value than the first and is not to be recommended. So minimizing loss of damped informational value version 1 recommends contracting to the consequences of EH $\vee$ $\sim$E which given the (suppressed) background information is known to be equivalent to H $\vee$ $\sim$E.

Thus insisting on minimizing loss of version 1 informational value frustrates contraction of K^{**} to the open corpus K. In contraction, X retains the information that either the coin was not tossed or it landed heads.

Informational Value in Contraction

Notice that K^{**} *should* contain "$\sim E \vee$ Lands on the Surface". But then again so should K. That is because X is committed to the proposition that this coin like other coins invariably lands on the surface of the Earth when tossed near the surface and regards this generalization as an explanatorily lawful regularity. Such explanatorily lawful regularities are prized as informationally valuable. X is or should be loath to give them up. "$\sim E \vee H$" is not an instance of an explanatorily valuable regularity. Giving it up does not incur the kind of loss that ensues in the other case. Minimizing loss of version 1 informational value cannot recognize the difference between the values of "$\sim E \vee$ lands on the surface" and $\sim E \vee H$ and the relevance of this feature to the satisfaction or violation of the Recovery Condition.

I do not have to claim that contraction in the belief-conforming case *must always* be the same as in the belief-contravening case even when statistical examples are involved. Perhaps retaining $\sim E \vee H$ is warranted in some contexts. I merely insist that in such examples, contracting from K^{**} to K ought not to be *prohibited* either. Advocates of partial meet contraction and Recovery are committed to such prohibition. This is also true of those who insist on minimizing loss of version 1 damped informational value.

I am always surprised when someone insists that conformity with Recovery is allowed in contexts where it is known that a statistical experiment has been run and recognized what the outcome is. I am astounded when they claim that Recovery is mandated in such cases. I do not need to insist on my surprise but only my astonishment to call Recovery into question and to undermine the claim that in deciding how to contract one should minimize loss of version 1 damped informational value.

4.8. Damped Informational Value: Version 2:

Damping, version 2:

> The intersection of a set of maxichoice contractions in a finite subset T of the set Ω of maxichoice contractions of K is a contraction from K incurring a loss of informational value

Informational Value in Contraction

equal to the greatest loss in informational value yielded by a maxichoice contraction in T. Equivalently stated, the informational value of the intersection of a set of maxichoice contractions in the finite subset T is equal to smallest informational value belonging to a maxichoice contraction in T.

Version 2 Damping Thesis:

If Damping version 2 is satisfied by a weak ordering over the set Ω' of potential contractions from K and S′ is the set of maxichoice contractions that are at least as good as a best maxichoice contraction removing h from K, the intersection of S′ is *an* optimal contraction removing h from K.

The following numerical measure of informational value satisfies Damping Version 2.

Damped Informational Value: Version 2:

Consider all potential contractions of K as defined relative to LK, $V_{LK,K} = U_{LK}$ and M^*.

(1) The version 2 loss in damped informational value incurred by shifting from K to a maxichoice contraction of K is equal to the loss in undamped informational value thereby incurred as represented by M^*.

(2) The version 2 loss in damped informational value incurred by shifting from K to an intersection of a set of maxichoice contractions of K is the largest loss incurred by any maxichoice contraction in the set.

Consider then a saturatable contraction removing h from K. The version 1 loss of informational value it incurs is equal to the loss of undamped informational value it incurs. That is equal to the sum of the M^*-values of the cells in U_K^* whose intersection with K constitutes the saturatable contraction in question. The version 2 loss is equal to the largest M^*-value among these cells.

Any potential contraction removing h from K is an intersection of a set S of saturatable contractions removing h. The loss in version

Informational Value in Contraction

1 (version 2) informational value incurred is equal to the largest loss in version 1 (version 2) informational value incurred by the members of set S.

Type 1 damped informational value is thus a hybrid. Saturatable contractions removing h are evaluated as required by assessments of undamped informational value. Intersections of such contractions are evaluated in the same way as damped information version 2. The two "pure" forms are undamped informational value that can be determined by summing over M^*-values in cells of U_K and damped informational value version 2 that can be determined by identifying the maximum M^*-value in the given set of cells.

The *loss* of damped informational value according to version 2 incurred by a contraction removing h from K is equal to the largest M^*-value belonging to an element of U_K^* in the subset of such elements whose intersection with K is the contraction in question.

Minimizing version 2 loss of damped informational value satisfies *the version 2 damping constraint* on deriving loss of informational value from LK, U_{LK} and M^*.

This procedure yields an ordering of all contractions from K regardless of what extralogical sentence in K is removed from K. The contraction strategies (including those that Makinson called "withdrawals") removing h from K are evaluated according to a restriction of the ordering of all contractions from K to those removing h from K. The weak ordering guarantees that x is an optimal contraction removing h from K if and only if x is an intersection of a set S of maxichoice contractions meeting the following conditions:

(a) S contains at least one member of U_K^* entailing $\sim$h that carries minimum M^*-value among elements of U_K^* entailing $\sim$h. Let that M^*-value be $M^\#$.

(b) S contains no cells in U_K^* carrying M^*-value greater than $M^\#$.

The Rule of Ties then stipulates that the weakest of these optimal contractions should be chosen. The weakest such contraction exists. It is the intersection of all and only maxichoice contractions carrying M^*-value less than or equal to $M^\#$.

Informational Value in Contraction

This contraction strategy is the intersection of the set of all maxichoice contractions carrying no greater M^*-values than the minimum M^*-value $M^{\#}$ carried by maxichoice contractions removing h from K.

MainThesis C:

> If the contraction recommended for removing h from K is the result of minimizing loss of damped informational value according to version 2 and the Rule of Ties, the contraction is the intersection of K with those cells of U_K^* that carry M^*-values less than or equal to the smallest M^*-value carried by a cell entailing $\sim$h.

> *Observation* $1''(2'', 3'')$: Under special assumption 1 (2,3), minimizing loss of damped informational value according to version 2 is an intersection of saturatable (but not necessarily maxichoice) contractions removing h from K. Recovery Fails.

> *Observation* $4''$: Under special assumption 4, minimizing loss of damped information value according to version 2 must be an intersection of a set of maxichoice contractions removing h from K. Recovery is satisfied.

Minimizing loss of damped informational value of version 2 is minimizing loss of informational value in a sense that extends the partial ordering of potential contractions generated by U_K^* (or potential contractions removing h from K) in conformity with the weak positive monotonicity condition. One can claim with good conscience that minimizing loss of damped informational value version 2 is minimizing loss of informational value just as one can in the case of undamped informational value and damped informational value version 1.

Version 2 of damped informational addresses sample space examples such as the case of the coin that is known to have landed heads in precisely the way presystematic judgment requires. In particular, it secures failures of Recovery under special assumption 1 and removes, thereby, an obstacle to assigning all cells in finite ultimate partitions positive M-value.

Informational Value in Contraction

In the belief-conforming version of the coin tossing example considered in the previous example, the dual ultimate partition consists of $\sim$E and ET. The candidate contractions removing E from K^{**} are EH $\vee$ $\sim$E and EH $\vee$ $\sim$E $\vee$ ET. The informational value of the first contraction cannot be less than that of the second by weak positive monotonicity. But if the informational value of EH is greater than that of $\sim$E, the two contractions must then carry equal version 2 damped informational value as long as the value of ET is no greater than that of EH. And I take it, in most settings inquirers will take these two propositions to carry equal informational value.

Thus, the only context in which $\sim$E $\vee$ H should be retained is when ET carries lower informational value (and higher M^*-value) than $\sim$E. This could very well happen if $\sim$E $\vee$ H were an instance of an explanatorily important regularity. There may be other reasons as well. In the case of statistical experiments this assignment of M^*-values to elements of U_{LK} does not happen precisely because the analogue of $\sim$E $\vee$ H is not an instance of something the inquirer takes to be a lawful regularity and does not regard this claim as carrying valuable information for some other reason. If losses of version 2 damped informational value are to be minimized, then $\sim$E $\vee$ H will be given up. Recovery will be violated. If losses in version 1 damped informational value are to be minimized, $\sim$E $\vee$ H will be retained and Recovery obeyed.

For any specific M^*-function, versions 1 and 2 are two ways of extending the partial ordering of potential contractions generated by U_K^* while keeping the faith with the weak positive monotonicity condition, the extended weak positive monotonicity condition, the intersection equality condition and, as a consequence of these three requirements on assessments of informational value, the damping constraint. Are there any other ways of evaluating informational value in conformity with the damping constraint?

Version 1 evaluates saturatable contractions removing h from K and maxichoice contractions from K in conformity with undamped informational value. Version 2 evaluates only maxichoice contractions from K in conformity with undamped informational value. The

Informational Value in Contraction

damping constraint is then applied to all intersections of maxichoice contractions from K.

One might explore various ways of partitioning the saturatable contractions removing h from K into a set evaluated according to undamped informational value of the constituent maxichoice contractions and a set evaluated by damping. The possibilities are legion. And they do not promise an improvement on what versions 1 and 2 provide. We might as well rest content with these two.

Or, more accurately, we should rest content with seeking to minimize loss of version 2 damped informational value.

My argument has been this. Anyone who embraces version 1 damped informational value is going to mishandle the counterinstances to Recovery in the case of stochastic experiments. Hence, if one is going to endorse minimizing loss of damped informational value, it had better be version 2.

Another argument may now be advanced. Version 2, like undamped informational value, determines the informational values of potential contractions from K removing h as a restriction of the assessment for potential contractions from K regardless of which extralogical sentence in K is removed. The assessment of losses in informational value no longer depend on what h is the "input" to contraction.

Should inquirers minimize loss of damped informational value when deciding how to contract? Consider someone who seeks to minimize loss of informational value in the sense of an evaluation satisfying weak positive monotonicity and extended weak positive monotonicity and wishes to do so in a manner that guarantees that using the Rule for Ties will minimize loss of informational value and avoid mandatory maxichoice contraction. Such an agent will require that informational value be damped.

Should minimizing loss of informational value be a common feature of the aims of contraction? I think so just as I think that seeking new error-free information ought to be the aim of deliberate expansion.

My argument has been directed at those who take the minimization of informational value seriously, who agree that maxichoice contraction ought not to be mandated in contraction and who recognize that requiring inquirers to obey Recovery when revising beliefs about stochastic processes is misguided.

Most contemporary writers on belief change have not considered justification of change of belief to require showing that the justified change is optimal or admissible all things considered given the specification of cognitive goals. And even if they have, they have not always taken seriously the need to spell out what are to count as the options available to the inquirer. Some commentators apparently cannot credit that considering beliefs about statistical experiments can so decisively refute the Recovery postulate as I believe it can. It would be pointless to examine all the ways in which the conclusions I have been advancing have been or might be avoided. I will focus on a project that I find more interesting.

Minimizing loss of version 2 damped informational value yields recommendations for contractions identical with the recommendations favored by Rott and Pagnucco (1999). Yet, I think that there are some important philosophical issues that separate the ideas of Rott and Pagnucco from my own. I would prefer to examine these differences that seem to be embedded within a framework of substantial agreement than to gaze uncomprehendingly across an abyss of misunderstanding at those whose dissents are more radical.

In the early 1990s, Rott had entertained the proposal for contraction that he and Pagnucco elaborated in 1999 and I am defending.

Rott (1991) introduced it as a useful aid in calculating AGM revisions. The AGM revision of K by adding h can be derived by first contracting using an AGM contraction removing h and then expanding by adding $\sim$h. The very same revision can be obtained by contracting using another AGM "revision equivalent" contraction that is not a partial meet contraction and then expanding by adding h. For reasons to be explained shortly, Rott thought that contracting in a manner that I would rationalize by minimizing loss of version 2 damped informational value is a user friendly way to obtain an AGM revision that can be obtained also by a revision equivalent partial meet contraction. The new type of contraction had an instru-

Informational Value in Contraction

mental value; but it was unclear how central it was conceptually to the understanding of contraction.

Rott and Pagnucco (1999) take the issue of rationalizing what they call "severe withdrawals" (I think they should be called "mild contractions") more earnestly than Rott apparently did in 1991. Although Rott and Pagnucco and I agree in taking severe withdrawals or mild contractions seriously, I support the proposal because, on the one hand, there is a clear type of aim (minimizing loss of version 2 damped informational value) relative to which it has a decision-theoretic rationale and because, on the other hand, the prescription that emerges conforms to requirements of presystematic practice. Rott and Pagnucco have not supplied a clear decision-theoretic rationale and, indeed, seem to take a stand against the kind of approach I adopt that urges minimizing loss of informational value of some kind. Yet, Rott has become an advocate of interpreting belief change as a problem for rational choice.

I believe that lurking behind the superficial agreement between Rott and myself in endorsing mild contraction or severe withdrawal, there are some serious differences concerning what we demand of a decision-theoretic grounding of belief change. Two philosophically interesting bones of contention may be considered:

1. What is to be required of a decision-theoretic rationale for a change in state of full belief? Rott (1993 and 2001) seems to offer a quite different answer than I have been advancing since the 1960s.
2. Should inquirers who are required to contract belief-state **K** represented by K relative to U_K^* by removing h seek to minimize losses of informational value at all or should they, as Rott and Pagnucco (1999) think, seek the most plausible contraction?

In the the following chapter, I shall compare the answers offered by Rott and Pagnucco or by Rott to these questions and those I favor.

Contraction, Rational Choice and Economy 5

5.1. Choice Functions and Selection Functions

In Levi 1967 and 1984, I sought to rationalize deliberate or inductive expansion from K relative to ultimate partition U_K in the following manner:

1. A roster of potential expansions of K is specified relative to U_K. These constitute the cognitive options. A cognitive option is representable by a subset of U_K each element of which goes unrejected according to that option. Let the set of such options be $P(U_K)$.
2. A specification of the aims is provided that was then represented by an epistemic utility function over relevant "consequences" of exercising one of the cognitive options given the specification of which element of U_K is true.
3. A credal probability distribution over U_K is given.
4. The injunction to maximize expected epistemic utility is deployed to determine the set of optimal options.
5. A Rule for Ties is invoked as a secondary criterion to select one of the optimal options.

Contraction, Rational Choice and Economy

Condition 4 yields a ranking of the available cognitive options in $P(U_K)$. One can, if one likes, extend the ranking to the set of all lotteries among the available cognitive options. Let $M[P(U_K)]$ be the "mixture set" of all lotteries over the elements of $P(U_K)$. The mixed options in this mixture set need not be available to the inquirer. Nonetheless, the inquirer can provide a ranking of $M[P(U_K)]$ that expresses the goals of inductive expansion were the lotteries in $M[P(U_K)]$ available for choice and on the assumption that the evaluation of the members of $P(U_K)$ is embedded in the evaluation of members of $M[P(U_K)]$.

Given these suppositions, the elements of $M[P(U_K)]$ should be ranked according to their expected values where these expected values are determined by assuming that the values of the "pure" options that are components of the mixtures are their expected epistemic utilities. The representation of the ranking of $M[P(U_K)]$ in terms of expected utility can be recharacterized as a weak ordering of the same domain that satisfies requirements equivalent to Von Neumann–Morgenstern axioms. Instead of representing the ranking of $P(U_K)$ by an expected epistemic utility function, we can represent it by such a weak ordering with respect to *categorical* weak preference over $M[P(U_K)]$ in which the weak ordering of elements of $P(U_K)$ is embedded. The embeddability of the weak ordering or preference over $P(U_K)$ in the weak ordering of $M[P(U_K)]$ permits a third method of representation in terms of a *choice function* that takes as arguments any finite, non-empty subset S of $M[P(U_K)]$ and delivers as value a non-empty subset $C(S)$ of S. $C(S)$ is the set of members of S each of which come out best according to the categorical weak preference over $M[P(U_K)]$ restricted to S. If x and y are elements of $M[P(U_K)]$, x is revealed to be weakly preferred to y if and only if there is a finite S containing both x and y such that x is a member of $C(S)$. Revealed preference is complete in the sense that for every x and y in $M[P(U_K)]$, either x is weakly preferred to y or y is weakly preferred to x. As long as the categorical preference is a weak ordering and the choice function takes as values the set of optimal options from the set S of available options, revealed preference and categorical preference should coincide.

Contraction, Rational Choice and Economy

It is possible, of course, that there is indeterminacy in the credal probability distribution or in the epistemic utility function that will lead to indeterminacy in the assessment of expected epistemic utility. In that case, categorical preference over $M[P(U_K)]$ will be a quasi ordering. The value of the choice function $C(S)$ is then the set of options in S that come out optimal in S according to some permissible expected epistemic utility function. These are *E-admissible* options. Revealed weak preference is defined in the manner indicated above. It remains complete but may lack other properties of a weak ordering such as transitivity of equipreference. The categorical weak preference does not coincide with the revealed preference defined by the choice function. It is incomplete and thus allows for noncomparability.

Many students of rational choice, including Hans Rott, construct the choice functions differently in the case of indeterminacy. $C(S)$ is the set of *maximal* options in S, i.e. those options that are not categorically strictly dispreferred to any members of S. Once more categorical and revealed preferences come apart. But they do so differently than when E-admissibility is used to define choice functions.[1]

We may also consider choice functions that incorporate the Rule for Ties. When there is no indeterminacy, the revealed preference relation no longer coincides with the categorical preference. The reason is that the weakest optimal expansion with respect to categorical preference is now revealed better than the other expansions that are optimal with respect to categorical preference. One may think of the new revealed preference as a lexicographical weak ordering. I prefer to think of the Rule for Ties as a rule for adjudicating between best (or E-admissible) options when the primary values fail to do so.

---

[1] For a discussion of the necessary and sufficient conditions that choice functions must satisfy in order to guarantee that revealed preference will be a weak ordering as well as the implications of weaker conditions see Sen (1971) and Herzberger (1973). I have related revealed preference to categorical preference and the properties of choice functions in Levi (1986). All of these references addressed the topic without regard as to whether the decision problem is a moral, political, economic, prudential, aesthetic or cognitive one. We are focusing on cognitive decision problems here. They are cognitive in two respects: the options are changes in doxastic commitment—commitment as to what to fully belief and the goals are characteristically cognitive.

Contraction, Rational Choice and Economy

The criteria invoked are secondary criteria that play no role when the primary criteria are decisive. And when ties are broken, the options recommended are not valued higher according to the primary criterion or all things considered. The choice function that incorporates the secondary criteria does not separate out the primary from the secondary considerations in the revealed preference. It is, therefore, too coarse-grained to use when studying primary and secondary preferences. (See Levi, 1986 for more discussion of these matters in the general case of practical decision-making.) But the choice function does summarize the conclusions reached as to which options are admissible taking all value commitments both primary and secondary into account. In this respect, the use of choice functions in connection with inductive expansion is just an instance of their use in decision-making under risk or uncertainty.

In set theory, choice functions are functions from non-empty subsets of objects in a given domain Ω to members of such sets (Barwise, 1977, 347). The notion of a choice function used in revealed preference theory and decision theory differs from the set theoretical notion in two respects:

1. Formally, a choice function is a function from non-empty, finite subsets of objects in a given domain Ω to non-empty subsets (not necessarily singletons) of these subsets.
2. The subset S that appears as an argument in a choice function *as this concept is used in accounts of decision-making* is a subset of a set Ω of *potential options for choice*.

The evaluation of S is assumed to be embedded in an evaluation of the potential options in Ω. $C(S)$ is intended to represent the set of options that *would be* optimal or admissible *were* the set S the options available for choice by the decision-maker while that evaluation is the operative one. Two illustrations of the distinction between evaluating a set of potential options and the evaluation of a set of options available for choice may be helpful.

In the use of indifference maps to characterize consumer demand, the potential options are the various "commodity bundles" represented by points on an indifference map. Not all the potential options

Contraction, Rational Choice and Economy

are options available to the consumer. Only those points below the budget line representing the given prices and the income of the consumer represent options the consumer faces. However, the evaluation of the consumer's options is embedded in an evaluation of the potential options that characterizes choices that the consumer would make were the consumer to have a choice between various sets of commodity bundles other than the set the consumer actually faces.

A decision-maker might face a choice between taking and leaving a certain lottery. The prizes and penalties that are outcomes of the lottery are not options available for choice. But in assessing the options actually faced, it may be helpful to assume that the values of the options actually faced is embedded in a valuation of a space of potential options consisting of the prizes (or lotteries where these prizes will be realized for sure) and all possible mixtures or lotteries of these. A choice function could then be defined on non-empty, finite subsets of the set Ω of potential options that represents the global evaluation of Ω and by implication the evaluation of the options actually available as well.

Logicians have often allowed for choice functions that satisfy (1) even when the values of these functions are not singletons. Often these functions are called *selection functions* and they do not satisfy requirement (2). Typically a selection function takes as arguments subsets of a set W of maximal elements, points, maximally consistent propositions or worlds. The value of such a function σ for some subset S of W is a subset of S. Condition (1) is satisfied. However, $\sigma(S)$ is typically understood to represent a proposition that is true if and only one of the worlds in $\sigma(S)$ is true.

Deciding how to expand in deliberate expansion and how to contract are two settings where it is possible to apply both choice functions relevant to decision-making and selection functions. However, the choice functions used in such settings are distinct from the selection functions used. Failure to take note of this leads to confusion.

In deliberate expansion, the options available for choice are represented by subsets of U_K belonging $P(U_K)$. For some purposes, the arguments of the choice function could be restricted to the set

Contraction, Rational Choice and Economy

of non-empty subsets of $P(U_K)$—the power set of U_K without the empty set. This type of choice function might serve to make comparative evaluations of all the cognitive options available to the inquirer when U_K is the ultimate partition.

If the aim is to use a choice function to derive a numerical representation of the expected utilities of the options actually available from a preference over potential options, the set of potential options should not be $P(U_K)$ but $M[P(U_K)]$ (or some suitable alternative). As long as the preference over this domain is a weak ordering, the argument S of the function C could be any finite, non-empty subset of $M[P(U_K)]$—including subsets of $P(U_K)$.

The best options in $P(U_K)$ are those that do not reject any element x of U_K for which $Q(x) > qM(x)$ while rejecting all such elements y for which $Q(y) < qM(y)$. Elements z for which $Q(z) = qM(z)$ may or may not be rejected by optimal potential expansions. If the Rule for Ties is invoked, the elements z go unrejected. But the other options carrying best expected epistemic utility rank as optimal. So for the purpose of representing evaluation of expected epistemic utility, the Rule for Ties may be ignored.

If the subset of $M[P(U_K)]$ contains mixtures of the "pure" options in $P(U_K)$, expected epistemic utility will identify a set of expected utility maximizing options. Choice functions are readily determined.

Thus, the choice function is determined by expected epistemic utility values for $M[P(U_K)]$ and offers what is required when the argument of the choice function is $P(U_K)$.

There is, however, another way to obtain functions that satisfy the formal requirement (1) for choice functions. U_K is a subset of U_{LK}. Other non-empty subsets of U_{LK} characterize other consistent potential belief-states. On the assumption that relative to LK we have a credal probability Q^* and an informational value determining probability M^* such that Q and M are obtained by ordinary conditionalizing K from Q^* and M^*, then for each subset U_K of U_{LK} we have an expansion K of LK that recognizes all and only cells in U_{LK} belonging in U_K as serious possibilities. Hence by the rules previously presented for inductive expansion, for each value of q, we have a definite subset $\sigma(U_K)$ of unrejected elements of U_K.

Contraction, Rational Choice and Economy

Formally σ has the structure of a choice function. But if we take into account the intended application of choice functions in decision-making, σ cannot be interpreted as a choice function.

Choice functions in the sense relevant to decision theory take as arguments sets of objects from a domain of potential options. The value of such a function is some subset of its argument. If U_K is the ultimate partition, the set of options from which a choice is to be made is the set $P(U_K)$ of potential expansions of K.

But according to the current proposal, the domain of the selection function σ is $P(U_{LK})$. That is to say, the argument for the function σ is U_K for some potential expansion K of LK characterizable by a subset of U_{LK}. The elements of U_{LK} are the strongest potential expansions of the minimal belief-state **LK** or the minimal corpus LK that expresses it. They are analogous to possible worlds, maximally consistent sets of sentences or models of a given language. σ takes sets of those possible worlds as arguments, whose elements are consistent with K.

To be a choice function determining the admissible subset of the available options for expansion from K, the argument of σ should be but is not a complete set of potential expansions of K. The argument for σ does not exhaust the cognitive options. σ fails as a choice function for inductive expansion. The arguments it takes could be regarded as sets of strongest consistent options available as expansions of K. When U_K is the argument of σ, the set of options available is the power set $P(U_K)$.

To be sure, σ could be interpreted as recommending that the inquirer come to full belief that exactly one of the elements of $T = \sigma(S)$ is true. T must then represent a single cognitive option—the coming to full belief that the true element of S is one of the elements of T.

If $\sigma(S)$ is so construed, it represents a cognitive option but not a member of its argument U_K. A member of U_K is a consistent expansion of K furnishing maximally consistent relevant information concerning the issue under study. The claim that the true element of U_K lurks in T is an expansion of K but is not maximal in this sense. On this reading, σ fails to satisfy even the formal requirement (1) for a choice function.

Contraction, Rational Choice and Economy

This last difficulty can be ameliorated by insisting that the value of σ is a subset of U_K so that the formal requirement (1) on choice functions is preserved. This would not, however, eliminate the fact that the argument of σ does not characterize all the available options and that the value does not identify all the admissible options.

However, even though σ is not a choice function representing the recommendations for inductive expansion, σ could be interpreted as an alternative means for representing the recommendations of such a choice function.

The value of σ is the recommended set of unrejected elements of U_K according to the choice function over all the potential expansions of K. According to the account of deliberate expansion I have proposed, these selected elements are the maximally consistent expansions of K according to U_K that fail to be rejected at the stipulated value of q. The Rule for Ties recommends suspension of judgment between these expansions (the intersection of the set $\sigma(U_K)$). At least this will be so if credal probability and epistemic utility are determinate and maximization of expected epistemic utility is supplemented by the Rule for Ties.

The function σ so construed is not a choice function satisfying (1) and (2). It is a function from a set of maximal elements (worlds, points or whatever) to subsets where the subsets are intended to possibilities that remain unrejected. But the set of points or cells in U_K that go unrejected represent the expansion of K by adding the proposition represented by that set of points. So the function σ has the qualifications to be a selection function.

The selection function σ and choice function begin at the same place. Given LK, U_{LK} and K, the ultimate partition U_K is determined. U_K determines the arguments of both the choice function and the selection function.

U_K determines the domain of the choice function to be the set $P(U_K)$. The valuation of the potential options is assumed to be embedded in an evaluation of the elements of $M[P(U_K)]$. And the value of the choice function for some subset of $M[P(U_K)]$ such as $P(U_K)$ is the set of options that are optimal or admissible according to the ranking of the elements of that subset. If the argument of the

Contraction, Rational Choice and Economy

choice function is $P(U_K)$, its value is the set of expansions each of which rules out elements x of U_K for which $Q(x) < qM(x)$, does not rule out elements y such that $Q(y) > qM(y)$ and rules out some subset of the elements z of U_K such that $Q(z) = qM(z)$.

By way of contrast, the argument of the selection function is U_K. And the value of $\sigma(U_K)$ is the subset of elements of U_K that are not ruled according to that optimal option among those identified by the choice function according to which none of the z's in U_K such that $Q(z) = qM(z)$ is eliminated. That subset represents the proposition that is recommended for addition to K in the expansion singled out by the Rule for Ties. The selection function states for each potential expansion K not only what U_K will be but determines the expansion of K that would be recommended as maximizing expected epistemic utility and using the Rule for Ties.

However, in order to show that the recommendation of the selection function does what is claimed, it is necessary to show that the recommended option does indeed maximize expected utility among the elements of $P(U_K)$ and is picked out from these by the Rule for Ties. The selection function does not do this. Indeed, the selection function does not show that the recommended expansion is best among all expansions of K available for choice. To do this, it is necessary to be given a ranking of the expansions available for choice. Nothing involved with the selection function does this. Embedding the ranking of the options available for choice in a mixture set does permit the derivation of the set of admissible expansions from an argument showing that these options best promote the goals of the inquiry. And given this embedding, the ranking of the options in the mixture set and each of the subsets can be characterized by a choice function.

Thus far I have been considering choice functions and selection functions for deliberate expansion. There is, however, a parallel distinction that bears on contraction removing h from K. This is the distinction that is relevant to a comparison of the views of Rott with mine.

Rott and I agree that contraction should be treated decision-theoretically. But the agreement is superficial. Rott fails to take seriously the differences between selection and choice functions and, as a consequence, tends to confuse choice functions with selection functions. This failure, in my judgment, undermines the decision-theoretic aspect of his approach to contraction.

The title of Chapter 7 of Rott's important recent book (2001) is *Coherentist Belief Change as a Problem of Rational Choice*. I overlook the qualification "coherentist" to the topic of belief change. There are, I concede, two kinds of belief change: changes due to efforts to fulfill doxastic commitments as when an agent attempts to recognize the logical consequences of what he or she already explicitly believes and changes in doxastic commitments. The former kind of change corresponds roughly to what Rott calls "vertical" changes whereas the latter are "horizontal" changes. Although Rott's distinction and mine are not precisely equivalent, the differences do not appear to matter in the current discussion. Rott, however, means to distinguish between two kinds of approaches to horizontal change or to change in commitment: foundationalist and coherentist.

I shall explain in Chapter 7 why I do not think this distinction helpful. It is not that I take sides with the coherentists against the foundationalists. I object to certain coherentist accounts of justifications for contraction—such as accounts defending AGM contraction—even though these accounts are coherentist. I also object to accounts that proceed by contraction from belief bases. And I do so for substantially the same reason. In both cases, restrictions are imposed on the range of available contraction strategies that are not warranted given the goals and aims of the problem under investigation. The coherentist AGM approach stipulates without justification that contractions should be partial meet contractions. Foundationalists often stipulate without justification that contractions should not be partial meet contractions. Neither approach is acceptable.

In Chapter 7 of his book, Rott adopts a coherentist approach and seeks to understand coherentist belief change as a problem of rational choice. Needless to say, I applaud Rott's intention. Since the 1960s I have advocated thinking of what I now call deliberate or inductive expansion as a problem for rational choice. Rott's discussion addresses the problem of how to contract among contractions removing h from K as a decision problem. I myself have thought about contraction this way since the 1970s although, thanks to the paper by Alchourrón, Gärdenfors and Makinson (1985), I came to realize that my early efforts to address this problem were too casually and carelessly conceived.

In spite of my admiration for Rott's intentions, I contend that his efforts also do not succeed.

Rott (1993 and 2001) has proposed to employ choice functions used to represent relations of revealed preference as in Herzberger (1973) and Sen (1971)[2] as a means of defining contraction functions whose values are contractions from fixed K given the stipulated removal of some sentence h. Rott deploys *selection* functions as the choice functions appropriate for this purpose.

In Chapter 6 of his book, Rott develops an account of choice functions where, as I have indicated, the arguments of the functions are options and the values are sets of what I have been calling admissible options. The presentation is interesting and useful even when Rott presents wrinkles of his own that are debatable. In Chapter 7, Rott brings the results of Chapter 6 to bear on the question of contraction. He claims to have reduced the principles of rational contraction and revision to principles of rational choice by the use of choice functions.

Rott (2001, 170) acknowledges explicitly that his choice functions are selection functions of the sort that had been used in supplying semantics for conditionals by Stalnaker (1968), Lewis (1973) and Chellas (1975) and that formally similar devices had been used in the 1985 AGM paper.

Rott's selection functions can be used to reveal a preference or ranking of cells of U_K^* (worlds or models). Given any subset

---

[2] Herzberger and Sen succeed in systematically presenting work on revealed preference that goes back to the 1930s. For a discussion by a sympathizer with the revealed preference approach, see Little (1950). I have discussed choice functions and choice consistency conditions from the point of view of someone who rejects the requirement that rational agents should have weakly ordered preference rankings of their options in Levi (1986).

Contraction, Rational Choice and Economy

constituting a dual ultimate partition U_K^* (and associated K), a subset $\tau(U_K^* \cap [[\sim h]])$ of most preferred or at least maximal (in the sense of Sen) elements of U_K^* that imply $\sim h$ is identified.[3] The selection functions are construed as if the cells or worlds were potential options and that various subsets like $U_K^* \cap [[h]]$ are "menus" of options for choice. These elements are not admissible contractions from K. Without an additional definition of contraction from K removing h, the selection function makes no recommendation of a contraction at all. Rott supplies a definition (2001, 174, Definition 6). It is the intersection of all the maxichoice contractions associated with cells of $\tau(U_K^* \cap [[\sim h]])$.

Rott goes on to give a 'syntactic' variant of his account of selection functions and the contractions determined by them. And he examines how various properties of these selection functions when these are construed as choice functions in formal choice theory are associated with various properties of contraction functions.

Rott fails to do, however, what seems minimally necessary to sustain his claim to have interpreted contraction as a "problem for rational choice".

In the first place, he does not derive his selection functions from choice functions properly so-called. The arguments of such functions are *sets* of potential contractions removing h that are optional for the inquirer when engaged in efforts at contraction removing h and whose values are the sets of admissible options.

Second, there is no indication as to how such choice functions would be rationalized on the basis of the goals of the inquirer and the principles of rational choice. To do so, it would have been necessary to identify a representation of the goals of the inquirer in terms of a preference or utility evaluation of the set of *all* contractions removing h from K available to the inquirer.

What Rott and AGM give us is a preference over the maxichoice contractions from K removing h or the cells in U_K^* implying $\sim h$. In terms of Grove diagrams, they give an ordering of worlds falsified by

---

[3] In this discussion, I shall use Rott's "[[h]]" to represent the subset of elements of U_{LK} (these correspond to Rott's "worlds") that entail h.

Contraction, Rational Choice and Economy

K. The preference for elements of U_K^* is not embedded in a larger preference ranking of the non-empty members of the power set of U_K^*. A rationalization of the recommendations for contraction yielded by Rott's selection function is not provided.

If the aim of efforts to contract removing h from K is minimizing loss of version 1 damped informational value, it is possible to rationalize Rott's way of defining a selection-based contraction function with the aid of the Rule for Ties. Using version 1 damped informational value, we have seen that under special assumption 1 the meet of all optimal maxichoice contractions removing h is optimal and is recommended by the Rule for Ties. The optimal maxichoice contractions removing h can be selected from the set of all maxichoice contractions in U_K and the intersection recommended as the contraction to endorse in efforts to contract removing h. The result is K_h^- according to the selection-based definition of contraction provided by Rott as definition 6 on 174. By showing that our decision-theoretic rationalization of partial meet contraction coincides with the prescription of definition 6, we have provided a way of assimilating the injunctions of partial meet contraction into what Rott calls "practical reason".

Rott makes no attempt to offer this rationale or an alternative to it. He offers a selection function selecting the best maxichoice contractions removing h from K. And the contraction removing h that is recommended is the intersection of this set of best maxichoice contractions. Why this should be so is based on semantics and not principles of rational choice. I, by way of contrast, insist that the semantics should be replaced by a decision-theoretic rationalization.

Rott has confused choice functions that express the prescriptions characterizing efforts to optimize relative to given goals with selection functions that do no such thing. The use of selection functions may be rationalized by practical reason; but as far as I can make out, Rott fails to do so. If the task were to choose optimal maxichoice contractions, Rott's selection functions could be used. And it is also true that whether undamped losses, type 1 damped losses or type 2 damped losses of informational value are to be minimized, such losses in informational value are uniquely determined by a weak ordering of the elements of U_K^*. But the derivations are different.

Contraction, Rational Choice and Economy

Each one depends on a different way of obtaining preferences over potential contractions from K. The preference elicited for the elements of U_K^* according to the techniques of revealed preference theory is insufficient for achieving the requisite derivation decision theoretically. No case has been made for seeing the problem of how to contract as a problem for practical reason unless the preference over maxichoice contractions removing h from K (or over elements of U_K^*) that is characterized by a choice function is extended to a preference over all potential contractions removing h from K.

The point I am belaboring is no mere matter of terminology.

In Rott (2001), there is a brief discussion of severe withdrawal and the case to be made for it. In that setting, Rott seems to concede that his decision-theoretic approach has failed to provide a warrant for severe withdrawal. Stated more accurately, the use of selection functions cannot yield severe withdrawals. In my view, this does not imply that a decision-theoretic rationalization for severe withdrawal cannot be offered but only that there is no representation of the recommendation by means of a selection function.

Here is the problem. In the context of determining how to contract by removing h from K, a selection function takes as arguments subsets of U_{LK} that are constituted by members of the dual ultimate partition U_K^* that imply $\sim$ h. If the contraction is a severe withdrawal, it is the intersection of maxichoice contractions from K at least as good as the best maxichoice contraction removing h. So the set of maxichoice contractions that constitutes the argument of the selection function is the set of members of the dual ultimate partition U_K^* whether or not these elements imply $\sim$ h or h.

Moreover, the subset of U_K^* selected by the selection function is not the set of most preferred elements of U_K^*. So not only is the selection function not a choice function taking a set of potential contractions as a set of options in the argument place, it does not select the set of most preferred maxichoice contractions in U_K^* or the most preferred maxichoice contractions removing h in that set.

A binary selection function can be introduced. It takes as arguments the subset of U_K^* entailing $\sim$ h and the subset entailing h. The value of this function is the union of the most preferred elements in the first set with all elements of the second set that are weakly preferred to these. The intersection of the elements of this set with K is a severe withdrawal removing h from K. The binary selection function is neither a choice function nor a selection function of the sort countenanced by Rott in Chapter 6 of his book.

On the other hand, if the domain on which choice functions operate is not restricted to maxichoice contractions but includes all potential contractions from U_K, a preference ranking can be obtained such that the best contractions removing h from U_K include mild contractions also known as severe withdrawals. To achieve this end, a preference over potential contractions according to version 2 damped informational value can be used.

Unlike the preferences associated with Rott's selection functions, these preferences are defined for options represented by sets of worlds or subsets of U_K^*. Neither comparisons between worlds with respect to comparative similarity, nearness to one another, relative value or the like can substitute for the weak ordering of sets of worlds that is required.

Whether assessments of losses in informational value are undamped, version 1 damped or version 2 damped, it is true that the ordering of sets of maxichoice contractions is uniquely determined by the ordering of the maxichoice contractions embedded in the ordering of sets. But how the ordering of such sets or sets of worlds is determined varies depending upon which kind of assessment is deployed. And that ordering is the one that determines which options are optimal or admissible.

Severe withdrawal is rationalizable decision theoretically if the goal of contraction can be understood as minimizing loss of version 2 damped informational value. To succeed, however, choice functions that can be used in such rationalization must be clearly distinguished from selection functions that cannot.

To sum up, the use of selection functions to characterize contraction functions where the selection function is based on a "preference" over worlds, models or cells in LK does not suffice to provide an assimilation of theoretical justifications for contractions to practical means-ends reasoning.

Contraction, Rational Choice and Economy

The project I have undertaken, by way of contrast, does at least gesture in the direction of such assimilation. One may disagree with the view I have taken of the aims of deliberate expansion and the aims of contraction. But if the conception I have proposed of what these aims should be is acceptable, then the models I propose do succeed in characterizing how to justify expansion and contraction in a manner that imputes the "theoretical" aspects of such reasoning to the specification of cognitive or epistemic goals and reduces all other aspects of the reasoning to practical rationality.

I do not mean to leave the impression that Rott and Pagnucco (1999) fail to mount an argument for severe withdrawal in their important paper. My point is that they do not defend severe withdrawal by showing that it is optimal among potential contractions removing h relative to a goal that they think worth pursuing. In this sense, their defense is not decision-theoretic. In the next section, I summarize what I take their argument to be in the 1999 paper.

5.2. Informational Economy, Indifference, Strict Preference and Weak Preference

Gärdenfors (1988) thought that a Principle of Informational Economy guided the account of belief change he and AGM favored. When applied in the context of contraction, Rott and Pagnucco (1999) interpret the Principle of Informational Economy formulated in its "unadulterated" form as a Principle of Conservatism.[4] The

---

[4] Both Gärdenfors (1988) and Rott and Pagnucco (1999) refer back to a principle of conservativism in Harman (1986). Harman writes "One is justified in continuing fully to accept something in the absence of a special reason not to" (46). Whether Harman intended to endorse the idea discussed by Gärdenfors, Rott and Pagnucco is obscure to me. Rott and Pagnucco, for example, do consider briefly the question of the conditions under which the inquirer might have a reason to give up belief that h. However, the focus of their attention is on the question as to what other sentences one should remove from K given that one is warranted in removing h from K. By way of contrast, Harman is concerned with the conditions under which one is warranted in contracting by removing h from K. Insofar as this is Harman's concern, Harman's conservativism might be understood as insisting that one should not contract by removing h from K without a good reason (which, according to Harman, is constituted by a threat to "coherence"—

several potential contractions of K are represented by intersections of K with subsets of cells in U_K^*.[5] A potential contraction K_1 of K carries less information than another such contraction K_2 if and only if $K_1 \subset K_2$. Such comparisons of potential corpora partially order the potential belief-states expressible in L.

Neither Gärdenfors nor Rott and Pagnucco explicitly extend this partial order to a weak order. This is one of the points I have belabored in the previous section. However, these authors do assume the availability of another weak ordering—to wit, of the domain of maxichoice contractions or of the associated worlds or cells in U_K^*.

We thus can distinguish two versions of the Principle of Conservativism:

Strict Conservativism insists that losses in *information* be minimized. Because potential contractions can only be partially ordered with respect to strength, every maxichoice contraction is admissible in the sense that no other potential contraction is rated better than it. But there is no basis for choosing between maxichoice contractions. The weak ordering of maxichoice contractions counts for naught.

Weak Conservativism recommends minimizing losses of hyper-undamped informational value. Conservativism so understood requires that losses of informational value be minimized in a sense according to which the extension of the partial ordering with respect to information respects strong positive monotonicity. Weak Conservativism provides an integration of the partial ordering with respect to losses

---

whatever that is (32). To be sure, Harman's view might also encompass the problem considered by Gärdenfors, Pagnucco and Rott. Harman's Conservativism could then also mean that if one does contract by removing h from K, one should do so with as minimal a loss of information as is feasible. I am sympathetic with some version of the first principle of conservativism. One needs good reasons for contraction just as one does for expansion. To that extent Harman is right although I find appeals to coherence in this connection obscure. When it comes to the second thesis, I am against minimizing losses of information—the core idea behind Harman's Principle of Conservativism. I am, instead, in favor of minimizing losses of damped informational value of type 2.

[5] Recall that the elements of the basic partition U_{LK} are the consistent expansions of LK expressing in L strongest potential answers to the question under investigation. They need not be maximally consistent expansions of LK. Nor need LK be the set of logical truths expressible in L. Rott and Pagnucco explicitly take their worlds to be maximally consistent sets in L (2000, n. 9).

Contraction, Rational Choice and Economy

of information and the weak ordering of maxichoice contractions into a single weak ordering of all potential contractions of K.

Moreover, the weak ordering of potential contractions from K and the weak ordering of potential expansions of LK in which the first weak ordering is embedded are both representable by a function $Cont^*(x) = 1 - M^*(x)$. The integrated weak ordering of potential contractions from K may then be construed as an ordering with respect to hyper-undamped informational value.

Here the set of admissible options will all be tied for optimality. Because all potential contractions removing h will be weakly ordered, the maxichoice contractions removing h will be so as well. The optimal options will be the best of the maxichoice contractions removing h. The intersection or meet of the best of maxichoice contractions removing h will not be optimal among the contractions removing h from K.

By exploiting the preference over U_{LK}, Weak Conservativism differs from Strict Conservativism in ruling out some maxichoice contractions as admissible for choice. But both forms of the conservative principle recommend maxichoice contractions.

Notice that the argument just offered to the conclusion that conservativism favors maxichoice contraction invokes at least a partial ordering of *all* potential contractions removing h and some criterion showing that maxichoice contractions removing h are optimal in that they minimize loss of information as compared to all other potential contractions removing h from K.

Rott and Pagnucco (1999) point out that AGM do not recommend maxichoice contraction. They favor partial meet contractions. A partial meet contraction removing h from K is the intersection of K with members of a subset S of the maxichoice contractions removing h. S is determined by a selection function of the sort discussed in the previous section that takes as its argument the subset $U_K^* \cap [[\sim h]]$. The intersection of each member of S with K is a maxichoice contraction removing h from K. The value S of the selection function is a subset of the argument set. The intersection of its intersection with K is a partial meet contraction removing h from K.

Contraction, Rational Choice and Economy

Unless S is a singleton, recommending such a partial meet contraction is incompatible with the principle of conservativism whether strict or weak. The intersection of two or more maxichoice contractions does not minimize loss of information in the set inclusion sense. It does not minimize loss of informational value in the hyper-undamped sense.

Rott and Pagnucco (1999) and Rott (2001) seem to think that the endorsement of partial meet contraction is a betrayal of informational economy. I have sought to show that under a sufficiently generous conception of informational value as urging minimization of informational value in a sense satisfying weak positive monotonicity, it is possible to recommend partial meet contractions as minimizing loss of informational value. Rott and Pagnucco and Rott do not consider this possibility. Nor apparently do AGM. Rott and Pagnucco explore ways of avoiding the choice of maxichoice contractions in a principled manner in the absence of a comprehensive weak ordering of the set of all potential contractions.

It is in this setting that the two rankings considered by Rott and Pagnucco—the partial ordering with respect to information, entailment or set inclusion and the weak ordering of maxichoice contractions are exploited.

Rott and Pagnucco reconstruct AGM as thinking of the selection function as processing the elements of $U_K^* \cap [[\sim h]]$ by partitioning into sets of elements that are not discriminated from one another. It appears that the partition is based on the ordering of maxichoice contractions. Elements that are not discriminated are considered to be indifferent. Rott and Pagnucco formulate a Principle of Indifference according to which "objects held in equal regard should be treated equally".

Suppose that one considers the partial ordering of potential contractions removing h from K in terms of set inclusion. The potential contractions that are maximal options are the maxichoice contractions removing h. No other contraction incurs a smaller loss of information than such a contraction does. Minimizing loss of information recommends "picking" one of these maxichoice con-

Contraction, Rational Choice and Economy

tractions removing h. This goes against the Principle of Indifference. Even though the several maxichoice contractions removing h are non-comparable and not equipreferred, the Principle of Indifference urges that they be treated equally. That is to say, the weak ordering of maxichoice contractions removing h ranks all of them together. Following the Principle of Economy, on the other hand, discriminates between the maxichoice contraction chosen and other maxichoice contractions removing h from K.

To meet the demands of the Principle of Indifference, the intersection of all such maxichoice contractions will be recommended. This intersection is weaker than any of the maxichoice contractions removing h. The Principle of Informational Economy in its guise as conservativism weak or strict is blatantly violated.

This intersection of all maxichoice contractions removing h from K is full meet contraction that AGM reject as vigorously as they reject maxichoice contraction. AGM plead for something intermediate between the extremes—to wit, partial meet contraction. This too deviates from Informational Economy but not so extremely as full meet contraction does.

For these reasons, Rott and Pagnucco recognize that AGM do not endorse the Principle of Conservativism; but they think that AGM still take Informational Economy into account.

In settling on partial meet we realize that the Principle of Economy and the Principle of Indifference are in a state of tension with respect to one another; Economy advocates the selection of a single element from $K \perp \phi$ [the set of $U_K^* \cap [[\sim h]]$ with K] while Indifference recommends giving up more than necessary if the selection mechanism does not single out a unique 'best' solution (Rott and Pagnucco, 1999, 504).

Notice that the two principles are not "in a state of tension" because Economy urges optimization by minimizing loss of information and Indifference urges optimization according to some other evaluation. Indifference does no such thing. There is tension because the two principles make differing recommendations. But Rott and Pagnucco do not recognize either principle as optimizing according to some value. Optimization is not an issue.

Contraction, Rational Choice and Economy

Rott and Pagnucco recognize that something more is needed than a Principle of Indifference to derive the recommendation of partial meet contractions. The set of potential maxichoice contractions removing h from K will be partitioned into at least two subsets if full meet contraction is not to be endorsed by the Principle of Indifference. A comparison of the maxichoice contractions removing h is invoked that is embedded in a weak ordering all maxichoice contractions from K.

Thus, Rott and Pagnucco are led to announce a Principle of Strict Preference that insists that "objects held in higher regard should be afforded a more favourable treatment" (504). Taking the "objects" here to be maxichoice contractions removing h from K, the instruction is to give such maxichoice contractions more favorable treatment. We have not reached a preference ranking of sets of worlds or of maxichoice contractions that might represent contractions that are not maxichoice. The Principle of Strict Preference requires the inquirer to contract using maxichoice contractions that are ranked best *among maxichoice contractions removing h*. If we consider all the maxichoice contractions determined by cells in U_K, there may be some that do not imply $\sim h$ that are as good or better than the best cells implying $\sim h$. These cells are ignored. Only the best among cells entailing $\sim h$ and thus determining maxichoice contractions removing h are considered.

The Principle of Indifference requires that these maxichoice contractions be treated equally. Their intersection is recommended. According to Rott and Pagnucco, this is done in violation of informational economy. The conjunction of the Principle of Indifference and the Principle of Strict Preference thus yields a recommendation to take the partial meet contraction of the optimal maxichoice contractions removing h from K.

Rott and Pagnucco then weaken the conjunction of the Principle of Indifference and the Principle of Strict Preference to the requirement that "if one object is held in equal or higher regard than another, the former should be treated no worse than the other" (504). According to Weak Preference we should consider the set of maxichoice contractions from K that are weakly preferred to the best maxichoice

Contraction, Rational Choice and Economy

contractions removing h from K. The recommended contraction removing h is the intersection of these selected maxichoice contractions. The advantage of the Principle of Weak Preference is that it enables us to consider the preference ranking over all maxichoice contractions from K and not merely those removing h from K.

Rott and Pagnucco take the preference for the maxichoice contractions from K removing h as the basis for applying Weak Preference. Weak Preference applied to this set selects out the set of maxichoice contractions at least as good as the highest ranked maxichoice contractions removing h (or the highest ranked elements of $U_K^* \cap [[\sim h]]$) as the set meriting most "favorable treatment" and then recommends equal treatment, i.e. taking the intersection of the selected elements.

Rott and Pagnucco then point out that Weak Preference avoids restricting in advance the roster of contractions to partial meet contractions removing h rather than considering all potential contractions removing h. Elements of U_K^* may imply h rather than $\sim h$. Given the nature of the problem for contraction, every potential contraction must be derived from the intersection of a subset of U_K^* containing at least one member implying $\sim h$. But as long as the subset contains at least one member implying $\sim h$, all other maxichoice contractions that are equipreferred to that one should be treated the same whether or not they imply h or $\sim h$. And Weak Preference insists that all maxichoice contractions that are preferred to these should be treated just as well.

Thus, Rott and Pagnucco enunciate principles for how to select maxichoice contractions from K without imputing values to subsets of U_K^* or to contractions they represent. Once the set of maxichoice contractions is selected, the intersection of these maxichoice contractions is recommended.

Thus, Rott and Pagnucco do not recommend choosing an optimal or at least an admissible contraction from the roster of potential contractions removing h. Nothing has been done to show that the principles they advocate are principles of rational choice or that they are derivable from principles of rational choice and some conception of what the aims of contraction should be.

Contraction, Rational Choice and Economy

If the impact of a Principle of Informational Economy is measured in terms of how effective it should be in preventing the recognition of more and more elements of U_K^* as serious possibilities as the result of contraction, I agree with the assessment advanced by Rott and Pagnucco that the Principle is standing on its last legs.

Nonetheless, I think that there is a principle that can reasonably be said to qualify as a Principle of Informational Economy that is very much worth pursuing. I have already suggested that modes of evaluation that extend the partial ordering of potential contractions with respect to losses of information to a weak ordering in conformity with the Weak Positive Monotonicity Requirement can qualify as evaluations of losses of informational value. Minimizing loss of undamped (but not hyper-undamped), version 1 damped or version 2 damped informational value may, on this view, be seen as conforming with the Principle of Informational Economy even though they both deviate in one way or another from the Principle of Conservativism. Optimizing according to Version 2 and the Rule for Ties yields precisely the recommendation offered by Rott and Pagnucco.

Rott and Pagnucco not only reject my interpretation of the Principle of Informational Economy. They seem to reject the three versions of the principle I have just listed as well. They replace them with the Principles of Indifference, Strict Preference and Weak Preference. Now the three versions of the Principle of Informational Economy I propose seek to extend to a weak ordering (with some modification) the partial ordering of potential contractions of K by removing h. To achieve this end, I assumed certain constraints that such an extension should satisfy such as Weak Positive Monotonicity. The principles deployed by Rott and Pagnucco do not seek to extend the partial order with respect to information to a weak ordering over the potential contractions. Indeed, it is unclear from what Rott and Pagnucco say whether they would be prepared to identify a weak ordering or a quasi-ordering over all potential contractions removing h from K. But they could be doing so. They could be seeking to extend the weak ordering over cells in U_K^* (or the corresponding weak ordering over maxichoice contractions from K) to a complete weak ordering over the power set of U_K^* (or the set of all contractions from K).

Contraction, Rational Choice and Economy

What is missing is any rationalization of the use of their principles based on some conception of the goals of contraction.

In spite of his protestations to the contrary, it seems to me that Rott (2001) and Rott and Pagnucco (1999) *reject* the view that the problem of contraction is a problem for rational choice. It is because Rott and Pagnucco do not take the assimilation of theoretical to practical reason as seriously as they should that I take exception to their dismissal of the Principle of Informational Economy. Our shared endorsement of mild contraction or severe withdrawal might leave the impression that our differences are primarily terminological. But because Rott and Pagnucco and I have different requirements for a decision-theoretic rationalization of belief change, our attitude towards informational economy is more than a verbal one. Rott and Pagnucco reject the view that damped informational value as I define it is or should be minimized in contraction. The Principle of Informational Economy as I think of it is rejected not only in name but in spirit.

Rott (2001,144–6), explores more closely what equal treatment might mean in the context of choice functions that specify a set of more than one option admissible for choice from a "menu" of available options. It might mean "picking" one of the equally valued options "at random". Or it might mean going for a "satisfactory compromise or combination or aggregation of the members of the choice set" (145). But surely what Rott is calling a "compromise" is an option distinct from those in the choice set as he has constructed it. Rott is partial to the second alternative and seems to regard intersections or meets of optimal maxichoice contractions as examples of such "satisfactory compromises". To repeat, Rott should then include such meets in the menu and in the choice set. Rott acknowledges (146) that such meets carry less information than their maxichoice constituents. He also acknowledges that such compromises are recommended only if they count as optimal. That should mean that the partial ordering of the power set of the set of "worlds" with respect to subset inclusion (i.e. with respect to information) does not represent the inquirer's preferences over that domain. So what ordering does represent the inquirer's preferences?

Contraction, Rational Choice and Economy

If the ordering ranks a meet of maxichoice contractions as optimal along with its maximal constituents, why is it a compromise? It would have been better to suggest that recommending it is the outcome of invoking a Rule for Ties as a secondary criterion.

In spite of the residual obscurity here, the main message of Rott and Pagnucco (1999) and Rott (2001) is quite clear. Given the set of maxichoice contractions at least as good as the best that removes h from K, the recommended contraction is the intersection or meet of this set.

I believe I can, in good conscience, say that this recommendation is a best option because a best option is one that minimizes loss of version 2 damped informational value. Can Rott and Pagnucco do the same?

There is one remaining issue of philosophical interest found in the Rott–Pagnucco account. Even if they were to accept my strictures on rationalizing the choice of contractions, they would not endorse my version of Informational Economy. As I reconstruct their view, the best contraction strategy removing h is the intersection of those maxichoice contractions that are at least as *plausible* as the most plausible maxichoice contraction removing h. This approach is consonant with abandoning Informational Economy. It makes sense to say that in contraction, we should open our minds to propositions at least as plausible as the proposition we are constrained to entertain and, indeed, the more such propositions are entertained the better. So, perhaps, in this way, severe contraction can be seen to be an optimizing strategy without appealing to the minimization of loss of damped informational value of any kind.

One can make this kind of claim. But I think it should be resisted. In the end, this disagreement between Rott and Pagnucco and myself turns on deep differences concerning the aims of inquiry. I shall elaborate on the issues in the next section.

5.3. Contraction and Plausibility

In the context of contraction from K by removing h, the ranking of maxichoice contractions from K determines the extent to which

Contraction, Rational Choice and Economy

members of K are vulnerable to being given up. There is some disagreement concerning how degrees of vulnerability or invulnerability to being given up are to be understood. The issues shall be taken up later on. Whatever the differences, degrees of entrenchment, degrees of incorrigibility and the like are widely acknowledged to be determined by the "preference" or "ranking" of maxichoice contractions in U_K^*.

But what features of maxichoice contractions are prized in evaluating elements of U_K^*?

I contend that the ranking is with respect to loss of informational value incurred in contraction from K. Pagnucco and Rott claim that it is a ranking with respect to *plausibility* (1999, 508). This view is echoed in Rott (2001). Consider all maxichoice contractions of K that are at least as plausible as the most plausible removing h from K. According to Pagnucco and Rott, the recommended contraction removing h from K is the meet of these maxichoice contractions.

What does plausibility mean here? Here is what Pagnucco and Rott write when illustrating how their method works with Grove models. Interpret possible worlds to be cells in U_K^*.

Essentially, a system of spheres centred on [K] orders those worlds inconsistent with the agent's epistemic state K. Intuitively, the agent believes the actual world to be one of the K-worlds but does not have sufficient information to establish which one. However, the agent may be mistaken, in which case it believes that the actual world is most likely to be one of those in the next greater sphere and so on. As such, a system of spheres can be considered an ordering of plausibility over worlds; the more plausible worlds lying further towards the centre of the system of spheres (506–7).

The set of points [[K]] is the subset U_K or set of seriously possible worlds. Plausibility is clearly intended to be an evaluation of all of the "worlds" in U_{LK} including both those in U_K and those in U_K^* with respect to some notion of likelihood. If the truth of a hypothesis is plausible, it is, at a minimum, possibly true in the sense of serious possibility. And the more plausible the hypothesis, the more likely it is to be true.

Keep in mind, however, that we are concerned here with evaluating the merits of contractions from a state of full belief where the truth of all consequences of that state is taken for granted. If an inquirer's belief-state is K, any hypothesis h incompatible with K is not a serious possibility. The coherent inquirer must regard every such hypothesis as certainly false *and maximally implausible*.

Pagnucco and Rott point out that the inquirer "may be mistaken" in believing that the actual world is one of the K-worlds. Of course, the inquirer can coherently acknowledge the logical possibility that his or her current full beliefs contain falsehood.

But logical possibility is not serious possibility. And one person's conviction is another person's doubt. The inquirer may acknowledge that he or she may cease being certain in the future and that his or her future (and past beliefs) may be (and often are) in error. In any one of these senses, the inquirer may be mistaken in believing that the actual world is one of the K-worlds. However, as long as the inquirer is in the state of full belief represented by K, the inquirer cannot coherently acknowledge the serious possibility of being mistaken in this belief. Any doubt the inquirer registers is, in Peirce's words, a "paper doubt".

This means that every element in the dual ultimate partition U_K^* is, from the inquirer's point of view when in the belief-state represented by K, impossible. Each and every cell in U_K^* is maximally and equally implausible. There can be no distinction between hypotheses incompatible with K with respect to plausibility. If plausibility is understood relative to K, all elements of U_K^* should be equipreferred. Equipreferred potential contractions are treated alike according to the Principle of Indifference. Either K should be contracted to LK or should not be contracted at all.[6]

---

[6] Many philosophers respond to this kind of observation by suggesting that no reasonable inquirer is certain of any extralogical or a posteriori truth. Items incompatible with K are not judged to be false with maximum certainty but only with more or less confidence. Whether such confidence is measured by probabilities or by variations on Shackle measures, as authors such as Spohn (1988) have done, K no longer represents a state of full belief. That is to say, K is no longer a state of information or evidence cum background information relative to which probability judgments or other judgments of uncertainty such as degrees of belief in the Shackle sense may be made.

Contraction, Rational Choice and Economy

This is not a quibble over the meaning of words. If X fully believes that h, X's judging that ∼h is probable to any positive degree (even if it is infinitesimal) conflicts with X's conviction. This incoherence is due to the fact that degrees of credal probability are fine-grained discriminations between serious possibilities.

Assessments with respect to plausibility are different from evaluations with respect to credal probability. (Rott and Pagnucco and I are, I think, in agreement on this point.) Even so, they too remain fine-grained assessments of serious possibility. Seriously possible hypotheses are divided into the surprising or implausible, those that are neither surprising nor plausible and the plausible. Plausible hypotheses are serious possibilities that would be added to K were the inquirer X to engage in deliberate expansion at some level of boldness q above 0. The more plausible the conjecture, the more surprising its negation and the less bold the inquirer needs to be to reject that negation.[7]

Cells in U_K^* are not serious possibilities. Relative to K, they are all equally and maximally implausible. The preference for cells in U_K^* cannot represent grades of plausibility relative to the agent's state of full belief **K** or corpus K.

5.4. Embedding Preference in Prior Plausibility

There is a more charitable way to interpret the remarks of Rott and Pagnucco. For the agent X to acknowledge that X might be mistaken is not to be taken literally. X is acknowledging the serious possibility

---

The only state of full belief allowed is the state of total ignorance where the corpus is the urcorpus consisting of logical truths and whatever passes for conceptually necessary truth. What happens to the study of belief change under these circumstances? We have returned to Parmenidean epistemology.

[7] I am assuming that Rott and Pagnucco are thinking of plausibility as degree of belief in Shackle's (1961) sense which is similar to expectation in Gärdenfors and Makinson's (1993) sense, Baconian probability in Cohen's (1977) sense or "plausibility" in Spohn's (1988) sense. The interpretation of degree of plausibility that h in terms of the degree of boldness needed to reject ∼h (or the corresponding degrees of caution) derives from my interpretation of Shackle measures in (Levi, 1967). The interpretation is summarized in ch. 3.5.

that at some future moment X will have good reason to contract K by giving up h. On the supposition (adopted purely for the sake of the argument) that this happens, the set of potential contractions available to X are the contractions associated with the subsets of cells in the power set of U_K^*. This does not imply that X has actually contracted by removing h from K. But in the context, X is choosing among various options for doing so. Instead of seeking to minimize loss of informational value, X might seek to contract so that only those elements of U_K^* become serious possibilities that are as plausible *when evaluated relative to LK* as the most plausible cell in U_K^* (relative to LK) that implies ~h.

How is such prior plausibility to be evaluated? I take it that the degree of plausibility that x satisfies the requirements of Shackle's b-measure of degree of belief. Relative to LK, b-values are assigned to the elements of the algebra generated by the basic partition U_{LK}—which in that setting serves also as the ultimate partition. The b-value = degree of belief = Baconian probability = degree of plausibility assigned an element x of U_{LK} should equal the degree of surprise = degree of disbelief = d-value assigned ~x = the smallest d-value assigned an element of U_{LK} that is in the disjunction equivalent to ~x. The degree of implausibility that x should equal the d-value assigned to x.

Thus, a single element x of U_{LK} will be assigned a pair of values {b(x), d(x)}. At least one of these values must be 0 although both may be 0. If one wishes, one can order these pairs in a one-dimensional series. If the b-value is positive, that is the value of the pair. If it is 0, the negative of the d-value is the value of the pair. Since at most one element of U_{LK} can carry positive b-value, if such an element exists it is ranked on top and all other elements are ranked in accordance with the negative of the d-value. Increase in d-value means decrease in plausibility. The ranking of the algebra generated by U_{LK} is then uniquely determined. This yields a ranking of U_{Lk} with respect to plausibility compatible with the proposal by Spohn (1988, 116).

Now the importance of the b-values (or the d-values) comes to the fore primarily in deliberate or inductive expansion. If the agent X exercises degree of boldness q, X should reject all elements of U_{LK}

Contraction, Rational Choice and Economy

whose d-value is greater than $1 - q$. This means that X should add to LK all members of the algebra generated by U_{LK} whose b-value or plausibility is greater than $1 - q$. That is to say, X should do so when X changes X's state of full belief from LK to an expansion responding to the question under consideration. Once, of course, X does this, all sentences added become full beliefs and, hence, maximally certain. *Prior to making this change* they are not fully believed. They carry plausibility greater than 1-q but less than 1.

Although I have made these remarks on the assumption that X is in belief-state LK and seeking to expand it using U_{LK} as the ultimate partition, what has been said applies *mutatis mutandis* to expansion from K with ultimate partition U_K.

I am suggesting as a possible interpretation of the remarks by Pagnucco and Rott implying that an inquirer concerned to remove h from K should select all worlds (elements of U_K^*) that are at least as plausible as the most plausible world implying ~h the assessment of plausibility on the supposition adopted purely for the sake of the argument that the state of full belief adopted is LK.

Construing plausibility to be relative to LK avoids ranking of elements of U_K^* in terms of losses of valuable information. The ranking of elements of U_K^* with respect to losses of informational value incurred by the corresponding contractions is uniquely determined by M^*. The ranking of these same elements according to the interpretation of plausibility I have proposed is uniquely determined by a function of Q^* and M^* in the case where credal and informational value determining probabilities are determinate. The rankings need not be the same. So Informational Economy even in the weaker and more generous version I have been defending is indeed abandoned when assessments are in terms of plausibility relative to LK. This is just as Pagnucco and Rott intend.

The proposed interpretation also avoids construing the ranking of elements of U_K^* in terms of plausibility relative to K—a position that remains, in my view, clearly untenable.

Finally, the difference between Pagnucco and Rott's proposal on this interpretation and my approach is not a verbal dispute but reflects rather different conceptions of the aims of contraction.

It could happen that the ranking of the elements of U_{LK} is the same with respect to both plausibility and M^*. If K is derived from LK via deliberate expansion at a given level of boldness, all elements of U_K^* will carry 0 b-values so that the plausibilities of the intersections of elements of the power set of U_K^* are ordered after the suggestion of Spohn in agreement with the ordering with respect to d-values. Under these conditions, the severe withdrawal of Rott and Pagnucco and my mild contraction will coincide. This is a possibility. However, in general, the rankings of the members of U_K^* determined by the function of Q^* and M^* appropriate to plausibility relative to LK and the ranking of the same elements determined by M^* alone that is appropriate to informational value will differ.

According to the interpretation I am now exploring, Rott and Pagnucco are advocates of what I shall call the *Embedding in Plausibility Thesis*:

> The ordering of elements of U_K^* with respect to preference for purposes of contraction is embedded in the ordering of elements of U_{LK} with respect to plausibility relative to LK.

By way of contrast, I favor the *Embedding in Informational Value Thesis*:

> The ordering of elements of U_K^* with respect to preference for purposes of contraction is embedded in the ordering of elements of U_{LK} with respect to informational value as represented by $cont^* = 1 - M^*$.

Both orderings of U_{LK} extend to the algebra generated by the basic partition in accordance with Shackle's calculus. Hence, the restrictions of these orderings to the potential contractions removing h give rankings of the potential contractions removing h. One of them is a plausibility ranking relative to LK restricted to the potential contractions removing h from K. The other is a ranking with respect to version 2 damped informational value for the algebra generated by U_{LK} restricted to the same set of potential contractions.

Judgments of plausibility, so I submit, are relevant to the context of expansion. A conjecture may be added to the body of full beliefs if

Contraction, Rational Choice and Economy

the degree of plausibility, Baconian probability, degree of expectation or degree of confidence of acceptance relative to the initial corpus K is sufficiently high. That is why such judgments are determined by a trade off between risk of error and informational value. But when the issue is contraction, risk of error in the sense of risk of importing false belief is not an issue from the inquirer's point of view. The inquirer is not adding any false beliefs because the inquirer is not adding any beliefs at all. In contraction, there can be no risk of error relative to the initial corpus K. No doubt there can be risk of error from some other point of view such as LK. But to suppose that risk relative to LK is relevant when contracting from K is to betray the belief state K. The inquirer X is committed to full belief—i.e. certainty—that each and every consequence of K is true. So the issue of risk of error relative to LK is moot. Only if X were in a state of doubt concerning the elements of K that are not consequences of LK could risk of error figure in the task of contracting from K.

But if X were in a state of doubt concerning the consequences of K, X would have already contracted from K. The exercise would have already been completed. The proposed interpretation of plausibility is inappropriate to the decision problem of choosing between rival potential contractions removing h from K.

5.5. Plain Belief

There is a response that could be made on behalf of Rott and Pagnucco—one which Wolfgang Spohn quite explicitly endorses. According to Spohn, an inquirer should not fully believe any extralogical proposition. X's minimal corpus LK should be restricted to logical truths and whatever conceptual necessities we may think required. Spohn thinks that belief change is concerned with change in deterministic yes or no "plain" belief. According to Spohn's view translated into my terminology, X plainly believes that h if and only if X believes that h to a positive degree = assigns a b-value greater than 0. Expansion, contraction and revision operate on corpora of positive beliefs and not full beliefs. With the possible exception of logical, mathematical and conceptual truths (if there be such), no propositions should be assigned maximum plausibility.

There are variants on this view. One might think of corpora of beliefs of degree above some threshold or other. We could speak of belief change concerning such states of plain belief.

On any such account, the only state of full belief would be **UK** with corpus UK. UK is the corpus of logical, mathematical and conceptual truths and, in this setting functions as the minimal corpus LK. There is no incoherence in evaluating elements of U_K^* with respect to plausibility relative to LK (=UK) when the truth of each and every element of the dual ultimate partition remains a serious possibility.

I do not have any difficulty in understanding the notion of a corpus of plain belief. But I do have some difficulty with the idea that rational belief change is change in state of plain belief. Spohn understands plain belief as whatever passes a certain threshold of plausibility (relative to LK). Assessment of plain belief so conceived may be relevant in the context of efforts to expand from LK to another corpus of full beliefs. Clearly items that carry 0 b-value or plausibility are not to be added to LK. Each element of U_K^* carries 0 b-value relative to LK. In that case, plausibility is ordered, according to Spohn's proposal, by negative d-value.

Spohn maintains that change in state of full belief is illegitimate. Whatever the minimal state of full belief might be, it is to remain fixed. This means that assessments of plausibility and plain belief lose their intended application. But in the absence of any concern to change the state of full belief, I do not understand what interest a state of plain belief does or could have. The importance of d-values, b-values and cognate notions is parasitic on the concern with deliberate expansion of states of *full* belief. Otherwise they play no role in inquiry.

5.6. Plausibility as Informational Value

There is yet another response available to anyone defending the Embedding in Plausibility thesis. The objections I have raised presuppose that in expansion of a state of full belief the aim is to

Contraction, Rational Choice and Economy

obtain valuable information that is free of error as assessed from the point of view prior to expansion. Many authors, however, seem to think that in both science and everyday life, inquirers aim at fixing belief without regard to the avoidance of error.

If that is so, plausibility or b-value understood as a satisficing measure of support according to which an inquirer X is warranted in adding any claim to full belief that is supported by the current information to a degree above a given threshold would be a decreasing function of M^*-values of the members of U^*_{LK} alone when expanding from LK. Given those values, the plausibilities of all potential expansions are evaluated in accordance with Weak Positive Monotonicity and the version 2 Damping Condition. Consequently, using plausibility relative to LK to evaluate contractions from K is after all equivalent to minimizing loss of version 2 damped informational value. The Embedding in Plausibility and Embedding in Informational Value theses are interchangeable.

This response too is unacceptable. It suggests that inquirers should ignore risk of error in inductive expansion. As long as risk of importing false belief (risk of error) is recognized to be a relevant concern in inductive expansion, this proposal should be firmly rejected.

In this and the previous two sections, I have considered different approaches to supporting the Embedding in Plausibility thesis and offered considerations that argue against each of them. None of these difficulties argue against the Embedding in Informational Value thesis. And, as I have suggested, minimizing loss of version 2 damped informational value provides a bona fide decision-theoretic rationale for severe withdrawal or mild contraction that avoids the pitfalls of minimizing loss of information or of undamped informational value while preserving the insights of those who have advocated principles of informational economy.

5.7. Severe Withdrawal = Mild Contraction

Rott and Pagnucco (1999) and I agree that contractions of the sort described in Main Conclusion C should be taken seriously. They call

Contraction, Rational Choice and Economy

such contractions "severe withdrawals". I prefer "mild contractions". Two reasons motivate my terminological predilections:

The first is a stubborn insistence that the problem of how to contract should look at all potential contraction strategies and not merely those that are partial meet contractions. Calling potential contractions that satisfy Recovery "contractions" and potential contractions that do not "withdrawals" suggests strongly even if it does not imply that the latter are second rate. I wish to resist using terminology that even suggests this view.

Second, contractions sometimes give birth to revisions so that an obstetric metaphor rather than one from the drug culture is not totally out of place. The only issue is whether the contractions are mild or severe. To answer this question, we must ask what sorts of values are of concern in contraction. I have been insisting that we ought to be concerned to minimize loss of informational value.

If the informational value is undamped informational value, the loss incurred would be considerable. Thinking of the contractions under consideration as severe seems entirely reasonable according to that reckoning.

Furthermore, assessing loss of informational value along the lines of version 1 of loss of damped informational value also implies that the contraction according to version 2 would be severe.

On the other hand, assessing losses of damped informational *value* according to version 2 yields the result that the contractions are mild. There is no more loss in informational value of this kind by adopting the severe withdrawal/mild contraction than there is in adopting the corresponding partial meet contraction.

To be sure, using the geometry of Grove modeling to represent alternative contractions makes it appear that the contractions are severe. But this seems to me to be one of the misleading aspects of Grove-think.

Consider the Grove diagram of contraction of K by removing E (Fig. 5.1).

Here the innermost circle represents the current corpus K. We shall suppose that the lower-case roman letters represent elements of U_K^*. Circle 1 minus the innermost circle consists of worlds carrying

Contraction, Rational Choice and Economy

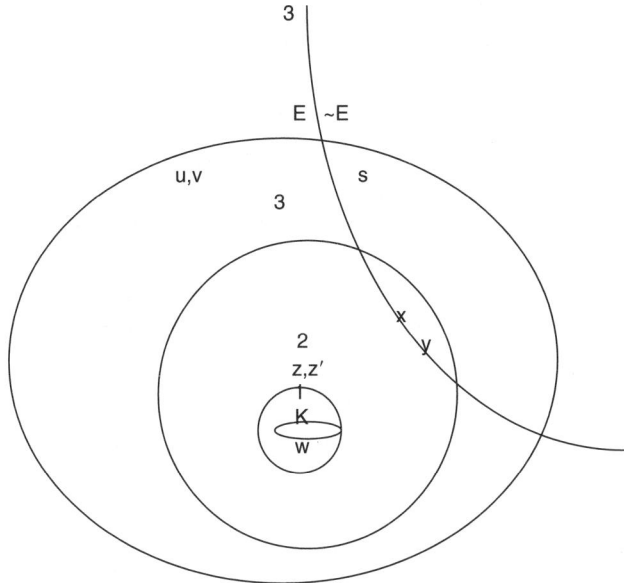

Fig 5.1

0 *M*-value. Circle 2 minus circle 1 includes worlds carrying positive *M* values no greater than worlds x and y which are worlds according to which E is false. Circle 3 minus circle 2 contains worlds carrying positive *M*-values greater than the *M*-values of x and y.

Minimizing loss of undamped informational value calls for contracting by choosing one of the two maxichoice contractions obtaining by forming the union of [[K]] and x or of [[K]] and y. Both of these incur a positive loss of undamped informational value. Hence, it is clear that the union of the two sets of points increases the loss. The partial meet contraction cannot be recommended.

If we calculate minimum loss in informational value incurred by removing E from K using damped informational value of the first kind, the optimal saturatable contractions are the unions of [[K]] and {x} and {w} or [[K]] and {y} and {w}. So is the union of these contractions. Recovery is violated. Of course, special assumption 2 obtains.

If the Rule for Ties is applied to the set of contractions minimizing damped informational value of the first kind, the union of the two saturatable contractions mentioned above is recommended. The loss in undamped informational value is equal to the total M-value assigned points in the intersection of the set of points $\sim$E and sphere 2 and to points in sphere 1. But the total M-value of points in sphere 1 is 0. Hence, the loss of damped informational value of the first kind incurred by the recommended contraction is equal to the loss of damped informational value of the first kind incurred by the corresponding partial meet contraction.

Recovery obviously fails as long as there are some points of U_K^* in sphere 1. But loss of informational value incurred by violating Recovery as compared to partial meet contraction is 0. The Rule for Ties clearly then recommends violating Recovery.

The geometry of the Grove model, however, suggests, even if it does not imply, that a genuine loss is incurred by violating Recovery; for it invites you to think of items in the first circle as incurring a genuine loss. We could, however, amend the modeling so that the items in circle 1 fell on the boundary of the sphere for K where K is now taken to be an open set. It then becomes clear that the difference in loss of both undamped and damped informational value of the first kind incurred by partial meet contraction and by minimizing loss of damped informational value version 1 is 0. Let us call contractions recommended by the injunction to minimize of loss of damped informational value *impalpable contractions*.

If we calculate damped informational value of the second kind and use the Rule for Ties, we form the union of the impalpable contractions just described with $\{z, z'\}$. The result is what Pagnucco and Rott call a severe withdrawal. Looking at the geometry of the Grove model it certainly looks severe. For it suggests an additional loss of informational value equal to the informational value of the contents of sphere 2 which would be positive. If we are measuring loss in undamped informational value, this claim is entirely correct.

However, there is no such loss in damped informational value of the second kind. There is no more loss incurred than if the maxichoice contraction represented by the union of |K| with $\{x\}$ were used.

Contraction, Rational Choice and Economy

Whether the contraction is mild or severe is clearly going to depend on the kind of loss that is of concern to the inquirer. This is the important philosophical point that I mean to belabor.

In the case of impalpable contractions, the loss is no greater than that incurred by the partial meet contraction whether the informational value is undamped, damped of the first kind or damped of the second kind. Mild contractions incur a greater loss than partial meet contractions when the loss is assessed with respect to undamped and damped informational value of the first kind. But mild contractions incur no more loss than partial meet contractions when loss in undamped informational value of the second kind is evaluated. From that perspective, the contraction is as mild as the corresponding partial meet contraction. It can only be taken as severe when we seek to minimize loss of undamped informational value or damped informational value of the first kind.

The Grove model diagram cannot reveal this for the simple reason that such diagrams represent the ordering of cells in the dual ultimate partition with respect to how "severe" the maxichoice contraction that is the union of $|K|$ and $\{x\}$, where x is a cell, happens to be. The Grove model diagram says nothing about how severe contractions are supposed to be that are unions of [[K]] with sets that are not such singletons.

If one thinks that somehow the more inclusive a sphere, the more severe the contraction will be, that is, indeed, a tacit commitment to undamped informational value—a commitment, so I have argued, no one should want to make.

Grove models rest silent with respect to this proposal as well as with respect to alternatives. And that is why Grove models are in the final analysis uninformative in revealing the structure of acceptable contractions.

Grove models can distinguish between maxichoice contractions and non-maxichoice but saturatable contractions. Within the latter category, Grove models can be used to distinguish between saturatable contractions removing E from K where the $\sim$E states are all in sphere 1, where the $\sim$E states are in sphere 1 or sphere 2 and where the $\sim$E states are all in sphere 3 and subspheres. We can even represent intersections of saturatable contractions. But there is no way to indicate how potential contractions of K other than maxichoice contractions are to be compared. The absence of such a standard seems to suggest to many that no systematic approach to critically examining such standards is available. I believe that by thinking of the goal of a contraction as minimizing loss of informational value of a certain kind and then exploring what kind it should be, we can add to the resources we have for coming to some non-arbitrary adjudication of the controversies concerning the character of contraction.

5.8. Revision and Recovery

As Makinson has correctly observed, every contraction function violating Recovery corresponds to a partial meet contraction that is AGM revision equivalent to it. That is to say, the contraction removing $\sim$h from K and then expanding by adding h yields the same corpus whether the contraction removing $\sim$h violates Recovery or is the partial meet contraction revision equivalent to it. For purposes of characterizing AGM revision, therefore, one might as well deploy partial meet contraction in defining contraction as an expansion of a contraction as any other contraction transformation corresponding to the given partial meet contraction. The results will be the same.

In belief change, this does not diminish the importance of studying types of contraction failing to satisfy Recovery; for not every contraction is followed by an expansion. But in suppositional reasoning where the success of a revision is stipulated, it may appear that doubts about Recovery are of less importance.

This is not so. In suppositional or conditional reasoning, the revision transformation ought not to be AGM revision but rather what I have called Ramsey Revision (Levi, 1996). Ramsey revision requires removing $\sim$h when $\sim$h is in K and removing h when h is in K where h is the supposition that is to be added subsequent to the contraction. Ramsey revision K_h^{*r} coincides with AGM revision K_h^* when the Recovery condition on contraction is satisfied. It also

Contraction, Rational Choice and Economy

coincides with AGM revision when h is inconsistent with K (the belief-contravening case) and when K is "open" with respect to the truth of K. But when K contains h and Recovery fails, AGM and Ramsey revision diverge.

In a situation where the agent is convinced that the coin was tossed and landed heads (E&H) so that E&H is in K, reasoning on the supposition that E requires that E be contracted from K and then restored before inferences from E are drawn. We want to consider whether on the supposition that the coin had been tossed, the coin would have landed heads. Presystematically, it is clear that in most contexts we are prepared to judge that because the coin had been tossed, it would have landed on the surface. We are not prepared to judge, however, that because the coin had been tossed, it would have landed heads. It might, after all, have landed tails. We do not think that the tossing explains why the coin landed heads.

AGM delivers an opposite verdict. In my judgment, this constitutes an argument from presystematic practice supporting the idea that revision in suppositional reasoning is not AGM revision but Ramsey revision without the Recovery condition for contraction.

Suppositional reasoning in "sample space" examples illustrated by the coin requires that contraction violate Recovery. If this is right, not only is failure of Recovery manifest in belief change but also in suppositional reasoning and in the logic of conditionals.

Some of the ramifications of this point were explored in Levi (1996). Both the postulates (K^*4) and (K^*8) for AGM revision were weakened to characterize Ramsey revision (40). However, the approach adopted there was predicated on the idea that in contraction loss in damped informational value of type 1 was being minimized and that, as a consequence, the contractions involved that violated Recovery were impalpable contractions. As Hansson and Olsson (1995) have correctly shown, all the postulates for AGM contraction except $(K - 5)$, which, in the light of the others, entails Recovery, are satisfied.[8] This is true for mild contraction (alias severe withdrawal) as well.

---

[8] Hansson and Olson (1995, 108) correctly point out the need for a special postulate stipulating that if $\vdash h$, $K_h^- = K$.

AGM (1985 observation 6.5) shows that (K−7) and (K−8) in the light of the other postulates for contraction except (K − 5) entail the following:

Ventilation (−V). $K^-_{h\&f} = K^-_h$ or $K^-_{h\&f} = K^-_f$ or $K^-_{h\&f} = K^-_h \cap K^-_f$.

Without (K−5), (−V) implies (K−7) in the light of (K−1)-(K−4) and (K−6). (K−8) is not implied although with the aid of (K−5) it is.

Ventilation holds for Ramsey as well as AGM contraction. For Ramsey revision, the following holds for cases where h&f is in K *whether or not Recovery with Ramsey revision held even though none of these revisions need be identical with K as they would be if AGM revision obtained.*

(a) $K^{*r}_{h\&f} = K^{*r}_h$ or $K_{h\&f} = K^{*r}_f$ or $K^{*r}_{h\&f} = K^{*r}_h \cap K^{*r}_f$.

Pagnucco and Rott (1999) point out that postulates for severe withdrawals or mild contractions imply the following stronger "factoring" condition from AGM (1985, 525):

Decomposition (−D): $K^-_{h\&f} = K^-_h$ or $K^-_{h\&f} = K^-_f$.[9]

Assume that damped informational value of type 2 is minimized in contraction and Ramsey revision is used. If K contains h&f, we have the following result:

(b) $K^{*r}_{h\&f} = K^{*r}_h$ or $K^{*r}_{h\&f} = K^{*r}_f$.

Hence, even though we cannot say, as in the case of AGM revision, that if f is not in K^{*r}_h, that $[K^{*r}_h]^+_f$ is a subset of $K^{*r}_{h\&f}$, we can say that either $[K^{*r}_h]^+_f$ or $[K^{*r}_f]^+_h$ is a subset of $K^{*r}_{h\&f}$.

Thus, whether under the sobriquet "mild contraction" or "severe withdrawal", contractions minimizing loss of damped informational value type 2 in conformity with the Rule for Ties do have a non-negligible effect on the formal properties of Ramsey revision. Because (for reasons already given) I now recommend mild contraction over impalpable contraction, I suggest strengthening the postulates for Ramsey revision to the extent just indicated.

---

[9] If damped information version 2 is being minimized, when $K^-_{h\&f} = K^-_h \cap K^-_f$, the right-hand term is identical to both K^-_h or K^-_f.

Contraction, Rational Choice and Economy

In this essay, I am arguing that the case for seeking to minimize loss of damped informational value of type 2 is also a case for violating Recovery. Pagnucco and Rott reach this conclusion by a different argument. I have suggested that their argument is not sufficiently loyal to decision-theoretic requirements. In particular, Pagnucco and Rott fail to show that the severe withdrawal (or mild contraction) is optimal because their principles do not allow for evaluating intersections of sets of maxichoice contractions as better or worse. When details are filled in by introducing version 2 of damped informational value and the Rule for Ties is invoked to arbitrate between optimal contraction strategies, their recommendations are obtained on a foundation more in accord with decision-theoretic principles.[10]

Rott and Pagnucco fail to recognize the importance of Ramsey revision as compared to AGM revision. For this reason, they do not recognize how significant the difference between severe withdrawal and partial meet contraction actually is in the context of suppositional reasoning and the logic of conditionals.

---

[10] In an interesting paper, Meyer, Labuschagne and Heidema (1998) have proposed an account of contraction they call "systematic withdrawal". Like Pagnucco and Rott, Meyer, Labuschagne and Heidema begin with an ordering of cells in U_K^* and seek to derive a recommended contraction. The partial meet contraction favored by AGM is the intersection of K with the cells entailing $\sim$h that are "nearest" K. Meyer, Labuschagne and Heidema argue that the intersection ought to be extended to cover cells in U_K^* that entail h that are nearer to K than the nearest cells entailing $\sim$h (1998, 15–17). Recovery is violated. The contraction is in general weaker than that yielded by minimizing damped informational value of type 1 but not of damped informational value of type 2. Let the ordering of elements of U_K^* be a "K-faithful" weak ordering (total preorder). According to the decision-theoretic approach I favor, the ordering should be extended to all potential contractions of K. The contraction of K by removing h to be recommended is a best such contraction according to the weak ordering that satisfies the Rule for Ties. One might achieve the desired result for contraction of K by removing h; but I do not see how this ordering can be made to cohere with contraction of K by removing f. Meyer *et al.* do not endorse my decision-theoretic program any more than Pagnucco and Rott do. As a consequence, the merits of the Meyer, Labuschagne and Heidema proposal for systematic withdrawal as compared with severe withdrawal can be compared only by consulting intuitions about the implications of the two proposals. I suspect such comparisons will prove inconclusive. But the fact that mild contraction or severe withdrawal has a decision-theoretic rationale while systematic withdrawal does not seems to offer a strong argument for the former over the latter.

Contraction, Rational Choice and Economy

If we think of contractions that are AGM revision-equivalent as equivalent for the intended applications in belief change and suppositional reasoning, the choice between AGM contractions and AGM revision-equivalent severe withdrawals looks like a matter of taste about which one may dispute without much argument.

I claim that the relevant notion of revision-equivalence is Ramsey revision-equivalence. This view undermines the claim that the difference between AGM and mild contraction is a mere matter of convenience and taste as Rott (1991 where mild contraction was originally considered) suggested.

Rott and Pagnucco (1999) make important contributions to providing an axiomatic characterization of severe withdrawal or mild contraction. And they make several interesting observations about severe withdrawal. For example, Observation 7 (518) states that given a partial meet contraction function for theory K, the smallest (in the set inclusion sense) withdrawal function that is AGM revision equivalent to the partial meet contraction function and satisfies the following condition is a severe withdrawal function:

(−8c) if $K^-_{h\&f}$ implies f, then $K^-_{h\&f}$ is a subset of K^-_h.

Unfortunately as long as Rott and Pagnucco continue to think of AGM revision as the central revision operator useful in suppositional reasoning, the ultimate significance of their ideas remains obscure.

Advocates of AGM contraction need to find a good argument insisting upon AGM as compared with impalpable and mild contraction. I have been insisting that such a good argument should identify goals for contraction that will yield a recommendation of AGM contraction. I have invoked the idea that in contraction one should seek to minimize loss of informational value just as I had done in 1980. I have offered a characterization of a family of conceptions of informational value that permit us to think of members of this family as expressions of what Gärdenfors calls the Principle of Informational Economy.

Arbitrarily restricting the options for contraction removing h from K to partial meet contractions removing h from K is an unacceptable way to justify partial meet contraction. Any decision-theoretic

Contraction, Rational Choice and Economy

justification of a recommendation for contraction should consider all potential contractions removing h from K relative to U_K^*. On this assumption, the following results have been announced.

Minimizing undamped informational value rationalizes maxichoice contraction removing h from K.

Minimizing damped informational value version 1 recommends AGM contractions under special assumption 1.

Minimizing version 2 damped informational value rationalizes mild contraction.

All three claims are based on the specification of a goal for contraction as represented by a determinate utility function, the requirement that an admissible option be optimal with respect to that utility function and the Rule for Ties.

The differences between the three prescriptions are taken to be differences in the values to be promoted in removing h from K. I have appealed to two kinds of considerations to justify my shift from advocating minimizing loss of version 1 damped informational value to minimizing loss of version 2 damped informational value.

(1) The version 1 damping condition is restricted to intersections of saturatable contractions removing h from K. Saturatable contractions are evaluated in terms of damped informational value. Why saturatable contractions should be evaluated differently from other intersections of maxichoice contractions remains obscure. Version 2 of the damping condition abandons the restriction.

(2) Ramsey Revision works well in suppositional reasoning applied to thinking about stochastic processes provided Recovery fails under special assumption 1—as it does when loss of version 2 damped informational value is minimized.

5.9. Entrenchment and Incorrigibility

Minimizing loss of informational value incurred by removing h from K requires identifying those potential contractions removing h from

Contraction, Rational Choice and Economy

K that carry maximum informational value. This calls for an evaluation of potential contractions of K with respect to informational value in some reasonable sense or other.

This evaluation carries with it another sort of assessment. Both K and all potential contractions removing h have other belief-states as consequences. Indeed, every potential contraction of K in the sense of a deductively closed subset of K containing the logical truths is such a consequence and all finitely axiomatizable subsets of this type are representable by sentences in K. Implementing a contraction removing h from K involves giving up some consequences of **K** and retaining others and this can be characterized as giving up some sentences in K while retaining others.

From this consideration, it becomes apparent that an assessment of potential contractions of K removing h also determines a comparison of consequences of K (or the sentences that represent them) with respect to how vulnerable they are to being given up when h is removed.

In Levi, 1980, I contended that although sentences in an inquirer's corpus K at time t are all maximally certain from the agent's point of view at that time, they may, nonetheless, differ from one another with respect to their degrees of incorrigibility (or degrees of corrigibility). I also claimed that discrimination with respect to incorrigibility depended on the losses in informational value that are incurred (62). Degrees of incorrigibility or vulnerability to being given up are not degrees of confidence, degrees of expectation, degrees of support by evidence. The more incorrigible or invulnerable it is to give up full belief that h, the greater the loss of informational value there is in doing so. Informational value is an epistemic utility reflecting the research project or other demands for information of the inquirer in the given situation. Judgments of degrees of incorrigibility are another expression of the same value commitments.

As already indicated, in Levi, 1980, I assumed that losses in informational value incurred in contraction are to be assessed as losses in undamped informational value. I have explained why I now think this is a bad idea. In any case, in 1980, I did not elaborate in detail on how grades of incorrigibility are to be derived from such assessments.

Contraction, Rational Choice and Economy

In Levi, 1991 and 1996 I sought to elaborate the idea of incorrigibility as derived from losses of damped informational value of type 1 and to compare it with Gärdenfors's notion of entrenchment (Gärdenfors, 1988). Here I shall reformulate the conceptions of incorrigibility and entrenchment in a manner that is neutral with respect to whether losses being assessed are losses of type 1 or type 2 damped informational value. I shall then consider the specializations of incorrigibility and entrenchment relative to losses of each of these two types.

Incorrigibility as I conceived it reflected the vulnerability of sentences to being removed from K conditional on some particular sentence being removed. g is more incorrigible than f in the context of contracting K by removing h if and only if the smallest loss in informational value among contraction strategies removing both h and g from K is greater than the smallest loss of informational value among the same set of contraction strategies that remove both h and f.

Sentences that are not in K are assigned 0 degrees of incorrigibility. So are h and all sentences in $[K/K_h^-] = $ the set of sentences in K that are removed when h is contracted from K. There is no loss of informational value incurred by removing sentences not in K since they are already removed. And there is no additional loss of informational value incurred by removing sentences in K but not in K_h^- once it is settled that a shift from K to K_h^- is to be made. Since assessments of this additional loss are what are at stake in evaluating incorrigibility, sentences in $\{K/K_h^-\}$ are minimally incorrigible just as are sentences not in K.

Consider the subset of potential contraction strategies removing h from K (relative to LK and U_{LK}) that also remove g. Whether assessments of damped informational value are of type 1 or type 2, there will be at least one potential contraction strategy of this kind that carries maximum damped informational value in that set. The existence of a maximum is insured as long as U_{LK} (and, hence, U_K^*) is finite and assessments of damped informational value induce a weak ordering over all potential contractions. Here we are also assuming that informational value is determined by a uniquely permissible M^* defined over U_{LK}.

Let $D(g/h, K)$ equal the damped informational value of a contraction of K that minimizes loss of damped informational value among all contractions of K removing h that also remove g. Depending on which version of damped informational value is being minimized, we may write $D_1(g/h, K)$ or $D_2(g/h, K)$.

$D_1(h/h, K) = D_2(h/h, K) = D(h/h, K)$ is equal to the damped informational value of K_h^-. Whether we are thinking of damped informational value of type 1 or of type 2, this damped informational value will equal the Cont-value of a maxichoice contraction removing h from K that carries maximum cont-value in this set and, hence, minimum M^*-value.

Def. The *degree of incorrigibility of g* relative to K, h, LK, M^* and $U_{LK} = in(g/h, K, LK, M^*, U_{LK}) = D(h/h, K) - D(g/h, K)$.[11]

In the following discussion, I shall abbreviate this as $in(g/h, K)$ assuming that LK, M^* and U_{LK} are given and held fixed.

$D_1(g/h, K) = D_1(h/h, K)$ in two cases:

(a) At least one maxichoice contraction removing h from K that carries minimum M^*-value and, hence, maximum undamped informational value among all maxichoice contractions removing h from K also removes g from K. This means that there is a cell in the dual ultimate partition U_K^* that entails both $\sim$h and $\sim$g and carries minimum M^*-value among cells entailing $\sim$h.

---

[11] Levi (1991, 143) offers a characterization of the relation "at least as corrigible as" consonant with the definition in the text. In Levi, 1996, the penultimate paragraph on 263 assumes the representability of incorrigibility by a real valued measure but imposes only ordinal constraints on the measure consonant with the 1991 formulation. The characterization at the bottom of the page contains a serious error and is inconsistent with the formulation one paragraph before. $in(g/h, K)$ is equated with $D(g/h, K)$ for cases where g is in K but not in all contractions. Everything around this passage presupposes what I intended to say—to wit, that $in(g/h, K)$ is a decreasing function of $D(g/h, K)$. As just indicated, I was not intending to specify a definite quantitative measure but to specify ordinal properties of any acceptable quantitative measure and to adopt the convention that incorrigibility be kept within the limits of 0 and 1. The specific measure proposed here satisfies these requirements as will any real valued measure that is a positive monotone transformation of the one given in the text.

Contraction, Rational Choice and Economy

(b$_1$) At least one maxichoice contraction removing g from K carries the same undamped informational value as K itself. This means that the minimum M^*-value assigned a cell in U_K^* entailing $\sim$g is 0. Consequently, the contraction removing h from K that minimizes loss of type 1 damped informational value and satisfies the requirements of the rule for ties recognizes that cell as a serious possibility and, hence, removes g as well.

D_1(g/h, K) < D_1(h/h, K) if and only if both conditions (a) and (b$_1$) fail.

D_2(g/h, K) = D_2(h/h, K) = D_1(h/h, K) if and only if either condition (a) or the following condition (b$_2$) holds:

(b$_2$) The minimum M-value assigned a cell in U_K^* entailing $\sim$g is no greater than the minimum M-value assigned a cell in U_K^* entailing $\sim$h. That is to say, D(g/g, K) $\geq D$(h/h, K).

D_2(g/h, K) < D_2(h/h, K) if and only if both conditions (a) and (b$_2$) fail. In this case D_2(g/h, K) = D_2(g/g, K) = D(g/g, K). By way of contrast, D_1(g/h, K) $\leq D_1$(g/g, K) = D(g/g, K).

According to the definition of incorrigibility, all sentences not in K as well as sentences in K but not in K_h^- carry minimum or 0 incorrigibility *whether or not loss of undamped informational value is of type 1 or of type 2*.

g is in K_h^- if and only if in(g/h, K) > 0. If instead of choosing a contraction removing h maximizing damped informational value when in(g/h, K) > 0, we choose one where the damped informational value is "good enough" in the sense that it is at least as great as D(g/h, K) and conforms to the requirements for the rule for ties among such satisficing contractions, the contraction sought removes h $\wedge$ g from K. The difference in damped informational value between this contraction and the contraction K_h^- that is the product of maximizing informational value and using the Rule for Ties is equal to in(g/h, K). If version 2 informational value is being minimized, the contraction is $K_{h \wedge g}^-$. If it is version 1, this need not be so.

Whether $D(g/h, K) = D_1(g/h, K)$ or $D_2(g/h, K)$, the corresponding incorrigibility measure satisfies the postulates laid down on 264 of Levi, 1996.[12]

Moreover, the values of $D(h/h, K)$, $D_1(g/h, K)$ and $D_2(g/h, K)$ are all determined by the M-function given K, h and U_K^*

Degrees of incorrigibility exhibit the formal properties of Shackle measures (Levi, 1991, 143 and Levi, 1996, 267). In particular, the degree of incorrigibility of a conjunction is the minimum degree of incorrigibility of a conjunct and for every consistent K, either the degree of incorrigibility of g or of $\sim$g is equal to the minimum or to 0 with respect to contractions removing h. Moreover, when giving up h contracts a corpus K, items with the lowest degree of incorrigibility (to wit, 0) are given up.

In these respects, they are formally similar to measures of what Gärdenfors (1988) has called degrees of entrenchment. But there are some differences. These differences derive from the difference between measuring vulnerability to being given up among contraction strategies removing some specific sentence h in K as I proposed in the case of incorrigibility and measuring vulnerability to being given up among all contractions removing some sentence or other from K. Entrenchment is, like incorrigibility, an evaluation of vulnerability to giving up sentences in a fixed K. The evaluation of incorrigibility is also relative to a fixed h that is to be removed from K. Entrenchment is not so relativized.

According to Gärdenfors, if both h and g are in K, g is no more entrenched than h if and only if g is not in $K_{h \wedge g}^-$. In that case, either h is in $K_{h \wedge g}^-$ or it is not. In the latter case, both h and g are equally well entrenched. In the former case, h is strictly more entrenched than g relative to K. Gärdenfors rightly insists that no items outside K differ

---

[12] Apart from some minor emendations needed because LK need not be restricted to logical truth, the conditions for degrees of incorrigibility relative to K and h run as follows:

(in1) If LK $\vdash$ g $\equiv$ g', in(g) = in(g').
(in2) in(f $\wedge$ g) = min [in(f), in(g)].
(in3) LK|-t if and only if in(t) = 1(= the maximin invalue).
(in4) in(g) = 0 or in($\sim$g) = 0
(in5) in(g) > 0 if and only if g is in K_g^-.
Corollary: in(h) = 0

Contraction, Rational Choice and Economy

in the vulnerability to being removed from K. In order to extend the assessment of entrenchment to all sentences in L, Gärdenfors assigns all sentences in L but outside K minimum entrenchment. And these are the only sentences assigned minimum entrenchment.

Gärdenfors does not relate degrees of entrenchment explicitly to losses of informational value incurred in contraction as determined by an M^*-function; but it is easy to do that. Whether we are thinking of the minimum loss of damped informational value version 1 or version 2 among contraction strategies removing $h \wedge g$, the optimal contraction removing $h \wedge g$ from K carries informational value $D(h \wedge g/h \wedge g, K) = \max(D(h/h, K), D(g/g, K))$. Hence, the entrenchment of g is less than that of h relative to K if and only if $D(g/g, K) < D(h/h, K)$.

$D(g/g, K)$ is the largest damped informational value assigned to a potential contraction of K that removes g among all potential contractions removing g from K. This is going to be the damped informational value of K_g^-. Informally, g is less entrenched than h in K if and only if the *loss* in damped informational value incurred by removing g from K is more than the loss incurred by removing h. The loss incurred by removing g from K is equal to the difference between the damped informational values of K and K_g^-. We then have the following definition of degrees of entrenchment.

Def: $en(g/K, LK, U_{LK}, M^*) =$ the difference between the damped informational value of K and $D(g/g, K)$ where $D(g/g, K)$ is equal to the maximum cont-value (1-minimum M^*-value) assigned a maxichoice contraction removing g from K.

So entrenchment is dependent upon the M^*-function just as incorrigibility is. But it is derived differently. All and only sentences not in K are assigned 0 entrenchment. All and only sentences not in K_h^- are assigned 0 incorrigibility. Moreover, the ordering with respect to entrenchment does not depend upon whether damped informational value is version 1 or 2. The ordering with respect to incorrigibility does.[13]

[13] The conditions on entrenchment relative to K stated in Levi (1996, 264) are given as follows:

These differences reflect another difference as well: Incorrigibility is relative to M^*, K, U_K^* and h. Incorrigibility can be determined uniquely by M^* and h (given K, U_K^*). Entrenchment is relative to M^*, K, U_K^* but not to h. M^* determines entrenchment uniquely (given K, U_K^*).

Suppose that $en(g/K) < en(h/K)$ where both h and g are in K. By the definition of entrenchment we have:

(1) $D(h/h, K) < D(g/g, K)$.

Suppose that we seek to minimize loss of version 2 damped informational value in removing h from K. (1) implies that condition (b_2) holds. As a consequence, we have the following:

(2) $D_2(g/h, K) = D(h/h, K)$.

By the definition of incorrigibility,

(3) $in(g/h, K) = in(h/h, K)$ if version 2 damped informational value is being minimized.

Suppose that we seek to minimize loss of version 1 damped informational value in removing h from K. (1) implies that the following holds:

(4) $D_1(g/h, K) < D(g/g, K)$.

(4) implies that (b_1) fails. Hence, $D_1(g/h, K) = D(h/h, K)$ only if there is a maxichoice contraction removing h from K that carries maximum undamped informational value and removes g as well—as condition (a) stipulates. Otherwise, $D_1(g/h, K) < D(h/h, K)$. Consequently we have:

(5) $D_1(g/h, K) \leq D_1(h/h, K)$.

(en1) If $LK|\text{-}g \equiv g'$, $en(g) = en(g')$.
(en2) $en(f \wedge g) = \min[en(f), en(g)]$.
(en3) $LK|\text{-}t$ if and only if $en(t) = 1$ (= the maximum en-value).
(en4) $en(g) = 0$ or $en(\sim g) = 0$
(en5) $en(g) > 0$ if and only if g is in K.

(6) Hence, $in(h/h, K) \leq in(g/h, K)$ if damped informational value is of type 1.

We started from the assumption that g is less well entrenched than h. We have shown that if the assessment of damped informational value is type 1, we cannot say that if g is less well entrenched than h in K, we should remove g when removing h from K (as Gärdenfors (1988, 87) does for AGM contraction). When condition (a) fails, g may be more incorrigible and, as a consequence, less vulnerable to removal when removing h.

On the other hand, if the assessment of damped informational value is of type 2, g must be as incorrigible as h so that removal of h will require the removal of the less well-entrenched and equally as incorrigible g as well.

5.10. A Dogma Vindicated (Sort of)

Rott (2000, 509) attacks the "dogma" of belief revision enunciated by Gärdenfors (1988) and Gärdenfors and Makinson (1988) that insists that partial meet contraction of most preferred maxichoice contractions removing h from K is minimal change. h may be removed from K through a contraction that is the intersection of K with a cell of U_K^* that entails $\sim h \wedge g$. There may be cells carrying lower M^*-value that entail $h \wedge \sim g$ so that g is less entrenched than h. Yet, g is retained in K_h^- according to impalpable contraction. The change cannot be minimal in the sense of removing only the sentences in K no more entrenched than h.

The situation parallels the case I have described where loss of version 1 damped informational value is minimized and where, according to the Rule for Ties, Impalpable Contraction is recommended. Under special assumption 1, partial meet contraction is recommended. In either case, it is true both for partial meet or AGM contraction and Impalpable Contraction removing h that minimizing loss does not mean restricting the sentences removed from K to those that are least entrenched relative to K.

Contraction, Rational Choice and Economy

But it does imply that the items in K that are removed are restricted to the least *incorrigible* relative to K and h.[14] Incorrigibility does what AGM wanted entrenchment to do.

More important, the recommended impalpable contraction and the corresponding partial meet contraction both are optimal in the sense that loss of version 1 damped informational value is minimized.

Minimum loss is retained in two senses. Loss in version 1 damped informational value is minimized and only the least incorrigible elements of K relative to h are removed.

Rott rightly points out that removing the least entrenched cannot be rationalized for AGM contraction (and by implication for or impalpable contraction). Removing the least entrenched can, however, be recommended for mild contraction or severe withdrawal. when loss of damped informational value version 2 is minimized and the Rule for Ties is invoked.

Gärdenfors, of course, thought of entrenchment as based on AGM partial meet contractions where the Recovery Condition is satisfied. Entrenchment so conceived cannot be derived from minimizing loss of type 2 damped informational value together with the Rule for Ties. And it cannot be derived from minimizing losses of undamped informational value (with the Rule for Ties) either as we have seen previously unless contraction is restricted to maxichoice contraction. If we wish to say, as Gärdenfors does (Gärdenfors, 1988, 87), that when K is contracted, the sentences removed are those carrying minimal unconditional entrenchment, minimizing loss of damped informational value of type 2 satisfies our requirements.[15] This is the

---

[14] Recall that $D_1(g/h, K)$ is the contraction removing g as well as h from K that carries greatest damped informational value version 1 among all contractions removing h that also remove g. Hence, incorrigibility of g can be construed as entrenchment of K on the condition that h be removed as well. In this sense, keeping losses to the minimally incorrigible is tantamount to keeping them to the minimally entrenched conditional on the removal of h. In this sense, minimality involves minimizing subject to a constraint.

[15] In Levi, 1991, I thought of entrenchment as a rephrasal of what I had in mind by incorrigibility as did Gärdenfors in 1988. Because of this, I insisted in modifying Gärdenfors postulate (EE4) which fails for incorrigibility and, hence, so I thought, for entrenchment. In Levi, 1996, I acknowledged the differences between Gärdenfors's idea and mine. Still the definition of entrenchment given on 265 (Gärdenfors, 1988) is unsatisfactory. I prefer the definition furnished here. In addition, I falsely asserted that K_h^- is the

Contraction, Rational Choice and Economy

important insight in Rott's attack on the second dogma of belief revision. Of course Recovery is abandoned.

Using damped informational value of type 2, it becomes apparent that whether one uses entrenchment or incorrigibility as a tool for representing appraisals of vulnerability to being given up is largely a stylistic matter depending on whether attention is focused on assessments of losses of informational value other than the losses that one is going to suffer by removing the stipulated sentence h or losses incurred by contracting from K alone are the center of attention.

What is substantive, so I claim, is that neither mode of assessment acquires any significance for either belief change or suppositional reasoning except when derived from a representation of the agent's demands for information. The specification of the minimal corpus, the basic partition and the informational value determining probability M^* are intended to give formal expression to such demands.

The interpretation of Shackle's formalism for potential surprise and belief in terms of inductive expansion rules supplies a way to understand potential surprise in terms of other ideas including subjective probability. In a similar spirit, deriving entrenchment or incorrigibility from the epistemic utility lost in contraction, i.e. in terms of loss in informational value, offers an understanding of entrenchment that merely taking it as a primitive idea constrained by postulates fails to provide. This is especially important since measures of entrenchment and incorrigibility are, except for minor adjustments, subject to the same formal requirements as Shackle's measure of potential surprise and belief. And because of this formal similarity, it may be (and has been) tempting to think of entrenchment and degree of belief as usefully embeddable in a single ordering. A careful look at their interpretations, however, should disabuse us of such temptation.

I am suggesting, in the first instance, that demands for information are representable by an informational value (or utility) determining

set of positively entrenched sentences in K minus the set of sentences carrying entrenchment at least as small as that of h. This is, indeed, true if damped informational value is of type 2; but in Levi, 1996 I was still using damped informational value of type 1 or, more accurately, had not clearly separated the two.

probability over L or, at least, over U_{LK} relative to LK. Undamped informational value and damped informational value of types 1 and 2 are defined in terms of it. In the most general setting, I argue that demands for information are represented by a convex set of such *M*-functions. The ramifications of considering such sets in assessing contraction strategies will be addressed in 5.12.

5.11. Categorial Matching

Many authors think that accounts of belief change that focus attention on transformations of states of full belief or corpora (belief sets) that represent them are inadequate. In determining how to contract, entrenchment plays a critical role. So the transformation of state that should be the locus of concern should be the corpus cum entrenchment ordering. In specifying a best contraction removing h from K, a recommendation concerning the new entrenchment ordering for the contracted corpus should be made. It is alleged that unless such instruction is given, the question of iterated revision cannot be adequately addressed.

Rott (2001, 44) declares that this attitude reflects a demand for conformity with the following principle:

> *Principle of Categorial Matching*: The representation of a belief state after a belief change has taken place should be of the same format as the representation of the belief state before the change.

The Principle of Categorial Matching seems to me misguided. A state of full belief is represented linguistically by a deductively closed set of sentences K in a suitably regimented language L. Given the demand to contract from K by removing h, widespread reliance is placed on the use of the entrenchment ordering to determine K_h^-. But the recommendation of a partial meet contraction or a mild contraction does not indicate what the new entrenchment of elements of K_h^- is going to be. Rott among many others thinks that the recommendation of K_h^- should come along with a recommendation of a new entrenchment.

Contraction, Rational Choice and Economy

Incorrigibility and entrenchment alike are determined by the inquirer's demands for information. I have suggested that demands for information are representable by (1) a minimal corpus LK, (2) a basic partition U_{LK} and (3) an informational value determining function M^*. In any series of investigations where these factors are held fixed, a change in the state of full belief **K** or the corpus K that represents it uniquely determines U_K^*, U_K, loss of undamped informational value, of damped informational value both in versions 1 and 2 and grades of entrenchment relative to K. If factors (1), (2) and (3) are changed while K is changed, the change in K will fail to determine the considerations relevant for assessing contractions.

But suppose one of the three factors held constant changes. In particular, let M^* change. Then the new entrenchment ordering will not be the same as it would have been had M^* remained fixed.

This circumstance ought not to lead us to insist that in giving an account of change in state of full belief, it is necessary to also give an account of how entrenchment should change with that change in state of full belief. Contractions of the state of full belief depend on the values for the factors (1), (2) and (3) prior to contraction. Whether the values for these factors remain fixed or change in some particular way has no bearing on what the recommended contraction should be. Changes in corpus and changes in these factors are independent variables.

Of course, the assumption of independence I am making may be controversial. Even so, we should not beg the question by insisting on a formulation of the state variable (the epistemic state) that precludes independent variation of the corpus and the three variables. The Principle of Categorial Matching begs the question in this objectionable manner.

There are many more degrees of freedom allowed in assessing changes in epistemic state when these factors are allowed to vary independently than there are if we insist on a theory that tightly links changes in full belief to changes in entrenchment and M^* as the Principle of Categorial Matching requires.

In genuine inquiry, it is often likely that demands for information as well as full beliefs will change in the course of investigation so that

Contraction, Rational Choice and Economy

the conditions for applying an account of iterated revision may be severely limited in such contexts. But iterated revision seems important in the context of suppositional reasoning. And, in suppositional reasoning, it is reasonable to assume that the demands for information (factors (1), (2) and (3)) are held fixed so that iteration can be systematically studied. In that setting, factors such as entrenchment will be changed in a definite fashion owing to the way in which demands for information are held fixed. This circumstance does not, however, require us to reject the separability of demands for information from states of full belief. It suggests rather that we acknowledge the special circumstances that surround the topic of suppositional or conditional reasoning.

In any case, nothing prevents those who wish to reduce the number of degrees of freedom in changes of contextual factors from mounting arguments in favor for their view. But they ought not to beg the question by building their view into the analytical structure they are going to deploy by the mere unargued for announcement of a general principle of categorical matching.

5.12. Indeterminacy in Informational Value

The main focus of the discussion to date has been on whether agents called upon to contract their state of belief seek to minimize loss of undamped informational value, damped informational value of type 1 or damped informational value of type 2. No matter which kind of loss is being minimized, the assessment of loss of informational value is itself a value judgment reflecting the inquirer's goals. Moreover, the assessment of loss of informational value is derivable from an assessment of informational value determining probability (as represented by an M^*-function relative to U_{LK} or by an M-function relative to U_K and K in the context of expansion).

No assumption was made, however, as to whether there is a M^*-value that everyone ought to adopt. I do not believe that there is such a standard. We should allow that inquirers may have honest disagreements concerning the choice of M^*-function.

Contraction, Rational Choice and Economy

On the other hand, the choice of M^*-function can make a difference in the way in which inductive expansions and in the way contractions are evaluated. Insofar as it matters to us how disagreements as to what to add via induction or to remove in contraction, we should give some account of how inquirers who do disagree can move to an evaluation of informational value based on the aspects of their conflicting assessments that they share in common.

Consider a context where inquirers are debating which of rival theories to add to their corpora. Sometimes the disagreements between such inquirers reflect differences in their research programs with respect to the explanatory virtues of the rival theories as much as differences in the assumptions they take for granted and the judgments of probability they base on them. Demands for informational value may seem to overwhelm assessments of risk of error as factors contributing to the dispute. In such cases, it is desirable that inquirers who have good reason for resolving their disagreements be capable of doing so without begging controversial issues including differences with respect to their research programs and, hence, their demands for information. There is a way to formally represent such shared agreements and how they relate to the critical assessment of expansion strategies.

Demands for information that are ingredient in the goals of inductive expansion are representable by measures of content or undamped informational value and the M-functions that determine them (Levi, 1967a, 1967b). In Levi, 1984, ch. 7 and 1980, I suggested that the shared agreements between inquirers who assess undamped informational value by different M-functions could be represented by the set of weighted averages of the several M-functions. Each of the "permissible" M-functions in such a convex set could be combined with the utility of truth through weighted averaging to form a permissible epistemic utility function after the proposals of Levi, 1967a, 1967b. A permissible expected epistemic utility of any potential expansion strategy in a set determined by K and U_K^* given a permissible credal probability function and a permissible epistemic utility function is then well defined. Each permissible expected epistemic utility function defines a set of potential expansion

205

strategies (potential answers) that are optimal with respect to that expected utility.

According to the decision theory I have advocated since Levi, 1974 and elaborated in Levi, 1986, a rational agent should restrict his choices to *E-admissible* options. An E-admissible option is one that ranks best in expected utility according to at least one permissible expected epistemic utility function in the set of permissible expected utility functions defined over the range of available options. The set of expected utility functions could be larger than a singleton because the agent's judgments of probability are indeterminate and, hence, representable by a set of probability distributions (over states).

Indeterminacy in expected utility may also be due to conflict or indeterminacy in the agent's values and goals that is representable by a set of utility functions. Problems of inductive expansion are situations where both kinds of indeterminacy can emerge. When the options are potential expansion strategies, these should be E-admissible. These are the expansion strategies that are optimal according to at least one permissible expected epistemic utility function.

In general, when more than one option is E-admissible, secondary value commitments may be invoked to recommend choice from a subset of the E-admissible options. In some contexts for example, an agent may place a premium on security and choose an E-admissible option that maximizes his level of security among the E-admissible options. Some such idea seems to make sense out of the violations of the independence postulate that are held to be manifested in the choices favored by experimental subjects when confronted with Ellsberg and Allais predicaments without interpreting the behavior as violations of independence (Levi, 1986, 7.7–7.8 and 1997, ch. 10).

What is true in general applies to deliberate or inductive expansion. When there is but one permissible expected epistemic utility function, there will always be a unique weakest optimal potential expansion strategy so that we can recommend breaking ties in expected epistemic utility by rejecting the smallest set of elements of the ultimate partition that maintains optimality. This is a special case where two or more options are E-admissible and a secondary

Contraction, Rational Choice and Economy

criterion is invoked to reduce the set of E-admissible options to a smaller set. When two or more expansions are admissible, a wise person tries to suspend judgment between their conclusions. This injunction is coherently acceptable when there is a uniquely permissible expected epistemic utility function and all E-admissible options are optimal options.

Can the Rule for Ties be extended to apply when more than one expected epistemic utility function is permissible? Can we recommend the *Strong Rule for Ties* that prescribes choosing the inductive expansion strategy that is the intersection of all the E-admissible ones? We could if that intersection were itself E-admissible. In that event, we can recommend choosing the uniquely weakest E-admissible expansion strategy.

Unfortunately we cannot always guarantee a uniquely weakest E-admissible potential expansion strategy when more than one expected epistemic utility function is permissible. When there is one, it can be recommended as in the case where there is a uniquely permissible expected utility function. Otherwise, the best we can do is to recommend selecting an expansion strategy that is (1) E-admissible and is such that (2) no other E-admissible expansion strategy is weaker than it is. Call this the *Weak Rule for Ties*.

The upshot is that in the context of theory choice and other types of inductive expansion where there is conflict and, hence, indeterminacy in assessments of undamped informational value and credal probability, we cannot guarantee a unique recommendation of a potential expansion strategy. We cannot say that the intersection of the admissible potential expansion strategies should be adopted; for that intersection may not be E-admissible.[16]

In inductive expansion, undamped informational value is aggregated with the utility of avoiding error to obtain an epistemic utility function characterizing the concern to obtain error-free information.

---

[16] If, however, we consider the result of reiterating the effort at inductive expansion via bookkeeping to a stable conclusion (see Levi, 1967, 1980 and 1996), it turns out that the conclusion will be univocal if we follow the Weak Rule for Ties as presented here and will coincide with the result of bookkeeping using a strong Rule for Ties.

Contraction, Rational Choice and Economy

In contraction, undamped informational value (or the M^*-function that defines it) is transformed into damped informational value (of version 1 or, as I now prefer, version 2). But just as the recognition of several M^*-functions as permissible is tantamount to recognizing several measures of undamped informational value and measures of epistemic utility as permissible, so too it requires recognition of several distinct measures of damped informational value as permissible as well.

In evaluating contraction strategies, however, we do not aggregate informational value with avoidance of error because in contraction the issue of avoiding error does not arise.

Aggregating informational value with the utility of avoiding error and worrying about uncertainty is unnecessary when attempting to identify optimal contractions relative to a single permissible evaluation of loss of damped informational value. Hence, any two evaluations that yield the same weak ordering of the potential contraction strategies will yield the same recommendations. One might argue that quantitative differences in assessment of informational value and, hence, in M^*-values are irrelevant to the assessment of contraction strategies.

Moreover, we are not really concerned with preserving the weak ordering induced by the M^*-function over its entire domain but only over elements of U_K^*; for the evaluation of damped informational value of the second kind is uniquely determined by this assessment. That is to say, the weak ordering of all potential contraction strategies with respect to damped informational value of the second kind is uniquely determined by the weak ordering of all potential maxichoice contractions.

Quantitative considerations cannot be so readily ignored in the case of inductive expansion. For one thing, interest in (undamped) informational value is weighted against the concern to avoid error. For another, the concern to avoid error implies a concern to minimize risk of error. When facing risk, quantitative dimensions of value become relevant.

Consider then an agent with corpus K concerned to remove h and facing a dual ultimate partition U_K^* with assessments of (un-

Contraction, Rational Choice and Economy

damped of type 2) informational value based on a convex set of M-functions. In particular, consider three elements x,y and z of U_K^*. Let the set of permissible M-functions be the convex hull of M_1 assigning values 0.1, 0.03 and 0.01 to x, y and z respectively and of M_2 assigning 0.01, 0.03 and 0.1 to the same elements. All other elements of the dual ultimate partition implying h receive higher M-values and, hence, could not qualify as optimal maxichoice contractions according to any permissible M-function. According to some permissible M-functions, meets of x and y and of z and y qualify as optimal contractions. But no permissible M-function recognizes the meet of all three as optimal. So it would appear that only the weak rule for breaking ties is operative in such cases. So the meet of three maxichoice contractions is not E-admissible and, hence, not admissible at all.

Keep in mind, however, that in contraction quantitative dimensions of informational value do not seem relevant. At least this is so when exactly one M-function is permissible. But in that case, we could just as well have adopted any other M-function preserving the same ordering over elements of U_K^*. We need not preserve the order over other subsets of elements of U_K.

Quantitative considerations do arise when we consider two M-functions such as our M_1 and M_2 to be permissible. We have supposed that the set of permissible M-functions is the set of all weighted averages $\alpha M_1 + (1 = \alpha) M_2$ (convex hull) of these two where $0 \leq \alpha \leq 1$. But if we had considered the set of weighted averages of all M-functions that are positive monotone transformations of these two (i.e. preserve the weak ordering generated by these two M-functions when restricted to elements of U_K^*), we would have had a much larger set of M-functions. In this set, it will turn out that potential contractions that are meets of maxichoice or saturatable contractions that recognize x, y and z as possibilities are optimal according to some permissible M-functions.

This result is quite general. If we are given n M-functions M_i as permissible, there are two ways to proceed:

Method 1: Take the convex hull C of the M_i's. Construct the set C^* of positive monotone transformations of members of C. These give the permissible weak orderings of potential contractions with respect to assessments of damped informational value of type 2.

Method 2: Form the set E of positive monotone transformations of the M_i's. Identify the "categorical" partial ordering of the elements of U_K^* according to which x is categorically weakly, strictly or equi preferred to y if and only if it is weakly, strictly or equi preferred to y according to each weak ordering in E. Consider the set D of extensions of the partial ordering to a weak ordering over U_K^*. $C^* \subseteq D$. D determines the permissible weak orderings of potential contractions with respect to assessments of damped informational value of type 2 in the sense of weak orderings that satisfy weak positive monotonicity and version 2 damping.

As illustrated above, method 1 does not guarantee that the recommendation of a strong Rule for Ties will yield an E-admissible contraction. According to the decision theory I favor for cases where there are multiple permissible rankings of the options, the use of the strong rule is then unacceptable as a general secondary criterion.

On the other hand, using method 2 does guarantee that the strong rule will always yield an E-admissible option.

Which method is acceptable given the supposition that loss of damped informational value of the second kind is to be minimized? Can we justify using method 2 rather than method 1 on the grounds that minimizing loss of damped informational value requires the use of ordinal information alone?

The answer to this question is not entirely clear to me. The pivotal difference between methods 1 and 2 concerns what count as potential resolutions of conflict between rival assessments according to each method. Method 1 takes the original quantitative assessments of undamped informational value or *M*-value, converts them into quantitative assessments of damped informational value of type 2, *considers potential resolutions of conflict between these rival assessments as weighted averages of the original quantitative assessments* and then ordinalizes the results. Method 2 *begins* by ordinalizing the quantitative assessments of damped informational value, finding the categorical preference and taking consistent extensions of that preference as the basis for a characterization of potential resolutions.

Contraction, Rational Choice and Economy

Method 1 takes the quantitative assessments of undamped informational value and the corresponding quantitative assessments of damped informational value seriously. Method 2 considers them irrelevant to assessing what is to count as a potential resolution of a conflict between different demands for informational value. I have argued that the quantitative dimension is important in addressing inductive expansion. Should we therefore respect it in dealing with contraction even though it plays no role in determining either entrenchment or incorrigibility orderings relevant for identifying recommended contractions?

There is a tension between two kinds of consideration: One may argue for method 1 on the grounds that the interest of expansion and contraction ought not to be divorced; method 2 may be supported on the grounds that only ordinal considerations are needed in contraction and that the strong Rule for Ties should be deployed whenever one can with good conscience do so.[17]

5.13. Fallbacks

When demands for information are conflicted in a manner that yields indeterminacy representable by a convex set of M-functions, each permissible M-function defines an assessment of damped informational value of type 2 and through that for each K a permissible entrenchment ordering of the elements of K. Each permissible entrenchment ordering yields a nested system of spheres in the sense of a Grove model. These spheres qualify as fallbacks in the sense of Lindström and Rabinowicz, 1990. If we consider all unions of the sets of fallbacks associated with each permissible ordering, we have a system of fallbacks of the sort considered by Lindström and Rabinowicz with an associated entrenchment ordering that allows for incomparabilities.[18]

---

[17] If we follow method 2, the choice function that emerges will allow for failures of Sen's property β and intransitivity of revealed indifference in choosing contraction strategies.

[18] Whether the entrenchment ordering is the categorical preference ranking of Levi, 1986 or the revealed preference ranking is unclear. And whether the permissible rankings are those allowed by method 1 or by method 2 is also unclear.

Contraction, Rational Choice and Economy

Lindström and Rabinowicz do not consider fallbacks to be contractions of K. But they are contractions in the sense in which I have used the term since 1974. Maximal ∼h permitting fallbacks in their sense are contractions of K removing ∼h that are E-admissible if permissible evaluations of losses of damped informational value are of type 2 so that an E-admissible contraction would have the properties of a mild contraction or a severe withdrawal. Lindström and Rabinowicz object to using mild contractions (and, by implication, damped informational value of type 2) on the grounds that contraction so conceived would be too drastic.

Part of their anxiety has been addressed previously by invoking coarse graining of potential contraction strategies with the aid of dual ultimate partitions and minimal corpora and another part has been addressed by pointing out that loss of damped informational value is not ordered by set inclusion.

Whatever their reservations with fallbacks might be in discussing contraction, Lindström and Rabinowicz have no reservation with using it in discussing revisions. That is because they still are following the tradition according to which revision of K by h when h is already in K is taken to be K itself. In that setting, it does not matter whether one uses a contraction function satisfying Recovery or not when considering revision. If it is advantageous to use mild contractions = severe withdrawals = fallbacks in discussing entrenchment—especially when considering failure of weak order, one can use it without raising any problems for revision other than the loss of weak order. Given their reservations when contraction does not lead to revision and their legitimate objections to Recovery, Lindström and Rabinowicz in effect distinguish two kinds of contraction of interest to them: One they call "fallback" and the other "contraction".

I, on the other hand, think that their fallbacks will serve the purposes of contraction very well. This becomes important when one takes Ramsey revision seriously as I do.

My concern here is with the issue of non-comparability. Lindström and Rabinowicz take the position that when two or more ∼h -permitting fallbacks are optimal according to some permissible

Contraction, Rational Choice and Economy

complete entrenchment ranking, no further recommendation is to be made.

In section 5.12, I conceded that one might be driven to the conclusion that two or more contraction strategies should end up as admissible all things considered if one uses method 1 for determining the set of permissible entrenchment rankings. I wish to emphasize, however, that this conclusion is quite an uncomfortable one. The instincts of Gärdenfors and Makinson to favor skeptical responses where one suspends judgment in such cases seem quite sensible.

The problem, as I have insisted, is that in order to cater to these sensible instincts one must show that doing so is not merely to choose an available option and not merely the intersection of admissible options, but is to choose an admissible option. One can overcome this problem with the aid of method 2 and do so in a manner that is in keeping with a principled account of rational choice when utility goes indeterminate. The cost of doing so, however, is that the link between the assessments of informational value relevant to inductive expansion and the assessments relevant to contraction are somewhat weakened.

The weakening may or may not be harmless. That remains to be seen. My reservation with the attitude of Lindström and Rabinowicz concerns the complacency with which they confront the prospect of abandoning the skeptical view. Even when entrenchment lacks a weak ordering, I would have thought the skeptical view an attractive one to endorse if one can honorably do so.

Some Problems with Infinity 6

6.1. Infinite Ultimate Partitions: Finite Intervals

Throughout this discussion of contraction, attention has been focused on basic partitions relative to LK containing finitely many cells and the finite ultimate partitions and dual ultimate partitions relative to K carved out of them. However, contexts arise where it is desirable to lift this restriction both for the purposes of inductive expansion and contraction. I shall summarize some partial suggestions regarding this topic by focusing on certain special kinds of cases where the need for thinking of infinity seems urgent.

Three kinds of problems where inductive expansion is called for will be discussed:

(a) Problems where the task is to estimate the value of a real valued parameter believed to take values in some finite (one-dimensional) interval.
(b) Problems where the task is to determine which of a countable set of alternative hypotheses is true.
(c) Problems where the task is to estimate the value of a real valued parameter on the real line.

Following the practice I adopted in Levi, 1980 and 1996, the recommendations made for these cases will be construed as limiting

Some Problems with Infinity

cases of certain sequences of recommendations for finite ultimate partitions based on the criteria of inductive expansion and stable inductive expansion I have sketched in 3.3 and 3.4. To use the techniques I propose successfully, the credal distribution Q^* and informational valued probability distribution M^* over the basic partition U_{LK} will have to satisfy certain conditions that will be indicated. But the distribution M^* used together with K to derive the measure M and $Cont = 1 - M$ over the ultimate partition U_K for use in inductive expansion is also used together with K to determine losses of informational value by shifting from K to some contraction that is representable by the intersection of K with the intersection of a set of elements of the dual ultimate partition when such losses are assessed by damped informational value. The use of the same M^* in the context of contraction as is adopted in the context of expansion is justified by principle called "Common Basis for Determining Gains and Losses of Informational Value" introduced in 4.3. The properties that M^* has in order to insure the successful use of the proposed inductive expansion criteria insure that the damping constraint introduced in 4.6 can be successfully extended to the infinite cases discussed here. The primary purpose of Chapter 6 is to obtain this result.

The first case concerns the problem of estimating a real valued parameter whose true value is believed to fall in some finite interval.[1] (Only one-dimensional parameters shall be discussed.) That is to say, with the exception of at most a subset of Lebesgue measure 0, all point estimates in an interval from a_* to a^* are countenanced as serious possibilities relative to K and are elements of an ultimate partition U_K relative to K.[2]

---

[1] Here the elements of the basic partition U_{LK} or the ultimate partition U_K constitute a non-denumerably infinite set. In the case under consideration, we not only have the set U_{LK} but the elements of U_{LK} form an interval having a certain length and contain subsets that are subintervals of the interval from a_* to a^* and have lengths. (Elements of U_{LK} have length 0.) Taking the class of all subintervals, we can form other (Borel) sets by taking countable intersections, and countable unions and by complementation and extend the measure of length to apply to these sets to form the set function known as the Lebesgue measure. Not all subsets of U_K will have a well-defined Lebesgue measure; but in this setting we will not need to rely on this point.

[2] Consider an interval from $x = 0$ to $x = 1$. There is nothing in logic or mathematics to prevent using the Lebesgue measure generated by lengths of subintervals of whose end

Some Problems with Infinity

Suppose the expectation determining probability distribution Q, the informational value distribution M and the Lebesgue measure are absolutely continuous in each other. That is to say, a subset of U_K has 0 Lebesgue measure if and only if it is assigned 0 Q-value and 0 M-value. (Both the Q-function and M-function are countably additive over the Borel sets and the cumulative distribution functions for Q and M are continuous to the right over U_K.)

Consider some real point estimate h_x asserting that x is the precise true value of the parameter in question. Let the hypothesis $h_{x,\varepsilon}$ assert that the true value is in the interval from $x - \varepsilon$ to $x + \varepsilon$. If $x = a_*$ or differs from a_* by an amount less than ε, $h_{x,\varepsilon}$ continues to make this claim but the background information precludes some of these points from being serious possibilities. If $x = a^*$ or differs from a^* by an amount less than ε, a similar remark applies.

Application of the inductive rejection rules to a partition of U_{LK} (or U_K) into finitely many intervals of positive length that includes $h_{x,\varepsilon}$ as an interval warrants rejection of $h_{x,\varepsilon}$ if and only if $Q(h_{x,\varepsilon})/M(h_{x,\varepsilon}) < q$.

If $h_{x,\varepsilon}$ is not rejected, however, at the level q, the question arises as to whether it is stably rejected (see 3.4, Levi, 1980, 1996 and 2001). Iterating deliberate expansion until no further information is obtained in this manner is sensitive to the way $\sim h_{x,\varepsilon}$ is divided into cells of an ultimate partition along with $h_{x,\varepsilon}$. The notion of stable rejection may be extended, however, by stipulating that $h_{x,\varepsilon}$ is robustly and stably rejected if and only if there is some partition of $\sim h_{x,\varepsilon}$ into finitely many cells that together with $h_{x,\varepsilon}$ constitutes an ultimate partition relative to which $h_{x,\varepsilon}$ is stably rejected at the level q.

Suppose at a given level of boldness q there is an ε^* such that for every $\varepsilon \leq \varepsilon^*$, $h_{x,\varepsilon}$ is rejected. h_x (which is an exact point estimate in the non-countably infinite ultimate partition U_K) is rejected at the given level of boldness q.

points are given by values of log x rather than by x to constitute the Lebesgue measure used in formulating the rules for rejecting elements of U_K. Using one gives us a finite Lebesgue measure for U_K and using the other an infinite one. I take the choice of one of these or some other alternative to represent the length of the interval values allowed by the basic or ultimate partition to be a feature of the inquirer's demands for information. As such it is a feature of the inquirer's cognitive goals.

Some Problems with Infinity

Suppose at a given level of boldness q there is an ε^* such that for every $\varepsilon \leq \varepsilon^*$, $h_{x,\varepsilon}$ is robustly and stably rejected. The exact point estimate h_x is *stably* rejected at the given level of boldness q.

If the cumulative distribution functions for the subjective probability Q and informational value determining probability M are differentiable so that they both define continuous density functions $f(x)$ and $m(x)$ respectively, h_x in U_{LK} is rejected at level q if and only if $f(x)dx < qm(x)dx$.

For a fixed partition of U_{LK} into finitely many cells including $h_{x,\varepsilon}$; $h_{x,\varepsilon}$ is stably rejected with $q = 1$ when $Q(h_{x,\varepsilon})/M(h_{x,\varepsilon})$ is less than the maximum of the ratios Q/M for cells of the given partition. If there is such a partition, $h_{x,\varepsilon}$ is robustly and stably rejected. Assuming the existence of the corresponding density functions, h_x is stably rejected when $q = 1$ if $f(x)dx/m(x)dx$ is not the maximum value for ratio of these two density functions for seriously possible point estimates in the interval from a_* to a^*.

Let us suppose that either the density function f for Q or the density function m for M is not everywhere continuous from a_* to a^* but has finitely many equally spaced points of discontinuity. Within each interval there is a continuous conditional f-function or m-function.

A simple case of this type would be one where the interval from a_* to a^* is divided into n subintervals and the density function m_i is constant over the ith subinterval but differs for each subinterval.

As before, for any point estimate, we can adopt the rejection rule formulated for the case where the Q and M distributions are continuous over the entire interval with the following modification: h_x is rejected if and only if $f_i(x)Q(i)/m_i(x)M(i) < q$ where f_i and m_i are the densities conditional on the true value being in the interval i. The same rejection rule can be extended to cases where U_{LK} or U_K does not consist of the points in a single interval but of the union of points in finitely many finite but non-overlapping intervals for each of which both the Q and M distributions are continuous.

The criteria for robust and stable rejection of $h_{x,\varepsilon}$ and stable rejection of h_x with degree of boldness q can be adjusted to the cases under consideration. If $q = 1$, h_x is stably rejected if $f_i(x)Q(i)/m_i(x)M(i)$ is less than the maximum that this ratio can take.

Some Problems with Infinity

We can have cases where a set of points of measure 0 belonging in the given interval may count as impossible according to LK (or K). In that case, the proposal is to reject all elements of U_K rejected according to the rejection rule on the assumption that all real values in the interval are serious possibilities and reject, in addition, all real values in the designated set of measure 0.

This proposal runs into trouble when the point estimate for which this ratio is a maximum is not a serious possibility. At $q = 1$, all serious possibilities would be rejected. This amounts to deliberate expansion into inconsistency. Even so, $f_i(x)Q(i)/m_i(x)M(i)$ would be bounded from above by this ratio. For values of $q < 1$, there would be a non-empty set of unrejected elements even if the set of points of measure 0 removed in advance as serious possibilities is non-denumerable. These considerations argue for forbidding $q = 1$.

However, $f_i(x)Q(i)/m_i(x)M(i)$ may not be bounded from above even when all points in the interval represent serious possibilities. Under the assumptions adopted here $f_i(x)Q(i)$ will carry a maximum. We can reasonably demand that $m_i(x)M(i)$ take positive values in the interval so that all elements of U_K can be rejected against some Q-distribution for sufficiently high positive q. But this requirement does not preclude 0 from being the lower bound for values of $m_i(x)M(i)$ or $f_i(x)Q(i)/m_i(x)M(i)$ being unbounded from above. When it is unbounded, attempting to reiterate inductive expansion could fail to yield a determinate solution. For this reason, we should require not only that $m_i(x)$ be positive for all i but that it be bounded away from 0. Then iteration with values of boldness $q < 1$ will lead to a non-empty subset of U_{LK} going stably unrejected.

Suppose the corpus is LK with U_{LK} structured in the manner just discussed. Inductive expansion has taken place so that the expansion K states that the true value falls in some subinterval from b∗ to b* or, perhaps, in the union of a set of subintervals of the interval from a∗ to a*.

Turn now to the topic of contraction from K as just specified. The dual ultimate partition U_K^* consists of all the rejected elements of U_{LK}.

In the cases of real valued parameter estimation under consideration, evaluating losses of informational value by contractions that

Some Problems with Infinity

restore points in U_K^* to the status of serious possibilities by the informational value determining probability function $M^*(x)$ seems unreasonable. Each such point carries 0 M^*-value. If we used the ordering determined by the M^*-function and employed assessments of losses of type 2 damped informational value, any contraction of K removing some sentence in K would automatically yield LK.

Suppose that an inquirer adopts demands for informational value that recognize finitely many distinct subintervals such that in each interval i, the density m_i^* conditional on the points falling in interval i of length L(i) should equal 1/L(i). The loss in undamped informational value of the interval is $M^*(i)$. The unconditional density in the interval is then the constant value $M^*(i)/L(i)$. $M^*(i)/L(i) > 0$ may replace $M^*(x) = 0$ as the loss of informational value for points x in the interval i. If the intervals are extremely small, the inquirer may not discriminate between the informational values of points within the interval. Even if the density f for the Q^*-distribution is continuous throughout the interval from a∗ to a*, the results of inductive expansion using this way of assessing informational value may not differ from the results of assessment using a continuous m^*-function over the entire interval in a manner that is of concern to the inquirer. If the differences do matter, the inquirer may refine the partition into intervals to a point that is satisfactory given the inquirer's demands for information.

With this *Finite Discriminability Condition for the Purpose of Assessing Informational Value* in place, the loss in undamped informational value of an interval i with uniform m_i^* density $1/L(i)_i$ will be $\int_i L(i) dx M^*(i) = M(i)$. The loss in informational value of points in the same interval will be $M^*(i)/L(i) > 0$. The loss of *damped* informational value version 2 of the interval would then equal the same $M^*(i)/L(i)$.

There is an important byproduct of the Finite Discriminability Condition. It is possible to contract K by removing a proposition h whose negation is representable by an open set of real values in U_K^*. If the informational values of such points could vary in infinitely many and, indeed, non-denumerably many ways, there might not be a saturatable contraction removing h that minimizes loss of damped

Some Problems with Infinity

informational value of either type 1 or type 2. This is so even though the informational value of elements of U_K^* that entail $\sim$h is bounded away from 0.

Finite discriminability with respect to informational value forestalls this possibility. Adopting the Finite Discriminability Condition on Assessments of Informational Value for both inductive expansion and contraction limits the generality of the proposals made here for inductive expansion but not in a serious way. It remains possible to invoke M^*-functions that are step functions with a finite number of steps but where the intervals into which the basic partition U_{LK}^* are as small as would be reasonably desired to gain an approximation to a continuous function. And in spite of the use of the Finite Discriminability Condition on Assessments of Informational Value, no such condition is mandated for credal probability distributions. Finally the inductive rejection rules that emerge still provide conditions for rejecting real valued point estimates belonging to U_K. The finitization proposed here is of the assessments of informational value.

6.2. Countably Infinite Ultimate Partitions

Let U_K or U_{LK} contain countably many cells. According to the criteria for inductive expansion proposed in Levi (1980 and 1996), rejection rules are formulated as follows:

> Cell d of U_K is *n-rejected* if and only if there is at least one subset of n elements A of U_K containing d, such that if the corpus specified that exactly one element of A is true, d would be *stably* rejected at the given level of boldness q.
>
> Cell d of U_K is rejected at the given level of boldness q if and only if there is an n^* such that d is n-rejected for every $n \geq n^*$.

The idea behind this rule is that d should be rejected provided that for all sufficiently large n, d is stably rejected relative to the n-fold subset A of U_K of which d is a member most favorable to rejecting d at the given level q. If d avoids rejection according to this test, it goes unrejected.

Some Problems with Infinity

In the countably infinite case, the Q and M functions can be either countably additive or finitely but not countably additive. Moreover, the finitely but not countably additive distributions can be "purely finitely additive" distributions that assign equal value to all cells and, hence, assign 0 value to all cells or they can be weighted averages of purely finitely additive and countably additive distributions (Schervish, Seidenfeld and Kadane, 1984).

In order to apply the rejection rule just given, conditional probabilities on finite subsets of U_K must be well defined even though the unconditional probabilities for the finite subset are equal to 0. As de Finetti argued, there should be no objection to such definability for subjective probabilities and the same, so I contend, is true for informational value determining probabilities.

Thus, even though two purely finitely additive probabilities assign 0 value to all elements of U_K, they may nonetheless differ in the conditional probabilities they assign conditional on a given finite subset A of U_k. One might assign equal probability 1/n to all elements of A whereas another might assign unequal probabilities.

The difference may be captured by means of a σ-finite measure defined over U_K, i.e. a countably additive measure F assigning positive values to the elements of U_K but where the countable sum need not be finite. One can use the F-function to define conditional probabilities in the usual way. $Q(d/A) = QF(d)/\sum_{d'\in A} QF(d')$ where A is a finite subset of U_K and $M(d/A) = MF(d)/\sum_{d'\in A} MF(d')$. When Q (or M) are countably additive, $QF = Q$ (or $MF = F$).

This means that it is possible to weakly order the elements of U_K with respect to the given probability. If d and d' are cells in U_K, let A be the join of the two cells. Given any finite set B that is a superset for A, the probability of d is at least as great as the probability of d' conditional on A if and only if the same holds conditional on B. Moreover, the comparison remains the same when the conditional probability is defined conditional on the true value falling in an arbitrary finite superset of A. This holds whether or not the probability measure is countably additive or merely finitely additive.

The inductive expansion rule or rejection rule for the countably infinite case has the following defect. There are Q and M distributions

Some Problems with Infinity

relative to which all elements of U_K are rejected for all positive values of q. To avoid this result, we may either abandon the inductive expansion rule or impose restrictions on the allowed Q and M distributions.

In my judgment, it is preferable to impose constraints on demands for informational value when otherwise serious methodological problems arise than it is to impose restrictions on credal probabilities or to abandon the inductive expansion rule. As it turns out, the inductive expansion rule may, for the most part, be retained by imposing relatively modest constraints on the range of M-functions.

It would be undesirable to rule out countably additive Q-functions playing the role of expectation determining probability distributions because they are commonly employed in applications. Moreover, it seems desirable to be in a position to assign equal (and, hence, purely finitely additive) probability to each element of a countably infinite U_K both when probability is expectation determining and informational value determining. Indeed, one of the motivations for introducing finitely but not countably additive Q-functions has always been to allow for probability judgments of this kind.

If an informational value determining M-function is countably additive over a countable domain and all elements of U_K carry positive M-value, there will be no smallest positive value for M. The greatest lower bound of such values will be 0. Otherwise the total probability for U_K would be infinite. Take any element d of U_K and let $M(d) = M^*$. Take the ratios $M(d'')/M^*$ for d'' such that $M(d'') < M^*$. These are also bounded by 0.

Suppose the inquirer's expectation determining probability function Q is finitely additive and is represented by a QF-function assigning equal positive value to each element of U_K. For any element x of subset A_n of n elements of U_K, the probability of d conditional on the true value falling in A_n, is $1/n$.

The use of a countably additive M-function together with such a Q-function must lead to inductive expansion into inconsistency for every positive value of q. Every element of U_K is 2-rejectable at every level of boldness $q > 1/2$. Just take any element d, identify a d'

Some Problems with Infinity

such that $M(d')/M(d)$ is very close to 0. (This is always possible under the assumption that the M-function is countably additive.) d is rejected on the assumption that d or d' is true for values of $1 \geq q > 0.5$. So d is 2-rejectable for values of q in that range. Add a d" to the set of alternatives that carries lower M-value than d'. d is rejected for values of q ranging from near 0.33^+ to 1 and, hence, is 3-rejectable. d remains n rejectable for increasing n and for values of q whose lower bound approaches 0 as n increases. So d is rejectable for every positive value of q. No matter what positive degree of boldness is exercised, it is possible for circumstances to arise where the rejection rule leads to inductive expansion into inconsistency.

The use of finitely additive Q-functions assigning equal probability to every element of U_K should not be prohibited in order to avoid this unattractive result. We should instead modify demands for information. I conclude that countably additive M-functions should not be used together with finitely additive Q-functions. Since we are allowing purely finitely additive Q-functions represented by constant QF-functions, we must disallow countably additive probability functions as informational value determining.

Given the same finitely but not countably additive Q-function, we should now consider finitely additive M-distributions. There are three cases to consider:

(a) The MF-function has a minimum in all subsets of U_K.
(b) The MF-function has no minimum but has a positive glb.
(c) The MF-function has no minimum but has a 0 glb.

Case (c) can be shown to lead to inductive expansion into inconsistency for all values of q by the same reasoning used in the countably additive case. Case (b) consists of cases where inductive expansion into inconsistency occurs for values of q less than 1 but greater than some specific positive value depending on the glb. Even so, any specific level of boldness can lead to inductive inconsistency provided the glb is low enough. We may be prepared to prohibit $q = 1$; but it is far from obvious that we want to prohibit any other

Some Problems with Infinity

positive value. So it may be concluded that cases (b) and (c) should be ruled out.[3]

Countably additive Q-functions always have a least upper bound. Provided that the M-functions are finitely additive and have MF-functions with positive minima, rejection rules avoid expansion into inconsistency as long as $q < 1$ and avoid expansion into inconsistency when $q = 1$ as well as long as the least upper bound is also a maximum.

In the case of purely finitely additive Q-functions, if the QF-function is bounded from above, no expansion into inconsistency is allowed for the case where $q < 1$ and if the upper bound is a maximum, in the case where $q = 1$. However, if the QF-function is unbounded, inconsistency is possible. This possibility cannot be prohibited as a demand for information. I am inclined to prohibit it anyhow but am not sure I can find a principled way to do so.

Inductive expansion into inconsistency is avoided provided that the M-function satisfies condition (a) and the Q-function is either countably additive or purely finitely additive with an associated QF-function bounded from above (or is a mixture of a countably additive and a purely additive function with a QF function bounded from above).

The chief reason for running through these considerations in connection with inductive expansion is to attend to the problem of contraction. Here we are concerned with the MF-function defined for U_K^*. This function is a restriction of the MF-function for U_{LK}. By reasoning already deployed for inductive expansion, the MF-function must have a minimum in every subset of U_{LK} including U_K^*. (U_{LK} must be well ordered by MF.) The upshot is that the ordering determined by the MF-function must have a minimum in U_K^* and in

---

[3] In Levi, 1996, 197, I contended that finitely but not countably additive M-functions should not assign elements of U_K more than finitely many different probability values. Otherwise they would be bounded by 0. That is true enough but irrelevant. In the context of n-rejection rules, the ordering of elements of U_{LK} with respect to M is replaced by the ordering with respect to MF. The question of relevance here is whether the σ-finite function MF should take on more than finitely many values. Every subset of U_{LK} should have a cell with a minimum MF-value in the subset. But there is no requirement needed that it have a maximum.

Some Problems with Infinity

every subset of U_K^*. Given that the ordering over U_{LK} is a weak ordering, the smoothness (Kraus, Lehmann and Magidor, 1990), stopperedness (Makinson, 1989) and limit (Lewis, 1973; Segerberg, 1996) conditions must be satisfied. Instead of imposing these conditions directly, I have proposed here and in Levi, 1996 to derive them from properties of the informational value determining M-function and the idea that inductive expansion rules should not allow inductive expansion into inconsistency.

6.3. Estimating a Real Valued Parameter Lying on the Real Line

If U_K consists of all real point estimates on the real line, rejection conditions for $h_{x,\varepsilon}$ appropriate for estimation in finite intervals spelled out in 6.1 are unhelpful. The complement of $h_{x,\varepsilon}$ receives Q and M-values equal to 1 and $h_{x,\varepsilon}$ receives 0 values for both.

The hypothesis $h_{x,\varepsilon}$ of 6.1 asserts that the true value of x is in an interval with a given length L. $\sim h_{x,\varepsilon}$ can be partitioned into intervals of length and, hence, Lebesgue measure L so that the entire real line is partitioned into countably many intervals of equal measure L. When facing a countably infinite partition, we can exploit the techniques of 6.2. Apply the inductive expansion rule specified there at a given level q. Those intervals that are rejected in this partition according to the criteria of 6.2 are L-rejected. A point estimate h_x at level q is rejected if and only if there is an L^* such that for all $L < L^*$, the point estimate is L-rejected at level q.

For reasons already rehearsed in 6.2, given any partition of the real line into intervals of positive fixed measure L, the MF-function used provides a well ordering of the cells of the partition. This does not mean that the points on the real line are well ordered with respect to losses of informational value. However, if demands for informational value are adopted that assign equal loss of informational value to all points lying in a cell of such a partition where L is very small, the density function, derived from MF as in 6.1, a well ordering of the points in U_K^* with respect to such losses in contraction. The situation parallels the Finite Discriminability Condition of 6.1 except we allow losses in informational value to be discriminated into denumerably but well-ordered many values.

As in 6.1, we proceed as if U_K^* consists of cells of U_{LK} incompatible with K of some fixed small Lebesgue measure. According to the restrictions imposed here, there should be a minimum M^*-value assigned to cells in $U_K^* = U_{LK}/U_K$. Smoothness, stopperedness or a limit assumption is secured by linking the assessments of losses of damped informational value of type 2 to assessments of undamped informational value in inductive expansion and worries about permitting expansion into inconsistency that arise of constraints implying such an assumption are not in place.

These reflections also furnish another more general reason to be suspicious of undamped informational value of type 1 in the context of contraction. The primary motivation for assigning 0 M^*-value to elements of U_{LK} concerns cases where the basic ultimate partition is infinite as it is in examples such as those considered here. Damped informational value of type 2 yields violations of the Recovery postulate only if the assignment of M^*-value of 0 is to be understood as the assignment of 0 to m(x)dx in the finite interval estimation task of 6.1 or 0 *MF*-value to an interval of positive Lebesgue measure in this section or 0 *MF*-value to a cell in the setting of 6.2. In these settings 0 means "impossible" in the sense of "incompatible with LK".

But as long as LK is the minimal corpus, contraction from the expansion K of LK forbids contractions allowing such impossibilities to be countenanced as serious possibilities. To do that calls for altering LK. Given the problematic of the inquirer, that possibility is not being contemplated. This consideration may be added to the others that support the use of damped informational value of type 2 rather than of type 1.

Base Contraction and the 7
Filtering Condition

Throughout this discussion, contraction has been understood to be a transformation of the current state of full belief to a weaker potential state of full belief relative to which consistent expansion to a potential state of full belief incompatible with the current state is available. I have focused attention on potential states of full belief only insofar as they are representable by deductively closed sets of sentences (*corpora or theories*) in some suitably specified language L. A contraction can be represented by a transformation of initial corpus K representing belief-state **K** to another potential corpus K_h^- representing belief-state $\mathbf{K}_h^-$. h is a sentence in L representing the potential state of full belief also represented linguistically by the $Cn(\{h\})$.

Several authors (most notably A. Fuhrmann, 1991 and S. O. Hansson, 1989) have objected to the use of deductively closed theories or corpora to represent potential states of full belief because they lack surveyability by means of finite resources. They suggest instead that attention be focused on contraction of finite sets of sentences whose closures represent potential states of full belief. Such a finite set A is called a base, basis or belief base for its closure K. $Cn(A) = K$.

There can be no objection to alternative equivalent representations of potential states of full belief. But those who explore the properties of base contraction do not seem to understand contraction of the base

Base Contraction and the Filtering Condition

A of a theory K by sentence h in a manner equivalent to contraction of K by h.

In both cases, h is taken to be a sentence in K. Otherwise, contraction is just an identity transformation. However, in contraction from a base, the *options* for contraction are restricted by the requirement that removal of h from K be representable as the deductive closure of some subset of the base A. For example, if K is the deductive closure of $h \wedge f$ and $A = \{h \wedge f\}$, the base contraction of K removing h is restricted to contraction that removes $h \wedge f$ and yields as corpus the set of logical truths. If, however, $A = \{h, f\}$ or $\{h \wedge f, f\}$, $Cn(\{f\})$ is also a potential contraction removing h that may be evaluated along with the set of logical truths with respect to their merits as potential contractions removing h from K with respect to the goals of contraction—such as minimizing loss of informational value in one of the senses discussed previously. (Notice that contraction to the logical truths violates the Recovery Condition. Contraction to the logical consequences of f does not.)

There are other bases available for the same K that impose different restrictions on contraction removing h. Suppose for the sake of simplicity that the minimal corpus LK is the set of logical truths and the dual ultimate partition consists of $h \wedge \sim f$, $\sim h \wedge f$ and $\sim h \wedge f$. Every potential contraction in the sense of a meet of saturatable contractions is representable as the deductive closure of the disjunction of $h \wedge f$ with a disjunction of some subset (including the empty set) of the elements of this dual ultimate partition. If every such disjunction is a member of a basis A^s, the set of available contraction strategies for contracting from K relative to A^s is identical with the set of meets of saturatable contractions. Relative to that basis (which is a finite basis) there is no restriction at all on the potential contractions relative to the dual ultimate partition that are optional for the inquirer. Relative to some such contractions, Recovery will be violated.

One can also consider as a basis all disjunctions with $h \wedge f$ of elements of the dual ultimate partition that entail $\sim h$ and no others. The set of contraction options will be restricted to partial meet contractions. Recovery must then be satisfied.

Base Contraction and the Filtering Condition

It is easy to see that contraction from a consistent, finitely axiomatizable corpus where the set of options is the set of all contractions of K removing h relative to finite U_K^* is a special case of contraction from a basis as conceived by both Fuhrmann and Hansson.

Let U_K be the disjunction of all elements of the ultimate partition U_K relative to the current corpus K. U_K implies LK. So does every element of the dual ultimate partition U_K^*. Every potential contraction of K is representable as the logical consequences of the disjunction of U_K with a subset S of elements of U_K^*. Assuming that K is finitely axiomatizable and that the basic partition relative to LK is finite, we have the finite surveyability sought by Fuhrmann and Hansson.

If K entails h, each such potential contraction will be a potential contraction of K removing h if and only if at least one of the elements of S entails $\sim$h. If members of a subset of such potential contractions are counted as the ones to be considered optional, the basis is constituted by a set of axioms for K consisting of U_K and each of the disjunctions of U_K with a subset S that represents an option in the subset. If the axiom system contains U_K or some sentence equivalent given LK with it as the sole axiom, we regard contraction to LK as the sole available option. The basis used could include all disjunctions of U_K with subsets S of U_K^* that contain at least one element entailing $\sim$h. That is to say, it could recognize all potential contractions as defined above to be available. It could be more restrictive and recognize only disjunctions of U_K with sets of members of U_K *all of which* entail $\sim$h. The available contractions would then be partial meet contractions. There are, of course, many other kinds of bases as well.

What I have been arguing here is that contraction from a basis is equivalent to contraction from a theory or corpus relative to a restriction of the set of contractions considered optional in some specific way. The case where no restriction is imposed except that imposed by relativization to the dual ultimate partition (or the basic partition) is a special case associated with a special kind of basis. So is the case where the restriction is to partial meet contractions.

Base Contraction and the Filtering Condition

I have urged that once the minimum corpus LK and the dual ultimate partition U_K^* are given, the available options for contracting K by removing h should be the meets of all subsets of saturatable contractions removing h from K. According to the understanding of a basis as specifying what the set of available options for contraction are to be, the basis should consist of the set of disjunctions of U_K with some subset S of members of U_K^*. No restriction should be imposed on contraction options except those introduced by reference to the minimum corpus LK and the dual ultimate partition U_K^*. Elimination of such options can be justified but the justification should show such options to be suboptimal. One should not eliminate such options by stipulation. Base contraction allows for eliminating contraction strategies by stipulation.

Insisting on base contraction because of a desire for surveyability misses the mark. Surveyability can be achieved by requiring finite axiomatizability and finite dual ultimate partitions. (I do not insist on such finitization as a general rule. But I see no reason to prohibit consideration of it.) There is no need to appeal to base contraction except in the degenerate sense in which contraction of a finitely axiomatizable theory relative to a dual ultimate partition is a base contraction.

In sum, if non-degenerate base contraction is to be taken seriously, the case for doing so will ignore the demand that restrictions on the options for contraction be justified by appealing to the goals of the inquiry.

Illustrations offered by Fuhrmann and Hansson suggest that they are committed to restricting the options for contraction for reasons having little to do with the aims of inquiry. Recently Makinson (1997) has been quite explicit about it.

Consider Hansson's famous example in (1989, 117–18) concerning someone looking for a hamburger in town on a public holiday. X knows there are two hamburger joints A and B in the town but at the beginning X is in suspense as to whether either one of them is open. X meets a friend eating a hamburger and concludes that one of the restaurants is open. X has a basis $\{A \vee B\}$. X then sees the light on in

Base Contraction and the Filtering Condition

restaurant A and concludes that it is open. X's basis is now {A, A∨B}. Upon reaching restaurant A, X finds the restaurant closed. He needs to replace his corpus by one containing ∼A. Should it contain A∨B? Hansson and Fuhrmann both think it should.

Change the story a bit. The person X looking for a hamburger does not meet anyone munching a hamburger. But X sees the lights of restaurant A. So X's basis is {A}. If X then sees the restaurant to be closed, X should not retain A∨B.

The point to emphasize here is that what seems to determine the constitution of the basis is that in some unexplained sense, certain beliefs are acquired directly. In the first scenario, A∨B is acquired directly (by seeing the person eating the hamburger). It is also deducible from A.

In the second scenario, A∨B is not acquired directly but only via deduction from A. A, on the other hand, is acquired directly.

I do not know what I am attributing to Fuhrmann and Hansson when I allege that they draw a distinction between beliefs acquired directly and those that are mere consequences of what is acquired directly. Neither Fuhrmann nor Hansson use the terminology I have used. They let their examples speak for themselves. What is clear is that the constitution of the base A is determined by how a belief is acquired or, perhaps, by how it is justified.

Given the base A, Fuhrmann goes further and introduces a "filtering condition" that stipulates that A∨B should be removed in the second scenario when A is removed because the only reason it is in the corpus K is the presence of A. Remove that reason and A∨B should be removed also (Fuhrmann, 1991: 184–6).

On the other hand, in the first scenario, A∨B should be retained because there is an independent reason for having A∨B in K additional to the reason for having A in K in the first place.

There is more than a whiff of epistemological foundationalism ingredient in the appeal to the filtering condition. It appears that when a consequence of the basis A is challenged (i.e. when a sentence h is to be removed from $K = Cn(A)$), we need to attend to the way in which an item gained entry into K in order to determine what is to be given up. This is so whether we are concerned with the causal factors that contributed to the entrance into K or with the reasons that justify such entry.

I follow C. S. Peirce in rejecting any such pedigree epistemology (see Levi, 1980, ch. 1.1). Deciding what to give up, according to my proposals, depends upon determining which contraction strategy minimizes loss of informational value. The approach to fixing belief I have advocated for three decades is neither foundationalist nor coherentist. I am a pragmatist. As Peirce insisted, in inquiry we seek to remove doubt. We should emulate scientific inquirers in seeking to remove such doubts in a manner that avoids error as well. But in giving up beliefs, avoidance of error cannot be an issue. From the point of view of the inquirer, all of his current full beliefs are true. In giving up beliefs, one cannot be importing error. So there is no risk of error. But doubts are introduced. Information is lost.

In Hansson's first scenario, one might indeed not give up $A \vee B$. The reason would be that in doing so one would have to call into question background assumptions like the circumstance that a person was seen eating a hamburger or that the presence of someone eating a hamburger is a reliable indicator of the fact that some hamburger joint is open. The loss of information incurred might seem too great to bear. This consideration has nothing to do with the way one acquired the belief that $A \vee B$. The point to consider is that the agent also believes that someone is eating a hamburger. In giving up A, one will either have to give up this claim (one form of loss of information), or give up the claim that $A \vee B$ so that the presence of such an agent is left unexplained, or retain $A \vee B$. The latter option incurs less loss of informational value than the other alternatives regardless of how the agent acquired his convictions in the first place.

In the second scenario, there is no need to explain the presence of a hamburger-eating agent or to call into question the reliability of the presence of such a person as a reliable indicator of the fact that some hamburger joint is open. The loss of type 2 damped informational value incurred by giving up $A \vee B$ together with A could very well be no greater than giving up A alone so that giving up both is to be recommended.

Hansson's example is thus accommodated without appealing to any reasons for coming to believe at all. Only *losses* in informational value are taken into account.[1]

Both Fuhrmann and Makinson (1997) seem to think that if one does not appeal to what Makinson takes to be a justificatory structure that is associated with a basis, one is not contracting from a basis but from a theory and in this setting the Recovery Condition should obtain. That is because the filtering condition cannot be applied. Why the fact that the filtering condition cannot be applied should justify insisting on Recovery is not clear to me. Neither Fuhrmann nor Makinson offer any considerations establishing this result. And

---

[1] A commentator on these remarks has suggested the agent whose beliefs are being contracted might retain $A \vee B$ in the second scenario because he or she is hungry. For present purposes, the dual ultimate partition consists of the deductive consequences of $\sim A \wedge B$ and the deductive consequences of $\sim A \wedge \sim B$. The current belief-state is the deductive consequences of the disjunction of $A \wedge B$ and $A \wedge \sim B$. To contract removing A while retaining $A \vee B$ calls for intersecting the current belief-state with the consequences of $\sim A \wedge B$. The commentator is in effect suggesting that the inquirer could attach greater informational value to this element of the dual ultimate partition than $\sim A \wedge \sim B$ because the inquirer was hungry. Nothing I have suggested in this essay precludes ranking the two elements of the dual ultimate partition differently or ranking them the same. Hungry or not, I would be strongly inclined to rank them the same and suspect that many others are like me in this respect but no dictate of rationality requires this to be so. It cannot be an objection against my proposal to point out that they might be ranked differently in the manner that leads to the retention of $A \vee B$. In the text, I merely pointed out that they could also be ranked the same. As to whether hunger might be the motive for rating $\sim A \wedge B$ higher, my profound ignorance of what motivates others to do what they do obliges me to concede that maybe the ratings go this way. Even so, I would have thought that whether $\sim A \wedge B$ and $\sim A \wedge \sim B$ are ranked together or not would have little to do with how needy the agent was for the provisions of a hamburger joint. Hunger would have lent some urgency to finding a hamburger joint *if there is one* but that is not enough to rate propositions acknowledging their existence as of greater informational value than propositions that do not. I agree that how M^*-values are assigned elements of the basic partition might be influenced by the agent's needs, hopes and desires *as long as weak positive monotonicity or, more strictly, the Damping Condition Version 2 is obeyed when assessing losses of valuable information*. These requirements act as a break on how an inquirer's moral and other value commitments can control his or her assessments of informational value but do not rule out consideration of these commitments from paying a role in determining the M^*-function. The same is true *mutatis mutandis* if losses in informational value are assessed according to damping condition version 1.

Base Contraction and the Filtering Condition

I have sketched here procedures whereby Recovery can be violated even though the filtering condition does not apply.

The point I wish to belabor is that justification is needed, when it is needed, for *changes* in belief and not for the beliefs the inquirer currently has. As a consequence, once it is settled that h should be removed from K, whether some item f in K is to be given up as well or not depends entirely on the inquirer's *demands for information*. These demands are expressed by the dual ultimate partition U_K^* and the assessments of these corpora for undamped informational value. These two modes of evaluation indicate which kinds of losses of information matter to the inquirer and how different losses that do matter to the inquirer compare with one another.

Why should one ever give up information? This and related questions are discussed in Levi, 1980 and 1991. In this essay, only one issue is under discussion. Given that h is to be removed from K, which of the many ways of contracting should be adopted? The salient difference between alternative contractions removing h is that different types of information are lost. Doubt is injected in different ways. The choice between alternative contraction strategies should be based on a consideration of which strategies minimize loss of valuable information or inject doubt in the least disturbing manner. The choice should not be based on the grounds invoked to add the information being considered for removal. Information is valuable if it contributes to explanatory intelligibility, to prediction, to the understanding of the subject matter under study. Such informational value is poorly correlated with the basis on which the information was acquired in the first place

In this essay, I have sought to remove some obscurities from the technical development of my views on contraction—views I have endorsed in broad outline since the early 1970s.[2] The important work

---

[2] My first elaboration of these ideas appeared in "Truth Fallibility and the Growth of Knowledge". I read this paper at several Universities from 1971 onward and finally at the Boston Colloquium for Philosophy of Science in 1975. The paper was not published by the Boston Colloquium until 1983. It was reissued as Chapter 8 of Levi (1984). Another essay of the period that emphasizes that in contraction loss of informational value is to be minimized is "Subjunctives, Dispositions and Chances" that appeared in *Synthese* 34 in 1977 and is reprinted as Ch. 12 of Levi (1984).

of AGM prompted me to elaborate my ideas in more technical detail than I had done hithertofore (Levi, 1991, 1996). Several errors and obscurities crept into these accounts calling for amendments. But the account of contraction I offer remains faithful to the philosophical perspective I have adopted for at least three decades. Contraction is not justified in virtue of the need to justify beliefs already held. And when it comes to evaluating contraction strategies, the concern is to minimize loss of valuable information. The pedigree of beliefs is irrelevant.

References

Alchourrón, C., Gärdenfors, P., and Makinson, D. (1985), "On the Logic of Theory Change: Partial Meet Functions for Contraction and Revision", *Journal of Symbolic Logic* 50: 510–30.

Adams, E. W. (1975), *The Logic of Conditionals*, Dordrecht: Reidel.

Arló Costa, H., and Levi, I. (1996), "Two Notions of Epistemic Validity: Epistemic Models for Ramsey's Conditionals", *Synthese* 109: 217–62.

Barwise, J. (ed.) (1977), *Handbook of Mathematical Logic*, Amsterdam: North-Holland.

Dubois, D., and Prade, H. (1992), "Belief Change and Possibility Theory", in *Belief Revision*, ed. by P. Gärdenfors, Cambridge: Cambridge University Press, 142–82.

Dudman, V. H. (1984), "Conditional Interpretations of If-sentences", *Australasian Journal of Linguistics* 5: 143–204.

Fuhrmann, A. (1991), "Theory Contraction through Base Contraction", *Journal of Philosophical Logic* 20: 175–203.

—— (1997), *An Essay on Contraction*, Stanford: CSLI publications and Folli.

Gärdenfors, P. (1988), *Knowledge in Flux*, Cambridge, Mass.: MIT Press.

—— and Makinson, D. (1988), "Revisions of Knowledge Systems using Epistemic Entrenchment", in M. Vardi (ed.), *TARK 88: Proceedings of the Second Conference on Theoretical Aspects of Reasoning about Knowledge*, Los Altos: Kaufmann: 83–95.

—— and Makinson, D. (1993), "Nonmonotonic Inference based on Expectations", *Artificial Intelligence* 65: 197–246.

Hansson, S. O. (1989), "New Operators for Belief Change", *Theoria* 55: 113–32.

—— (1991), "Belief Base Dynamics", Ph.D. dissertation at Uppsala.

—— and Olsson, E. J. (1995), "Levi Contractions and AGM Contractions: a Comparison", *Notre Dame Journal of Formal Logic* 36: 103–19.

Harman, G. (1986), *Change in View: Principles of Reasoning*, Cambridge, Mass.: MIT Press.

References

Herzberger, H. (1973), "Ordinal Preference and Rational Choice", *Econometrica* 41: 187–237.

Jeffrey, R. C. (1965), *The Logic of Decision*, New York: Wiley.

Kraus, S., Lehmann, D., and Magidor, M. (1990), "Nonmonotonic Reasoning, Preferential Models and Cumulative Logics", *Artificial Intelligence* 44: 167–201.

Levi, I. (1967), *Gambling with Truth*, New York: Knopf; reissued as paperback, 1973 Cambridge, Mass: MIT Press.

——(1974), "On Indeterminate Probabilities", *Journal of Philosophy* 71: 391–418.

——(1980), *The Enterprise of Knowledge*, Cambridge, Mass.: MIT Press. Reissued as paperback 1983.

——(1984), *Decisions and Revisions*, Cambridge: Cambridge University Press.

——(1986), *Hard Choices*, Cambridge: Cambridge University Press.

——(1991), *The Fixation of Belief and Its Undoing*, Cambridge: Cambridge University Press.

——(1996), *For the Sake of the Argument*, Cambridge: Cambridge University Press.

——(2001), "Inductive Expansion and Nonmonotonic Reasoning", in *Frontiers in Belief Revision*, edited by M-A. Williams and H. Rott, Dordrecht: Kluwer, 7–56.

——(2003), "Contracting from Epistemic Hell is Routine", *Synthese* 135: 141–64.

Lewis, D. (1973), *Counterfactuals*, Cambridge, Mass.: Harvard University Press.

Lindström, S. (1990) "A Semantic Approach to Nonmonotonic Reasoning: Inference Operations and Choice", unpublished manuscript.

—— and Rabinowicz, W. (1990), "Epistemic Entrenchment with Incomparabilities and Relational Belief Revision", *Uppsala Philosophy Reports*, 2, Department of Philosophy, Uppsala, Sweden.

Little, I. M. D. (1950), *A Critique of Welfare Economics*, London: Oxford University Press, 2nd ed. 1957; paperback 1960.

Makinson, D. (1987), "On the Status of the Postulate of Recovery in the Logic of Belief Change", *Journal of Philosophical Logic* 16: 383–94.

——(1989), "General Theory of Cumulative Inference", in *Non-Monotonic Reasoning*, edited by J. de Kleer, M. L. Ginsberg and E. Sandewall, 1–18. Lecture Notes on Artificial Intelligence 346. Berlin: Springer-Verlag.

——(1997), "On the Force of Some Apparent Counterexamples to Recovery", *Normative Systems in Legal and Moral Theory*, ed. by E. G. Valdés,

References

W. Krawietz, G. H. von Wright and R. Zimmerling, Berlin: Dunker & Humboldt.

Meyer, T. A., Labuschagne, W. A., and Heidema, J. (1998), "A semantic weakening of the recovery postulate", unpublished manuscript.

Olsson, E. (2003), "Avoiding Epistemic Hell: Levi on Pragmatism and Inconsistency", *Synthese* 132: 119–140.

Peirce, C. S. (C.P.), *The Collected Papers of Charles Sanders Peirce*, 8 vols., Belknap Press. References in the text take the form (CP.n.m) where n is the volume and m the paragraph number.

Quine, W. V. (1970), *The Web of Belief*, New York: Random House.

Rott, H. (1991), "Two Methods of Constructing Contractions and Revisions of Knowledge Systems", *Journal of Philosophical Logic* 20: 149–73.

—— (1993), "Belief Contraction in the Context of the General Theory of Rational Choice", *Journal of Symbolic Logic* 58: 1426–50.

—— (2000) "Two Dogmas of Belief Revision", *Journal of Philosophy* 97: 503–22.

—— (2001) *Change, Choice and Inference*, Oxford: Oxford University Press.

—— and Pagnucco, M. (1999), "Severe Withdrawal (and Recovery)", *Journal of Philosophical Logic* 28: 501–47.

Schervish, M. J., Seidenfeld, T., and Kadane, J. G. (1984), "The Extent of Nonconglomerability of Finitely Additive Probabilities", *Zeitschrift für Wahrscheinlichkeitstheorie und verwandte Gebiete* 66: 205–66.

Segerberg, K. (1995a), "Belief revision from the point of view of doxastic logic", *Bulletin of the JPL* 3: 535–53.

—— (1995b), "Three Recipes for Revision", in *The Parikh Project*, Uppsala: Uppsala Prints and Preprints in Philosophy 18: 102–12.

Sen, A. K. (1971), "Choice Functions and Revealed Preference", *Review of Economic Studies* 38: 307–17.

Spohn, W. (1988), "Ordinal Conditional Functions: A dynamic theory of epistemic states", ed. by W. Harper and B. Skyrms, *Causation in Decision, Belief Change and Statistics,* Kluwer Academic Publishers, 105–34.

Stalnaker, R. C. (1968), "A Theory of Conditionals", in *Studies in Logical Theory*, Oxford: Blackwell, 98–112.

Suppes, P. (1994), "Some Questions about Adams' Conditionals", in *Probability and Conditionals*, ed. by E. Eells and B. Skyrms, Cambridge: Cambridge University Press, 5–11.

Zadeh, L. (1978), "Fuzzy Sets as a Basis for a Theory of Possibility", *Fuzzy Sets Syst.* 1: 3–28.

Index

abduction 46–7, 53–5
abductive expansion 87
AGM 121, 124, 125, 134, 146, 157, 159, 163–7, 187–90
AGM revision 16–17
Arló Costa, H. vii
Alchourrón, C. 67
avoidance of error 15–16, 70, 77–80

Baconian probability 175
Bain, A. 4
Bar Hillel, Y. 98, 99
Barwise, J. 152
basic partition, U_{LK} 49–53, 56, 164
   and maximally consistent corpora 47, 55–7
   infinite cases ch.6
belief change as a problem of rational choice 2.1, 158–64
belief as commitment 5–8
belief as disposition 4
belief as theoretical primitive 4
boldness index q 86–9, 175–8

Carnap, R. 98, 99
Principle of categorical matching 202
categorical preference 159–50

certainty, absolute 8–9
certainty, almost 9–10. ch.6
choice functions 5.1, 151.
cognitive goals 40, 68–9, 76–80, 125
Cohen, L. J. 91–93, 176
commensurability thesis 16, 68
commensuration requirement 16, 2.5
commitment and performance 1.2, 44–5
common basis for determining gains and losses of informational value 110, 215
conceptual framework 41
conditional modal judgment 1.7
   belief conforming 29
   belief contravening 29
   iterated conditional modal judgment 34
   lacks truth-value 33
   open 29
   supported by belief states 33–4
consensus revision 35
consistent expandability 30–1
   and closest worlds analyses of conditionals 31–2
constant marginal returns in informational value of rejection 83

Index

content measure Cont 84–5, 99–102
context dependence and the Curse of Frege 3.7
contraction 12
  base contraction 227–33
  coerced contraction 19–22, 23–4
  contraction from inconsistency 19–22, 72
  deliberate contraction to give a hearing 22–3, 72–3
  how to contract 24, 38–9
  impalpable contraction 182–4
  maxichoice contraction of K relative to U_K^* 60, 164
  maxichoice contraction removing h from K relative to U_K^* 60
  mild contraction 39, 5.7
  partial meet contraction 24, 2.4, 135–41
  potential contraction 57–59
  potential contraction condition 61, 67
  saturatable contraction of K removing h relative to U_K^* 60, 125, 128–9, 131–2
  severe withdrawal 39, 5.7
corpus 13–14, 41–3, 47, 227–8
  minimal corpus LK 49
credal state 103
cross product rule 103
Curse of Frege 95–7

damping constraint 128
damping constraint version 2 129, 142
damping, version 1 131, 233
damping, version 2 141, 233
degree of belief or plausibility 3.6, 173–5, 5.4
degree of surprise 3.6
degree of unrejectability of $h = q(h|K, U_K, Q_K, M_K)$ 89
dual ultimate partition U_K^* 55–61
  infinite case ch. 6
Dubois. D. 91

E-admissibility 104, 150
embedding in informational value thesis 178, 181
embedding in plausibility thesis 179, 182
entrenchment and incorrigibility 1.4, 1.6, 5.9, 200–3
epistemic utility 86–8
epistemology:
  foundationalist 11
  coherentist 11
  naturalized 11
  parmenidean 10–13, 19–23
  pedigree 11, 231–2
expansion 13–15
  coerced or inadvertent expansion into inconsistency 17–18, 19, 23
  inductive expansion 12–13, ch.3
  rule for inductive expansion 87–8
  stable inductive expansion 88–9

Index

expectation 175
expected utility rule 103
extended weak positive monotonicity 126, 128

fallbacks 5.13
filtering condition 232–4
finite and countable additivity in expectation and informational value determining probability 221–5
finite discriminability condition for the purpose of assessing informational value 219–20
full belief 1–3:
  corrigibility of 10–12
  need for justification of change of 1–3
  potential state of 13–14, 41
Fuhrmann, A. ch.7

Gärdenfors, P. 17, 18, 19, 40, 67, 91, 121, 123, 124, 200
Grove models 182–6

Harman, G. 163–4
Hansson, S.-O. 18, 187, ch.7
Heidema, J. 189
Herzberger, H. 151, 158
hypothetic inference 54

inadvertent expansion into inconsistency 17–18, 19–22, 71–2, 106
incommensurability of points of view 16
inconsistency as epistemic hell 19–22
induction 54–5
information 70–1, 81
  information, informational value and positive monotonicity 81–2
informational value 40, 70–1, 79–80,
  damped informational value, version 1 129–30, 4.7, 141–2, 182, 184–5, 191
  damped informational value, version 2 129–30, 4.8, 182–7,191
  hyperundamped informational value 115
  undamped informational value 84, 99–101, 4.3, 122–5, 184–7,192
intersection equality 125–6

Jeffrey, R. C. 19, 91

Kadane, J. 221
Kelly, K. 21
Kraus, S. 225
Kuhn, T. 16

Labuschagne, W. A. 189
Lehmann, D. 225
Levi Identity 73
Lindström, S. 121, 134, 212–4

Main Claim A 122, 125
Main Thesis B 133–4
Main Thesis C 143–4

Index

Magidor, M. 225
Makinson, D. 40, 61, 67, 88, 91, 124, 134, 186, 199, 225, ch.7
maximal options 150
maximally consistent corpora in L 47, 55–6
method of authority 3
minimal belief state **LK** 49–53
mixture set 149
Meyer, T. 189
modal judgment conditional and unconditional 1.7

Olsson, E. 21, 72, 106, 187

Pagnucco, M. vii, 39, 40, 87 n.4, 146–8, 5.2, 174–6, 179, 180, 189–90
Peirce, C. S. 1,4, 53–5, 232
permissible probability 103
permissible utility 102–3
plain belief 93–5, 5.5
plausibility 173–5, 5.3, 5.4
Popper, K. R. 54, 98
potential contraction condition 61, 67
Prade, H. 91
principle of conservativism 163–7
principle of expected utility 103
principle of informational economy 123, 125, 5.2
principle of indifference 166–8
principle of strict preference 168
principle of weak preference 168–70
prior plausibility 5.4

probability 9
  credal probability as expectation determining 84, 4.1
  indeterminate probability 4.2
  informational value determining 84, 4.1
  permissible probability 103

Quine, W. V. 54–5

Rabinowicz, W. 212–4
Ramsey, F. 4
Ramsey revision 29–30, 186–91
Ramsey test 26
  AGM revision based 29
  consensus-based pseudo 35–7
  Ramsey revision based 30
real and living doubt 6
  see also serious possibility
realism
  messianic 15
  secular 15
  visionary 15
recovery 29–30, 61–7, 122, 130, 133–40, 143, 145
  recovery and revision equivalence 5.8
Reiter, R. 88
replacement 14, 20
residual shift 14, 20
revealed preference 150–1
Rott, H. vii, 39, 40, 121, 125, 134, 146–8, 156–63, 5.2, 5.3, 5.4, 179, 189–90, 199
rule for inductive expansion 87
rule for ties 87, 119–21, 125, 133–4, 150, 207

Index

Schervish, M. 221
secondary criteria 150–1
Seidenfeld, T. vii, 221
selection functions 5.1, 152
serious possibility 1–2, 10–1
Sen, A. K. 151, 158
Shackle, G. L. S. 90–1, 176, 179
Shackle measure 40
   damped informational value 101
   degree of unrejectability of h, $q(h)$ 88–9
   degree of potential surprise of h, $d(h)$ 88
   degree of belief that h, $b(h)$ 88
Spohn, W. 19, 40, 92–5, 176, 180–1
stable inductive expansion 3.5
   stable inductive expansion and non-monotonic consequence relations 88 n.5
strong min 127
strong positive monotonicity 82, 4.4
suppositional reasoning 1.7

systematic withdrawal 189

theoretical and practical rationality 18
theoretical and practical goals 18–9, *see* cognitive goals

Ullian, J. 54–5
ultimate partition 47–9, 51–3
   infinite case, ch.6
utility of new valuable error-free information 80, 86–7

value structure 93, 102
version 1 damping thesis 131
version 2 damping thesis 141
V-admissibility 104

weak min 127
weak positive monotonicity 82, 4.4, 167, 233
withdrawals 142

Zadeh, L. 91